South America
into the 1990s

Published in cooperation with
the Center for Strategic
and International Studies
Washington, D.C.

South America into the 1990s

Evolving International Relationships in a New Era

EDITED BY

G. Pope Atkins

Routledge
Taylor & Francis Group

LONDON AND NEW YORK

First published 1990 by Westview Press, Inc.

Published 2019 by Routledge
52 Vanderbilt Avenue, New York, NY 10017
2 Park Square, Milton Park, Abingdon, Oxon OX14 4RN

Routledge is an imprint of the Taylor & Francis Group, an informa business

Copyright © 1990 by the Center for Strategic and International Studies

Library of Congress Cataloging-in-Publication Data
South America into the 1990s : evolving international relationships in a New
  Era / edited by G. Pope Atkins.
    p. cm.
  ISBN 0-8133-7515-0
  1. South America—Foreign relations—1948–   . I. Atkins, G. Pope,
1934–
F2237.S68   1990
327.68′009′049—dc20   89-48772
                                                                              CIP

ISBN 13: 978-0-367-28795-5 (hbk)

Contents

Contents

Preface

The altered international and domestic circumstances of South America require a reevaluation of that region's international relations. The geographic scope of the subject is defined as South America beyond the Circum-Caribbean, excluding the states of Colombia, Venezuela, Guyana, and Suriname. The region thus defined—essentially what is often called the Southern Cone of South America and Brazil—forms an international subsystem with distinct characteristics that present special challenges to the various state and nonstate actors involved, both inside and outside the region. Although a great deal of attention over the past decade has been focused on events in Mexico and the Caribbean area, particularly Central America, South America beyond the Caribbean has received comparatively little consideration by both analysts and policymakers. This is unfortunate considering the sheer weight of South American states, the magnitude of the problems they and their external partners face, and the profound changes that are occurring in the region.

This book undertakes a multifaceted examination of South American international relations. Emphasis is placed on the continent's new era of domestic and international politics and the implications of the evolving South American environment for the policies of the many actors participating in the region's international politics. It grows out of a program of research, analysis, and discussion under the auspices of the Center for Strategic and International Studies supported by a grant from the Tinker Foundation.

A basic premise of this study is that profound changes in the South American subsystem and in its relationships with the outside world require fundamental reevaluation on the part of the United States. The region has grown dramatically in importance and represents a pressing set of items on the U.S. foreign policy agenda—fragile democratization, external debt crisis, domestic economic development management, and the traffic in narcotics (which also holds the dangers of narco-terrorism) being only the most obvious among them. The rapid pace of regional transformation, however, has outgrown the quality of attention that the United States has devoted to the area.

The authors of this study share a recognition of the importance of South America to U.S. interests and a desire for the United States to pursue an effective policy on the continent. They also agree that an effective pursuit of U.S.–South American relations requires a revitalized agenda that takes into account not only regional realities but also the implications of a South America now increasingly part of a wider global community. The chapters in this volume draw out various dimensions of the new South American environment and outline the interests and actions of the broad array of key regional and external actors.

A variety of substantive topics are taken up by a recognized authority in each instance. The authors take a common approach inasmuch as each makes some general conceptual commentary about the particular theme being pursued, compares the situation in the 1980s with that of the 1960s and 1970s in terms of both continuity and change, and identifies trends that seem likely to project into the 1990s. Other than that, however, all of the analysts have been encouraged to bring to bear individual expertise and experience with no prescribed conformity or orthodoxy of interpretation, conclusion, or prescription. Given the breadth of the subject examined and the dearth of relevant up-to-date materials, the research and writing tasks were undertaken on an individual basis.

As in any complex endeavor, the credit for bringing the book to a successful completion rests with several individuals and institutions. The Center for Strategic and International Studies and its Latin American Program provided a hospitable environment in which to undertake this kind of initiative. The technical support provided at the Center by Mary Donlan, Patricia Pickerall, and Carmen Pinelli in particular must be noted. Virginia Atkins Wilson drew the map. The editor thanks especially the Tinker Foundation, whose financial support was instrumental in the carrying out of the project. Ultimately, however, this book is the result of the professionalism, patience, and cooperation of the individual authors.

G. Pope Atkins

About the Contributors

G. Pope Atkins is Professor of Political Science at the United States Naval Academy and Senior Associate in Latin American Studies at the Center for Strategic and International Studies (CSIS). He has written extensively on Latin American international and comparative politics, including *Latin America in the International Political System* (2d ed., 1989). Dr. Atkins has been a visiting professor or researcher with the Institute for Latin American Studies at the University of London, El Fondo para el Avance de las Ciencias Sociales in Santo Domingo, the International Relations Department of the London School of Economics and Political Science, and other institutions.

Morris J. Blachman is Professor of Government and International Studies at the University of South Carolina, where he chairs the Coordinating Council for the Western Hemisphere in the James F. Byrnes International Center and serves as Associate Director of the Institute of International Studies. He is also Associate Director of Regions of the International Studies Association, headquartered at the university. Dr. Blachman has written widely on U.S. policy toward Latin America, including the editing of two books dealing with the subject.

Jack Child is Professor of Languages and Area Studies at The American University and former Associate Dean of the School of International Service. Born in Argentina, he pursued a career in the U.S. Army as a foreign area specialist officer in the Latin American region; his last assignment was on the faculty of the Inter-American Defense College. Among his many writings, Dr. Child is the author of *Geopolitics and Conflict in South America* (1985) and *Antarctica and South American Geopolitics* (1988).

Georges A. Fauriol is Senior Fellow and Director of Latin American Studies at CSIS. He has worked at the Inter-American Development Bank and the U.S. International Communications Agency; from 1977 to 1979 he was personal assistant to Ambassador Anne Armstrong. Dr. Fauriol has written in the areas of Latin American international relations,

Caribbean Basin affairs, Third World politics, and various aspects of U.S. foreign policy. His most recent publication is *The Third Century: U.S. Latin American Policy Choices for the 1990s* (1988).

Wolf Grabendorff is executive director of the European Community-sponsored Institute for European–Latin American Relations in Madrid. Formerly senior Latin American analyst for the Stiftung Wissenschaft und Politik, he is currently a commissioner of the International Commission for Central American Recovery and Development. Among his many publications on Latin American subjects, Grabendorff is co-editor of *Latin America, Western Europe, and the United States: Reevaluating the Atlantic Triangle* (1985).

William Guttman is a consultant to the International Monetary Fund and the Latin American Program at CSIS. He has previously advised the World Bank, the OECD, and various offices of the U.S. Department of State. Guttman's writings on economic development have appeared in a wide variety of academic journals. He is a graduate of the University of California at Los Angeles and Oxford University.

Roberto Russell is Director of the Facultad Latinoamericana de Ciencias Sociales (FLACSO), Programa Buenos Aires. He has taught at the University of Belgrano in Buenos Aires, the Johns Hopkins University School of Advanced International Studies, and Georgetown University. His recent writing has focused on Argentine foreign policy and South American international relations.

Wayne A. Selcher is College Professor of International Studies at Elizabethtown College, where he chairs the Department of Political Science and serves as Director of International Studies. Dr. Selcher has specialized in inter-American relations and Brazilian politics and foreign policy. He has conducted extensive field research in Brazil; his many publications include four books on that country's political system and foreign policy, including *Political Liberalization in Brazil: Dynamics, Dilemmas, and Future Prospects* (1986).

Howard J. Wiarda is Professor of Political Science at the University of Massachusetts (Amherst). He has been an associate of the Center for Hemispheric Studies at Harvard University and Resident Scholar and Director of the Center for Hemispheric Studies at the American Enterprise Institute. His extensive research and writing record includes pioneering works on Latin America's developmental tradition; he has recently focused on varied aspects of Latin American international relations and U.S. policy in the region. His latest books are *The Democratic Revolution in Latin America: Implications for United States Policy*, to be published for The Twentieth Century Fund, and *Latin American Politics and Development* (co-editor), 3d ed., to be published in 1990 by Westview Press.

South America

1

South America in the International Political System

G. Pope Atkins

This chapter presents a general overview of South American international relations, with the aim of coordinating the specialized chapters that follow. It attempts to establish a general framework for analysis and identify the various categories of relationships that are analyzed in the rest of the book. It also provides some historical background so that other authors may concentrate on current trends. The overall focus is on international structures and processes, especially the distribution of international power and influence.

The first part of the chapter defines South America beyond the Circum-Caribbean as an international political subsystem, pointing out its distinguishing characteristics and the essential levels for analysis. The second section is an historical evaluation of the subsystem's progression, noting major events at the various levels previously identified and how they contributed to an increasingly separate South American identity. The third portion summarizes the subsystem's elements as it has entered a new era (the primary subject of this volume), and briefly introduces the chapters that follow.

South America as an International Subsystem

Geographic Scope and Setting

In terms of international politics, the region of South America beyond the Circum-Caribbean includes the actions of states located in the Southern Cone (Argentina, Chile, Peru, Uruguay, Paraguay, and Bolivia), constantly involves Brazil as a key actor, and sometimes draws in Ecuador. Thus the northern tier states of Colombia, Venezuela, Guyana, and Suriname are excluded; they overlap with some of the concerns addressed in this book, but the thrust of their international relations are essentially part of the Circum-Caribbean subsystem. South America thus defined, while a part of the larger Latin American region, forms a separate subsystem with a number of characteristics that distinguish it from Mexico and the Circum-Caribbean.

A principal characteristic of the South American subsystem is its relative isolation from the mainstream of international politics. The region has been relatively shielded from the global mainstream of great power politics and, during the twentieth century, largely beyond their spheres of influence. It has a unique political-geographic situation that fundamentally affects both relations with external states and its own intraregional relations. The region's isolated geographic position at great distances from Europe and the United States has combined with other factors, especially the relative strength of the key local states, to exclude the area for the most part from global balance of power rivalries. This is in dramatic distinction from the northern portion of Latin America. Consequently, the Southern Cone states and Brazil have developed a distinct set of relationships with external actors, as well as intraregional structures and processes, largely outside the context of global power politics.[1]

Levels of Analysis

The South American international subsystem may be specifically defined on several levels that involve different kinds of relationships. They are categorized as follows:

1. The Local State Level. The leading South American states are, in a relative sense, internally institutionalized and independent in international politics, especially in comparison with most Caribbean countries. They have critical domestic problems, often related to their international environment, but the political systems and decisional outcomes of most of them rely less on personal relationships and more on institutional interactions than do the "crisis countries" of much of northern Latin America. Brazil is the leading nation in Latin America and in the South American subsystem. It stands apart in several respects, to the extent that it could be considered a distinct subsystem in its own right. By several measures of size—territory, population, economy, and others—Brazil ranks in the upper strata of the world's nation-states.[2]

2. The Extrahemispheric Level. South American relations with extrahemispheric states have been particularly important. Unlike the presence of Mexico and most Caribbean countries in a bilateral U.S.

economic network, the Southern Cone states and Brazil form a multi-lateralized trading and investing area. They also have long-standing cultural and military ties with Europe; the region's recent trade with Europe has included arms transfers. Brazil especially has diversified its economy and developed a broad network of bilateral relationships. Its multilateralized trade structure includes ties in Europe, the Middle East and Africa, and Japan, in addition to those with the United States. Argentina trades heavily with the Soviet Union. Peru has purchased a large volume of armaments from the Soviet Union and France. South American west coast states see themselves as part of a Pacific Basin trading system; Japan has become an important economic force in the region, notably with Peru, Bolivia, and, especially, Brazil.[3]

3. The Inter-American Level. Southern Cone states and Brazil have important interactions with the United States and other Latin American states, and have belonged to the Inter-American System since 1889. The United States, by and large, has been one of several competitors in South America, only briefly (after World War II) approaching a position of primacy as in the Circum-Caribbean or Mexico. While the U.S. presence in the subsystem remains important and should not be underestimated, the United States in its Latin American relationships has had the least interest and influence in the Southern Cone (with temporary exceptions), and its leverage with Brazil has declined dramatically over the past two decades. Furthermore, as noted above, these states have important linkages outside the hemisphere that balance U.S. influence.[4]

4. The South American Intraregional Level. The regional states have important sets of international issues and patterns of interactions among themselves. The South American region has long been an area of local conflict, with roots in the colonial period. The legacy includes a long list of territorial boundary disputes, national power struggles that have led to warfare and threats of war, and claims of sovereignty and competition for resources. They have been defined and shaped by regional conflicts with minimal reference to outside great power influence. Relative isolation in global politics has allowed important local rivalries and ambitions to operate. Indeed, those processes have largely been the consequence of the fact that outsiders have rarely played the role of local policeman. Isolation of the small states from extraregional influences, however, has increased their dependency on local great powers. The three weak states in the Southern Cone—Uruguay, Paraguay, and Bolivia—have been caught up in rivalries between Argentina, Brazil, Chile, and Peru; "buffer status" has been accorded them in the subregional game of power politics.

Subregional international politics have resulted in strategic components to several local states' foreign policies, and they have developed geopolitical and balance-of-power thinking toward their own region.[5] The espousal of geopolitical strategic perspectives further distinguishes the South American subsystem from the rest of Latin America. Particularly ominous is the introduction of nuclear questions into intraregional international relations, with advanced capabilities on the part of Argentina and Brazil. On the positive side, Argentine-Brazilian rapprochement since 1979, and successful Argentine-Chilean efforts to settle territorial disputes, have established a cooperative mood in intraregional politics.

5. *The South Atlantic–Antarctic Level.* Several of the subregional states extend their international concerns beyond the South American continent to the South Atlantic Ocean and to the Antarctic. From their perspectives, the issues in their own subregional interstate rivalry are linked to competition for resources in the sea and seabed and territorial claims in the South Atlantic and Antarctica. The South Atlantic zone includes the special case of Anglo-Argentine conflict over the Falkland/Malvinas Islands and other insular territories. The Antarctic involves a broad array of states around the globe; it has been regulated by a treaty regime since 1961. The South American states often interact in the South Atlantic and Antarctica from geopolitical perspectives; many local geopoliticians define the Southern Cone to extend to these contiguous zones.[6]

6. *The Transnational Level.* Nonstate actors—especially multinational corporations (MNCs), international labor organizations, transnational political parties, and churches with transnational linkages—are important components in South America's international relations. In certain economic, political, and social areas they are possibly becoming more significant than the external states, both in relations with their South American counterparts and with South American governments. This is true more for European-based entities than for those headquartered in the United States, with the exception of MNCs (especially commercial banks). U.S. labor is conservative and protectionist; U.S. political parties are not organized on international bases; and U.S. churches (including the Roman Catholic Church) have focused on Central American issues. European actors, on the other hand, have historical ties and increasingly intimate relations in the current era.[7]

7. *The International Economic System Level.* Special considerations of economic policies and interactions form a layer of analysis that relates to but cuts across the other levels. Although South America is politically isolated in global terms, external economic penetration has been intense. Foreign trade and investment are crucial to the well-being

of all regional states and comprise a salient element for the policies of the external states. South American foreign policies, in all cases, aim to maximize export opportunities, protecting and expanding markets as best they can. Economic policies tend to be highly pragmatic; many external relations revolve around economic needs, which in turn temper ideological positions and nationalist sensibilities. Current economic debilities bearing on the South American states, with much of their debt owed to U.S. banks, have raised suggestions of a new dependency relationship on outsiders, especially the United States. At the same time, South Americans have purposely developed a multiplicity of external economic interactions aimed at diversifying their dependency.[8]

Evolution of the South American System

The South American international subsystem has passed through five general historical stages or phases. Transitional periods involved events that signalled the end of one era and initiation of the next phase.[9]

Phase One (to 1860)

Although independence came in Spanish South America between 1808–1825, and to Brazil in 1822, the South American subsystem did not emerge as a coherently formed unit in world affairs until the latter part of the nineteenth century. Many of its elements, however, were evident in earlier times. The roots of the subsystem lie in the colonial and immediate post-independence periods, and further in events during the early national experience.

In domestic politics, most of the new South American states were characterized by disunity and fragmentation. Unlike Spanish America, Brazil escaped destabilizing post-independence dislocations when a member of the royal Braganza family joined with Brazilian nationalists, gave up his claim to the Portuguese throne, and, as Pedro I, ruled as Brazilian sovereign from 1822–1831. He was succeeded by his son, Pedro II, who reigned until 1889. They were effective constitutional monarchs who played the role of "moderating power" above partisanship, forcing political parties to alternate in office. Chile was the first Spanish American state to work its way out of chaos, and did so relatively soon after independence in 1818. In the early 1830s, Chile entered a two-decade period of consolidating "oligarchical democracy" in which suffrage was limited but leaders were chosen through the electoral process and the armed forces were subject to civilian authority.

Elsewhere, Spanish American difficulties included church-state disputes, financial dislocations, factionalism among the ruling elites, regionalism, violence, and caudillismo (a system of regional strong men with private armies and political ambitions). In addition to internal strife that prevented the creation of stable polities, unclear national boundaries and chaotic public finances produced conditions that invited conflict with neighboring states and intervention by European states. Argentina did not become a unified nation until after 1861; until then it was characterized by extreme regionalism and caudillismo. From 1829 to 1852, the dictator Juan Manuel de Rosas imposed an artificial "unity" on Argentines, although the regional caudillos enjoyed considerable autonomy. Peru was slow to consolidate as a nation after achieving independence, not doing so until the mid-1890s. After independence in 1822, Ecuador until 1830 was a part of the larger entity of Gran Colombia with Colombia and Venezuela; it then followed a path similar to that of Peru. Both states were characterized by political fragmentation, regionalism, disunity, and authoritarianism until near the end of the century. Bolivian politics were similarly dominated by caudillismo, a system surviving there until about 1880. After Paraguay gained independence in 1811, its political life was dominated by authoritarian personalist strongmen: José Gaspar Rodríguez de Francia was appointed "ruler for life," and so acted from 1816–1840; Carlos Antonio López then ruled from 1844–1862. Uruguay was born as a nation out of warfare between Brazil and Argentina, and was subject thereafter to their constant meddling, a situation exacerbating severe internal political strife involving considerable violence.

The new South American states played passive roles in international politics and were subordinate to the outside powers. Their independence from Spain and Portugal stimulated rivalry among the other European powers to gain regional influence or control. Chaotic conditions in Spanish South America raised serious questions in the minds of Europeans as to the viability of the new nations. As Harold Davis points out, the first priorities of the South American governments in their extraregional relations were to make peace treaties with their respective former colonial states, secure international recognition of other countries, and adjust their relations as Roman Catholic nations with the Holy See on church-state relationships; these problems persisted for many years.[10]

Great Britain was the primary external power. Its merchant fleets and superior naval force dominated the Atlantic, supported British commercial objectives, and denied expansion to other external states. France had imperial as well as commercial designs, but its attempt to recolonize Spanish America in the 1820s was frustrated by British opposition. Spain sought to recover its former colonies from time to time, but it was then a minor European power and did not figure prominently in regional affairs. The only post-independence territorial acquisition by an external state was Great Britain's Falkland Islands Colony in the South Atlantic, taken from Argentina in 1833.

British preeminence characterized Brazil's foreign relations. While Great Britain emphasized commercial interests, its attempt to suppress the international slave trade was an important factor in its relations with Brazil. All of the South American states, but Brazil especially, had to confront the questions involved in the abolition of the international slave trade, an issue inescapably raised by the independence movements and by British nineteenth century policy.[11] Brazilian relations with the United States were friendly, on the whole, and involved no really serious issues. The United States had been first to recognize Brazil's independence.

Relations among the subregional states were essentially conflictual. They found themselves continuing the old colonial territorial rivalries between Spain and Portugal, at the same time that they were determined to establish independent polities. The Spanish American states had to agree among themselves about national boundaries, indeterminate within the old Spanish empire, and to recognize the independence of new states. The intensity of the problem was dramatically illustrated by Chile's boundary and territorial disputes with all of its neighbors, and by the failure of the Viceroyalty of La Plata to achieve unity as a single nation. Brazil had borders with all of the new Spanish American states except Chile, a situation giving rise to numerous conflicts.

Intra-South American conflict also arose from rival ambitions for subregional leadership. This rivalry often drew in European involvement. The competition between Argentina and Brazil for dominance in the Rio de la Plata region revolved around conflict over Uruguay, a continuation of the prior contest between Portugal and Spain, which was in turn resisted by Uruguayan patriots. An indecisive Argentine-Brazilian war broke out in 1825 but Britain, its commercial interests disrupted, pressured Argentina and Brazil into signing a treaty in 1828 in which they agreed to recognize Uruguayan independence.

From 1838–1840 France blockaded the Rio de la Plata and asserted the claims of French citizens. Five years later France was joined by Britain in another blockade of Buenos Aires, from 1845–1850, this time in the context of the unsettled Uruguayan question. A siege of Montevideo from 1841–1851 involved the alliance of Argentine and Uruguayan factions on both of the opposing sides; the Anglo-French blockade aimed to support Uruguayans. After the French and British withdrawal in 1850, Brazil joined Uruguayan and Argentine factions to drive Argentine caudillo Juan Manuel de Rosas from power in Buenos Aires.

Important conflicts on the west coast of South America also developed in the early independence period. Chile, intent on dominating the Pacific coast, pursued aggressive policies toward Bolivia and Peru. In 1836 Bolivia and Peru formed a confederation; Chile responded by going to war in 1839 and breaking it.

A minority of Spanish American states attempted to organize among themselves, on the theory that presenting a united front toward the outside world was more effective than bilateral approaches. This organizational tactic took the form of four conferences between 1826 and 1865 that attempted to install mutual security agreements. Participation, inspired by fear of external threats, declined once those threats receded.

The new South American states established commercial relations with Europe and, to a lesser degree, the United States. Britain immediately dominated South American finance and commerce, a position it maintained throughout the nineteenth century. All of the South American states entered sovereign life with large foreign debts relating to their wars for independence; they immediately began to add to their debt burdens. South American governments sold most of their bonds in the London market, and a few in France and the United States. By 1827 every bond obligation was in default; consequently, little additional investment capital was attracted to South America until the 1860s.

Phase Two (1860–1914)

After mid-century the first era of South American international relations was coming to a close and a separate South American subsystem began to take more definite shape. The succeeding phase, from about 1860 to the beginning of World War I, brought changes in the relations of the regional states with each other and with outside powers. The South American subsystem was further set apart by U.S. domination of the Circum-Caribbean following its military victory over Spain in 1898 and the subsequent opening of the Panama Canal under U.S. control, and by the nature of Mexico's external relations under the Díaz dictatorship (1876–1910) and the country's virtual retirement from international politics after the Revolution of 1910.

The major South American states developed more consolidated national structures and viable political systems. Brazil continued its vigorous growth under Pedro II until his abdication in 1889; it then moved to a decentralized system that lasted until 1930 (now referred to as the Old Republic), in which politics continued to reflect an oligarchic, highly class-conscious system but with power decentralized to the state level. From 1851–1891 in Chile, upper class elites directed a republican system in which five civilian presidents regularly succeeded each other through elections. After a brief civil war in 1891, Chile established a parliamentary republic that lasted until 1925 with power asserted in the national legislature. Argentines finally overcame extreme regionalism in 1862, when they achieved a troubled unity under a national constitution prescribing federalism and republicanism. Politics was initially led by the upper classes in which suffrage was limited but civil rights generally respected; a new middle-class reformist movement (the Radical Civic Union—UCR) emerged in the 1890s, and won the presidency in the elections of 1916.

The other South American states took longer to evolve stable systems. Peru's military-civilian conflict lasted until 1895, when it entered a period of elected civilian rule that lasted until 1919. Ecuador, likewise, continued its authoritarian disunity until 1895, when it also entered a period of elitist civilian republican government. Until 1880, Bolivian political life was dominated by regional caudillos; they were discredited by their behavior in the War of the Pacific (see below) and were superseded by new conservative economic-social elites, who established a formal democracy led by oligarchies who often clashed violently among themselves. The situation in Uruguay improved marginally after mid-century in that the nation suffered much less from Brazilian and Argentine interventions and internal violence; but the new system was directed by shifting alliances of civilian elites and military leaders.

Southern Cone international relations determined the Paraguayan political system. Personalism, paternalism, and authoritarianism prevailed as Francisco Solano López succeeded his father as dictator in 1862 and ruled until he was killed in battle in 1870 in the War of the Triple Alliance (see below). Allied armies from Brazil, Argentina, and Uruguay occupied Paraguay from 1870–1876, enforcing a liberal constitution prior to their departure. Thereafter, Paraguayan elites coalesced into opposing sides: Conservative inheritors of the strongman tradition and Liberal elements who supported a new republican order. A great deal of Argentine and Brazilian meddling in Paraguayan politics occurred throughout this period.

Numerous South American leaders consciously sought extensive outside assistance in their quest for development in terms of "modernist" nationalism. They strongly desired to modernize their economies, military establishments, and social systems, and looked to foreign models and resources, especially European, to do so. South American remoteness took on importance as the external great powers concentrated on their imperialism in other parts of the world. Secure from most threats of European intervention, and later that of the United States, South Americans were able to concentrate on national development and regional rivalries. Spain's brief war with Peru and Chile in 1865 was an exception to the rule.

South Americans had extensive cultural, political, economic, and military ties with several European countries, and encouraged relations with Europe through immigration, investment, and cultural affinities. In South America the increasingly powerful United States was only one of several competitors, important primarily in commercial affairs. U.S.-Brazilian relations in time took on a new character. Brazil emerged from under British primacy and, after the turn of the century, sought more autonomy in an "unwritten alliance" with the United States.

All European states and the United States pursued predominately commercial interests. Germany and Italy entered the South American scene with their respective national unification in the 1870s. By the end of the century, Germany occupied third place in total Latin American trade, behind Great Britain and the United States but well ahead of France.

South American cultural relations with Europe, including the movement of peoples, were profound and persistent; those with the United States were much less significant. South American intellectuals and other elites had admired French culture for decades. Italy sent large numbers of immigrants, especially to southern South America and to Argentina in particular. Spain, after its military defeat by the United States in 1898, articulated a cultural policy called *hispanismo* that asserted a common hispanic civilization but backed it with few resources. Portugal had a substantial portion of its trade with Brazil and continued to send most of its immigrants there. Germany had ties with its ethnic populations in Brazil and southern South America.

Germany and France also played leading roles in the development of South American armies, thereby extending to the Americas their worldwide competition. They were responding to decisions by South American states in the late nineteenth century to seek foreign military missions for advice and training. Germany was predominant with the armies in Chile and Argentina, France prevailed in Peru, Brazil, and Uruguay, and the two states competed in Bolivia and Paraguay. Great Britain and the United States pursued their naval relations essentially as commercial ventures in support of their shipbuilding industries. Armaments contracts were entered into with European firms as well.

The Inter-American System was established in 1889 under U.S. leadership, primarily to promote expanded inter-American trade and procedures for the peaceful settlement of disputes. The United States refused to consider Latin American proposals for nonintervention and mutual security, insisting on unilateral application of the Monroe Doctrine. U.S. interventions in the Caribbean area after the turn of the century under the Roosevelt Corollary to the Monroe Doctrine produced a wave of anti-Americanism in South America, and led to efforts to unite all of Latin America in an anti-interventionist stand in the inter-American System; they were not successful until the late 1920s.

Eighteen of the twenty Latin American states—including all of those in South America—attended and played active roles at the Second Hague Peace Conference in 1907. Chile and Brazil were especially active participants. This was an indication that they were playing an increasing and more global role in international affairs.

In intraregional politics, unsettled and unmarked boundaries still plagued intra–South American relations and the period witnessed wars, threats of war, and other forms of conflict within the subsystem. These disputes were part of Southern Cone balance-of-power politics.[12] The Paraguayan War, or War of the Triple Alliance (1864–1870), pitted the alliance of Brazil, Argentina, and Uruguay against Paraguay. The alliance resisted the expansionist moves of Paraguayan dictator Francisco Solano López and ended with Paraguay's complete defeat. Chile's tense relations with Peru and Bolivia led to the War of the Pacific (1879–1883). Chile's victory resulted in its occupation and annexation of the Bolivian territories of Atacama and Tarapaca (leaving Bolivia a landlocked nation) and the Peruvian territories of Tacna and Arica. Various boundary disputes in the region were also prosecuted. They were settled either by direct negotiation or through third-party involvement. Those between Argentina and Chile were among the most important. In 1881 they agreed to a vague boundary settlement but it was contested in 1895 and almost led to war. A resolution of part of the dispute was arrived at in 1899 through U.S. arbitration; the British Crown handed down a further award in 1902 regarding another portion of the boundary.

In economic relations, British capital again financed large South American bond issues in the 1860s and 1870s. More than half of them were in default by the late 1870s but debt servicing improved in the 1880s. French investors in Argentina and Peru especially suffered heavy losses. Direct foreign investment was also important. Britain was exceptionally well entrenched in Argentina; it also had important levels of investment in Brazil. U.S. capital investment increased after the Civil War, especially to Chile. France favored Chile and Brazil as the main South American recipients of its external investment capital. With the dramatic development of several South American economies, their ability to trade increased.

Phase Three (1914–1943)

A new period opened with the beginning of World War I, continued through the global depression, and ended during World War II. South America entered the post–World War I period faced with profound changes in international relations and world power politics, followed by the collapse of world trade and credit structures in the Great Depression, and then by the further wrenching events of World War II.[13]

Dramatic events and changes occurred in the South American political systems. The Old Republic ended in Brazil in 1930 when Getulio Vargas seized power through coup d'etat and established a populist (and popular) corporatist dictatorship that lasted until his overthrow in 1945. Argentina's liberal democracy lasted until 1930, when the country had the first of its many military golpes de estado. A corporatist-fascist military regime (1930–1932) was forced to sponsor restricted elections, which resulted in a conservative restoration that lasted until 1943 through intimidation and fraud. In Chile, young reformist politicians forced the end of the Parliamentary Republic in 1924 and ushered in a half-century political period of mass participation and polarization. Communist and Socialist parties were founded in the 1920s to join the traditional Conservatives and Radical parties in providing a full range of ideological spectrum. The military enjoyed political influence from 1924–1932, a Conservative government ruled until 1938, and a Popular Front coalition of the center to the Marxist-left led by the Radical party from 1938–1947.

In Peru, President Augusto Leguía ended the shaky democracy in 1919 by forcing his own continuation in office; he was overthrown in 1939 to be followed by elected governments representing the staus quo and elite sectors and supported by the armed forces. Ecuador continued to be ruled by elected civilian but rigidly conservative governments into World War II. Bolivia also continued its formal but often violent oligarchic democracy until 1930. The system ended with the Chaco War (see below), after which almost continual violent struggle occurred among conservative, reformist, and social revolutionary advocates. In Paraguay the Chaco War also left in its wake social ferment and political turmoil among similarly competing groups. Uruguay began its remarkable democratic transformation after the turn of the century, due primarily to the efforts of José Battle y Ordóñez in creating a broadly based, reformist-centrist and pragmatic political party that came to dominate the political system.

On the extrahemispheric level, the United Kingdom continued to play a major role in South America during the interwar years but its influence steadily declined. Britain yielded first position to the United States as the major source of foreign capital for South America. In international military relations, France at first seemed free from serious military competition in South America, since the Versailles Treaty prohibited Germany from sending military missions and instructors abroad and abolished all German military educational institutions that might receive foreign officers. The treaty proved to be ineffective, however, and Germany soon returned to a position of influence. French and German interbellum military relations were built on pre-war foundations: Germany recaptured its relationships with Argentina and Chile, and France, with Peru and Brazil. Competition increased in the 1930s, however, when South America received training missions from Italy, Great Britain, the United States, and even Switzerland and Spain. Air and police missions were added to the traditional military (army) and naval missions.

The Soviet Union became a participant after the Bolshevik Revolution of 1917 when it created and attempted to control Latin American Communist parties. Like Tsarist Russia before it, however, the Soviet Union did not make the region prominent in its calculations. In 1935 the Comintern ordered Latin American Communist parties to join popular fronts; its only success was in Chile. At the same time, Fascist Italy and Nazi Germany sought to mobilize overseas communities in support of their foreign policies. After 1939 the Franco government in Spain melded *hispanismo* with *falangismo* and called it *hispanidad*; its appeal in Spanish America was limited mostly to reactionary elements.

In inter-American relations, World War I had led to a troubled hemispheric neutrality; some governments in South America favored the central powers, others the allies and the United States. This was followed in the 1920s with a crisis in inter-American relations based on continuing Latin American outrage over U.S. interventionism. The U.S. Good Neighbor Policy in the 1930s involved, among other things, the acceptance of the nonintervention principle. While this may not have directly affected South American nations, it did enhance U.S. relations with them. The United States also adopted the policy of reciprocal trade agreements that South Americans accepted (with the important exception of Argentina, which agreed to a special trade arrangement with the United Kingdom). As the European crisis evolved into World War II, all Latin American states participated in creating a regional mutual security structure within the Inter-American System.

Many of the extant South American boundary, territorial, and power conflicts continued throughout the period. The dispute between Bolivia and Paraguay over the Chaco region led to an exceptionally bloody war from 1932–1935, the first major South American war in half a century. The origins of the Chaco War lay in conflicting jurisdictions during the colonial period and the subsequent undetermined national frontier, and in Bolivia's loss of its Pacific coastline in the War of the Pacific that led it to turn to the east for an outlet to the Atlantic. The war ended only by the exhaustion and devastation of both sides, with Paraguay as the military victor gaining most of the disputed territory in the settlement.

Antarctica became a salient part of the South American subsystem after the turn of the century. In the nineteenth century the surrounding waters had been of commercial fishing and scientific interest but no territorial claims had been made. The United Kingdom made the first formal claim in 1908; Argentina and Chile did not make their territorial claims until 1940 and 1943, respectively. In the meantime, expanding interest in exploration and scientific expeditions began that have continued to the present day. The first was a Scottish expedition led by the scientist explorer William Bruce, who established the first permanent base in the Antarctic in 1902. Annoyed by the lack of support extended by the British government, Bruce turned over the base to Argentina in 1902. Argentine geopoliticians were already asserting that Antarctica was an extension of Patagonia.[14]

World War I had cut off European trade with South America; trade soon recovered after the war. U.S. investment increased the most during the decade, British investments remained stable until they began to decline after 1928, and German and French investments declined during the 1920s. Regional trade and foreign investment shrank drastically during the world depression beginning in 1930. The lack of capital and the decline of purchasing power in markets around the globe were exacerbated by protectionist policies adopted by South America's principal trading partners.

Phase Four (1943–1965)

The fourth era of the South American regional subsystem began during World War II and continued throughout the postwar period until the mid-1960s. By the middle of the war the United States had replaced all of the other external powers as the primary external influence throughout the hemisphere. Subsequent hemispheric relations were further shaped by the advent of the cold war in 1947, and in 1959 by the Cuban Revolution and its subsequent attachment to the Soviet Union. Even during this period of U.S. hemispheric primacy, however, the United States did not dominate South American affairs to the extent that it did those in the Circum-Caribbean.[15]

War-exhausted European states retreated from strong competition. They did not view Latin America, even South America, as closely related to their primary interests. They were first absorbed with their own reconstruction and then preoccupied with European affairs, relations with the superpowers, and new arrangements in their empires. Nor did the Soviet Union show strong interest in Latin America; it was more concerned with contiguous areas and the cold war, and regarded all of Latin America as inevitably a U.S. sphere of influence. Soviet policies were mainly clandestine, operating directly through local Communist parties (the Comintern had been abolished in 1943).

By the end of World War II, the United States had replaced all foreign powers throughout Latin America as the principal foreign power. It was the largest trading partner and capital investor and monopolized military relations. Since the United States enjoyed a dominant position in South America and perceived little threat to the region from communism, it devoted little policy attention to the area. South America simply did not figure prominently in the global Cold War criteria that were fundamental to U.S. foreign policies. The United States prevailed in converting the Inter-American System into an anti-communist alliance, although South American states resisted the U.S. efforts to draw them into Cold War orientations. The system was strengthened with the Inter-American Treaty of Reciprocal Assistance (Rio Treaty—1947) and the Charter of the Organization of American States (1948), but application of mutual security provisions centered on Caribbean conflicts, and economic cooperation (the primary South American interest) lagged until the late 1950s.

The South American states joined the rest of those in Latin America in playing active roles in the United Nations System. They organized a caucus to ensure the representation of their interests and maximum voting strength. Latin Americans also enthusiastically embraced economic integration among themselves, but on subregional rather than region-wide bases. One such organization involved all of the South American states: the Latin American Free Trade Association (LAFTA), organized in 1960, was subscribed to by Mexico, Brazil, and the nine Spanish American states on the South American continent.

In the wake of the Cuban Revolution of 1959, the United States elevated Latin America in its global priorities and adopted developmentalist assistance policies toward the region. Rudimentary developmentalism commenced during the last part of the Eisenhower presidency; President Kennedy extended and multilateralized the policies under the Alliance for Progress, and President Johnson continued them during the first part of his administration. The United States defined security to include national development, coinciding with Latin America's primary concern with national development. Aid was linked not only to economic development, but to social change, military reform, and democratic advancement as well.

The alliance's proposed democratic underpinnings were undercut by a series of military coups. Toward the end of the Kennedy administration and throughout the Johnson presidency, the United States accommodated to the military governments, expressing a preference for constitutional democracy but holding that reformist military regimes could offer paths to development and alternatives to communism.

South American activities in the Antarctic were regulated by the Antarctic Treaty, which was signed in 1959 and entered into force in 1961. Argentina and Chile were among the twelve original signatory states (the others were Australia, France, New Zealand, Norway, the United Kingdom, Belgium, Japan, South Africa, the United States, and the Soviet Union). The treaty was designed to avoid territorial conflict in the Antarctic, internationalize and demilitarize Antarctica, prohibit nuclear testing and radioactive-waste disposal on the continent, and ensure that the region was used for peaceful purposes (including, most prominently, cooperative exploration and scientific investigations). Signatory states agreed to set aside (but not renounce) their territorial claims during the life of the treaty. Seven states had claimed sovereignty over some part of the Antarctic continent—with considerable overlapping of the Argentine, Chilean, and British claims.

Economic issues were primary considerations for the Southern Cone states and Brazil. World War II had stimulated Latin American international trade, especially with the Allies, who purchased the region's raw materials in large amounts for their war efforts; but new investment capital did not flow into the region until after the conflict was settled in 1945. In the postwar period, South American governments vigorously retired bonds and a number of them repatriated certain foreign enterprises. Argentina, for example, appropriated British railways and other transportation facilities; other governments acquired foreign-owned public utilities. Nevertheless, direct foreign investments increased; U.S. business was the main source of funds. In fact, U.S. economic dominance was evident for much of the period. Most of the South American states conducted at least one-third (often more) of their total trade with the United States. U.S. investments accounted for about 40 percent of the total invested in Brazil, about half in Peru, and almost 75 percent in Chile. Germany and Japan became the strongest competitors to the dominant U.S. position. British investments and trade fell off sharply, and France had a low level of trade.

Phase Five (1965–1980)

Beginning in the mid-1960s and continuing until the end of the 1970s, the South American subsystem passed through another period of its international life along several dimensions. South America recaptured its contours as an independent subsystem, which had been eroded but not destroyed during the post-war period of U.S. hemispheric dominance. Challenges to U.S. primacy accelerated after the mid-1960s, essentially the result of increased activities by extrahemispheric states and intensified South American assertiveness in international politics. During this period, the United States played an important but diminishing role.[16]

After the mid-1960s the United States again placed a low priority on Latin America, clearly evident in its South American relationships.[17] The Soviet-Cuban threat seemed to recede in the Americas and other parts of the world assumed greater importance (notably preoccupation with the war in Vietnam). The Johnson administration greatly reduced funding for the Alliance for Progress, and President Nixon explicitly abandoned developmentalism and trade concessions that had been promised were not forthcoming. A new attitude was adopted toward arms transfers. In 1967 Congress severely limited the amount of direct arms sales to Latin America, and prohibited shipments of "sophisticated arms," on the grounds that funds should be applied to economic and social development. The ceiling on the value of arms sales to Latin America was eliminated in 1974 because Latin Americans did not reduce their expenditures but simply went to other suppliers; transfers of sophisticated weaponry, however, were still prohibited.

U.S. policy largely ignored South America except for specific issues. The Nixon administration did not change the pragmatic approach to military governments. Strong overt and covert measures were brought to bear on the Marxist government of Salvador Allende in Chile, elected in 1970 and overthrown in 1973 to be replaced by a military regime headed by General Augusto Pinochet. President Ford continued general U.S. policies in South America, and bilateral relations remained essentially the same.

President Jimmy Carter adopted policies that further strained U.S.-South American relations. Carter considered human rights to be the fundamental tenet of U.S. foreign policy; he reduced the role of military instruments of policy and sought to reduce nuclear proliferation. U.S. relations with Brazil and the Southern Cone states were reduced to low levels of activity. The United States banned the military regimes in Argentina, Chile, Paraguay, and Uruguay from receiving further arms transfers and certain forms of economic aid. Although the United States did not ban arms transfers to Brazil, its criticism of the human rights situation there prompted Brazil to refuse acceptance of any more U.S. assistance. Brazil was further offended by U.S. opposition to its acquisition of a nuclear reactor from West Germany, which it insisted was

for energy development purposes entirely divorced from weapons proliferation.

South Americans continued to diversify their external relationships.
Almost all of them sought expanded markets and sources of investment
capital. Although they could become politically more independent with
little risk, they could not isolate themselves from the international
trading system and required close relations with major industrial nations.

Numerous nonhemispheric states and organizations responded to the
South American desires to broaden the range of bilateral relationships.
Europeans again assumed important roles, joined by Japan and other
states and organizations. The Socialist International and the Christian
Democratic World Union began to pay more attention to their Latin
American colleagues. German cultural institutes and political-party-
sponsored foundations were particularly active. Germany invested heavily in Brazil and increased its trade with Argentina. France also enlarged
its trade with Brazil. The United Kingdom was by now a minor player
in the trade drama, despite its position as a principal arms supplier.
Arms sales were an important component of trade relations. During
the decade after 1966, about 75 percent of all Latin American military
orders (excluding those of Cuba) were placed in Europe, mainly with
the United Kingdom, France, and West Germany. Six South American
states—Argentina, Brazil, Chile, Colombia, Peru, and Venezuela—placed
some 97 percent of the orders. During this period, Brazil developed a
self-sufficient arms industry and drastically reduced its imports.

The European Community (EC) during this period began to develop
Third World policies, including a Generalized System of Preference
(GSP) giving concessional terms of trade for certain developing-country
exports. South Americans especially complained that the GSP covered
only a small portion of their trade with Europe. They also complained
that the Lomé convention of 1974—in which the EC gave further
concessions to former European colonies—further discriminated against
their export products.

South America in a New Era

Subsystem Characteristics

By the early 1980s, South America appeared to have entered a sixth
phase of subsystem evolution that promises to project into the 1990s.
While a number of the characteristics of this current era continue from
the previous one that commenced in the mid-1960s, it also has important elements that distinguish it as a newly emerging age in South

American international relations. Certain continental and global trends have converged to alter the nature of international relationships and foreign policy issues. A more open international environment and diffused external influences have allowed local actors greater latitude in the conduct of their foreign relations and permitted extraregional actors—both state and transnational—to institutionalize substantial involvement, some building on traditional relationships and others evolving into new ones. This new era of South American international relations raises a number of complex issues.[18]

In domestic politics, all of the South American states except Chile and Paraguay have continued or moved away from military regimes to constitutional democracies. Internal political, technological, and economic developments have to some degree changed the traditional foundations of all South American polities. A majority of Chileans, in a 1988 referendum, indicated disillusionment with the military government (although a substantial minority favored its continuation), and the aging dictator of Paraguay will probably leave the scene soon. Guerrilla insurgency has all but disappeared except for Peru, where the problem is very serious. The democracies are faced with fundamental challenges to their legitimacy, however, as they must resolve severe dilemmas regarding, variously, the external debt, social and economic equity, justice for past regime abuses, the narcotics traffic, and, in general, other social problems and the consolidation and institutionalization of democratic gains on a sustained basis.[19]

Among the international consequences of redemocratization are: (1) until changes in the late 1980's, the isolation of Chile and Paraguay in the subsystem; (2) easier relations with the United States and Europe for the other states, with the softening of vexing human rights issues; and (3) a significant retreat from the geopolitical bases of foreign policies on the part of most South American governments.

Extensive domestic political change is clearly a salient part of the new South American picture, but it raises a number of thorny questions. What is the nature of Latin American democracy in terms of its traditions, values, and national idiosyncracies, and how enduring is the current trend? More to the point for this book, what is the foreign policy connection? What has been the relationship of democracy to foreign policy formulation and the consequences for their relations with each other and the outside world? How different are democratic and military governments in their international orientations? To what extent has there been a retreat from or continuation of geopolitical bases for policy and what does this mean for the various sets of relationships? Does it portend a more peaceful and cooperative and less conflictual set of relationships? If so, how enduring will the new situation be?

New developments have occurred in South American relations with the extrahemispheric actors. In addition to revival of the longstanding ties to Europe, closer relations have been established in certain cases with the Soviet Union and Japan as well as in the Middle East and Africa. There is nothing new in the extrahemispheric presence—a multiplicity of outsiders has almost always been the norm; what is new is the shifting importance of the extrahemispheric actors. Brazil especially has diversified its economy and developed a broad network of bilateral relationships. Its multilateralized trade structure includes ties in Europe, the Middle East and Africa, and Japan, in addition to those with the United States. Argentina trades heavily with the Soviet Union. Peru has purchased a large volume of armaments for its army from the Soviet Union, in addition to aircraft from France. The European Community's interest in Latin America is heavily South American; its importance dates from the late 1970s and, with its role in the Anglo-Argentine conflict of 1982, has been extended to the political arena. West Germany has significant investment in Brazilian manufacturing industry and France has a weighty commercial trading relationship there. Spain and (to a lesser degree) Portugal, with their own redemocratization and new membership in the European Community, have indicated ambitions to be the "bridge" between Europe and Latin America. The Holy See has revived its presence in South America, more than in other parts of Latin America, with the extended visits of Pope John Paul II and the successful mediation of the Beagle Channel dispute between Argentina and Chile. Japan has extended its volume of trade and commerce and continues to rely on the assistance of Japanese communities in South America, especially in Peru and, most notably, Brazil.

Current relations with the United States were shaped by the inauguration of President Ronald Reagan in 1981. The new administration sought to reorient U.S. policies toward the region, reformulating the priority placed on human rights under President Jimmy Carter and attempting to restore viable relations with the dominant military-led regimes in the region. Policy attention came to be focused overwhelmingly on the broader concept of redemocratization as well as on the debt issue. In tandem, there was a waning U.S. interest in an expanded security policy. South American governments are not deeply involved in East-West issues. The Argentine security involvement in Central America in cooperation with the United States was a temporary aberration. South American states have joined in the Contadora Support Group challenging U.S. actions in Central America, but it reflects foreign policy principles more than action, involves little cost or risk, and provides another way to signify autonomy from the United States.

Brazil is especially notable in this regard. Once the junior partner in a cooperative alignment with the United States, it has increased its ability over the past two decades to pursue an independent foreign policy. Brazil has successfully diversified its external relations and is not prepared to reemerge as subordinate in any future relationship. For a time, under the military government, Brazil was striving for world power status; those ambitions have receded, but Brazil's determination to pursue an independent foreign policy continues as part of its current calculations.

The U.S. presence in South America and relations with individual states remains important, however, and should not be underrated, especially with regard to economic relations. Local states' freedom of action are diminished because of their severe debt burdens. The United States remains the single largest trading partner for several of them, including Brazil. Any further U.S. collaboration with South American states, however, will require some sort of resolution of the debt problem, in the sense of satisfactory agreement about the future of the debt structure and repayment.

Two questions regarding the roles of extrahemispheric actors and of the United States in the new era seem to stand out: (1) To what degree, in fact, has the United States been supplanted in the region and what are the trends in this regard? (2) To what extent have all of the outsiders changed the perceptions of their interests in the new South American environment and adjusted their actions to the new realities?

Intra–South American relationships have undergone dramatic evolution, particularly in the relationships of Argentina with both Brazil and Chile. Power balances within the region have changed, with forces at work that both promote and erode their stability. A cooling of local conflicts and tensions, with the Brazilian-Argentine rapproachment that began in 1979, survived the Anglo-Argentine war and changes of governments in both countries, and has been extended since. Settlement of the contentious and persistent Beagle Channel dispute between Argentina and Chile has further reduced tensions in the region. These are both historic changes, given the traditions of Southern Cone rivalries.[20]

The key question about subregional relationships is this: How enduring is the new climate of cooperation and what are the prospects that it will be sustained?

The South Atlantic environment is colored primarily by the aftermath of the Anglo-Argentine war of 1982, and that of the Antarctic by anticipation of a treaty review beginning in 1991. Anglo-Argentine military conflict and the subsequent continuing British military presence in the South Atlantic is a major new factor. Issues related to the

South Atlantic and Antarctica are also of U.S. and extrahemispheric interest. What does the new era in South America mean for South Atlantic rivalries and for the globally-oriented Antarctic treaty regime as it deals with its own changing environment?

The question of the external debt for all South American countries dominates the economic system level. Debt emerged as the single most important international issue with deep and long-term implications. This problem promises to affect many aspects of South America's domestic and international politics for many years to come. Does the debt crisis portend a new dependency relationship with the United States; or does the "mutual hostage" consideration, along with expanded and diversified multilateral relationships allow them to continue to pursue relatively independent foreign policies? Again, how enduring is this reality?

Organization of the Book

In sum, South America presents a complex mix of factors in political, security, and economic fields and distinct difficulties and opportunities for state policies. The entire panorama of these factors needs analysis in terms of the special subregional environment and of how they bear on South American, U.S., and extrahemispheric interests and actions. The authors of the following essays bring to the subject a variety of experience, expertise, and perspectives.

The next two chapters deal with South American foreign policy formulation. Professor Howard J. Wiarda presents a broad overview of South American domestic politics and foreign policy. He extends his comments to assess the implications of South American domestic change for U.S. policy. Professor Jack Child analyzes the current status of geopolitical thinking on the part of South American policy makers.

Professor Wayne Selcher shifts analysis to the intraregional level with an examination of international relations within the Southern Cone. Among other things, Selcher draws sketches of individual regional country foreign policies toward their neighbors, complementing the efforts of Wiarda and Child.

The next two chapters focus on the orientations of the major actors outside of South America. Professor Morris Blachman engages in an original examination of the bases of U.S. policy in terms of the concept of the national interest. Dr. Georges Fauriol then shifts attention to extrahemispheric interests and actions. He deals with a broad array of entities—in Europe (the individual states, European Community, and transnational entities), the Soviet Union, Japan, and the Third World.

William Guttman follows with an analysis of the international political economy of the current South American external debt crisis. His topic involves a substantive set of economic issues that run through the actions and interactions of virtually all of the actors previously analyzed; in the current subsystem they clearly merit separate analysis. The final chapter is a dual effort. Wolf Grabendorff comments on the meaning of current triangular European–United States–South American relationships, from a European point of view; and Roberto Russell analyzes the South American domestic and international environments and their implications for both South American and United States policy formulation, from a South American perspective.

Notes

1. For overviews of Latin America's international relations from a subsystem perspective, see G. Pope Atkins, *Latin America in the International Political System*, 2d ed. (Boulder: Westview Press, 1989), Chapter 2; and Yale H. Ferguson in Werner Feld and Gavin Boyd, *Comparative Regional Systems* (New York: Pergamon, 1980).

2. Foreign policy analyses of the South American states are found in Harold E. Davis, Larman C. Wilson, and others, *Latin American Foreign Policies* (Baltimore: Johns Hopkins University Press, 1975); Gerhard Drekonja K. and Juan G. Tokatlian (eds.), *Teoria y Práctica de la Política Exterior Latinoamericana* (Bogotá: Universidad de los Andes, 1983); Jennie K. Lincoln and Elizabeth G. Ferris (eds.), *The Dynamics of Latin American Foreign Policies* (Boulder: Westview Press, 1984); Heraldo Muñoz and Joseph S. Tulchin (eds.), *Latin American Nations in World Politics* (Boulder: Westview Press, 1984); Juan Carlos Puig (ed.), *América Latina: Políticas Exteriores Comparadas* (Buenos Aires: Grupo Editor Latinoamericano, 1984); and Luciano Tomassini (ed.), *Relaciones Internacionales de la América Latina* (México: Fondo de Cultura Economica, 1981).

3. William Perry and Peter Wehner (eds.), *The Latin American Policies of U.S. Allies: Balancing Global Interests and Regional Concerns* (New York: Praeger, 1985) is a valuable collection of essays on the foreign policies of the nonhemispheric states toward Latin America. Excellent general treatments of European interests are Wolf Grabendorff and Riordan Roett (eds.), *Latin America, Western Europe, and the U.S.: Reevaluating the Atlantic Triangle* (New York: Praeger, 1985); and Esperanza Duran, *European Interests in Latin America* (London: Routledge and Kegan Paul for the Royal Institute of International Affairs, 1985). Alfred Glenn Mower, Jr., *The European Community and Latin America: A Case Study in Global Role Expansion* (Westport: Greenwood, 1982) discusses EC policies toward the South American states. The best analyses of the Soviet Union's policies are Cole Blasier, *The Giant's Rival: The USSR and Latin America*, rev. ed. (Pittsburgh: University of Pittsburgh Press, 1988); and Augusto Varas (ed.), *Soviet–Latin American Relations in the 1980s*

(Boulder: Westview Press, 1987). See also Gustavo Lagos Matus (ed.), *Las Relaciones entre América Latina, Estados Unidos y Europa Occidéntal* (Santiago: Instituto de Estudios Internacionales de la Universidad de Chile, 1979).

4. For recent survey histories of U.S. policies, see Graham H. Stuart and James Tigner, *Latin America and the United States*, 6th ed. (Englewood Cliffs: Prentice-Hall 1975); and Harold Molineu, *U.S. Policy Toward Latin America: From Regionalism to Globalism* (Boulder: Westview Press, 1986). Recent political science surveys are by Cole Blasier, *The Hovering Giant: U.S. Responses to Revolutionary Change in Latin America*, rev. ed. (Pittsburgh: University of Pittsburgh Press, 1985); Margaret Daly Hayes, *Latin America and the U.S. National Interest: A Basis for U.S. Foreign Policy* (Boulder: Westview Press, 1984); Michael J. Kryzanek, *U.S.-Latin American Relations* (New York: Praeger, 1985); Abraham F. Lowenthal, *Partners in Conflict: The United States and Latin America* (Baltimore: Johns Hopkins University Press, 1987); and Lars Schoultz, *National Security and United States Policy Toward Latin America* (Princeton: Princeton University Press, 1987).

5. Jack Child, *Geopolitics and Conflict in South America* (New York: Praeger, 1985) is the best presentation of geopolitical thinking in Brazil and the Southern Cone; Howard T. Pittman, *Geopolitics in the ABC Countries: A Comparison* (5 vols. Ph.D. dissertation, The American University, 1981), makes a valuable contribution with his exceptionally broad review of the regional literature.

6. Jack Child, *Antarctica and South American Geopolitics: Frozen Lebensraum* (New York: Praeger, 1988) is an excellent description and analysis.

7. Richard W. Mansbach, Yale H. Ferguson, and Donald E. Lampert, *The Web of World Politics: Nonstate Actors in the Global Political System* (Englewood Cliffs: Prentice-Hall, 1975) includes two chapters by Ferguson on nonstate actors in Latin America. On MNCs, see Donald P. Irish (ed.), *Multinational Corporations in Latin America* (Athens: Ohio University Press, 1978); and on guerrilla movements, consult Michael Radu and Vladimir Tismaneanu, *Revolutionary Organizations in Latin America* (Boulder: Westview Press, 1986).

8. Broad treatments on the debt problem, in which the South American states loom large, include Andres Bianchi, Robert Devlin, and Joseph Ramos, *External Debt in Latin America: Adjustment Policies and Renegotiation* (Boulder: Lynne Rienner Publishers, 1985); Jonathan Hartlyn and Samuel A. Morley (eds.), *Latin American Political Economy: Financial Crisis and Political Change* (Boulder: Westview Press, 1986); Antonio Jorge and Jorge Salazar Carrillo (eds.), *Foreign Investment, Debt, and Economic Growth in Latin America* (London: Macmillan), 1988); Robert A. Pastor (ed.), *Latin America's Debt Crisis: Adjusting to the Past or Planning for the Future* (Boulder: Lynne Rienner Publishers, 1987); Rosemary Thorp and Laurence Whitehead (eds.), *Latin American Debt and the Adjustment Crisis* (Pittsburgh: University of Pittsburgh Press, 1987); and Howard J. Wiarda, *Latin America at the Crossroads: Debt and Development Strategies for the 1990s* (Boulder: Westview Press, 1986).

9. This section is a specialized (South American) version following the lines of a region-wide analysis of the Latin American subsystem and its several subregions by Atkins, *Latin America in the International Political System*

(1989), Chapter 2. An international history by Harold Eugene Davis, John J. Finan, and F. Taylor Peck, *Latin American Diplomatic History: An Introduction* (Baton Rouge: Louisiana State University Press, 1977), emphasizing Latin American points of view, is divided into similar time periods.

10. Davis in Davis, Finan, and Peck, *Latin American Diplomatic History* (1977), pp. 17 and 65.

11. Harold Davis in Davis, Finan, and Peck, *Latin American Diplomatic History* (1977), p. 65.

12. The most authoritative treatment of the South American balance of power system in the nineteenth century is by Robert N. Burr, *By Reason or Force: Chile and the Balancing of Power in South America, 1830–1905* (Berkeley: University of California Press, 1967).

13. For a general overview of this period, see Glen St. John Barclay, *Struggle for a Continent: The Diplomatic History of South America, 1917–1945* (London: Whitefriars, 1971).

14. Child, *Antarctica and South American Geopolitics* (1988).

15. Valuable surveys are provided by Samuel L. Baily, *The United States and the Development of South America, 1945–1975* (New York: New Viewpoints, 1976); and F. Parkinson, *Latin America, the Cold War, and the World Powers, 1945–1973* (Beverly Hills: Sage, 1974).

16. David Collier (ed.), *The New Authoritarianism in Latin America* (Princeton: Princeton University Press, 1979); Howard J. Wiarda (ed.), *The Continuing Struggle for Democracy in Latin America* (Boulder: Westview Press, 1980); and Howard Handelman and Thomas G. Sanders (eds.), *Military Government and the Movement toward Democracy in South America* (Bloomington: Indiana University Press, 1980).

17. Abraham F. Lowenthal articulates the U.S. "hegemonic presumption" and the decline of U.S. influence in "The United States and Latin America: Ending the Hegemonic Presumption," *Foreign Affairs*, 55 (October 1976), pp. 199–213.

18. Helio Jaguaribe, *El Nuevo Escenario Internacional* (México: Fondo de Cultura Económica, 1985), a leading Brazilian analyst, evaluates the new international scene and Latin America's place in it. Abraham F. Lowenthal, "Ronald Reagan and Latin America: Coping with Hegemony in Decline," in Kenneth A. Oye, Robert J. Lieber, and Donald Rothchild (eds.), *Eagle Defiant: United States Foreign Policy* (Boston: Little, Brown & Co., 1983) extends his theme of degenerating U.S. authority. Robert Wesson (ed.), *U.S. Influence in Latin America in the 1980s* (New York: Praeger, 1982) also considers decreasing U.S. leverage; he applies the same theme to Brazil in his *The United States and Brazil: Limits of Influence* (New York: Praeger, 1981).

19. Guillermo O'Donnell, Philippe C. Schmitter, and Laurence Whitehead (eds.), *Transitions from Authoritarian Rule: Prospects for Democracy* (Baltimore: Johns Hopkins University Press, 1986); James M. Malloy and Mitchell A. Seligson, *Authoritarians and Democrats: Regime Transition in Latin America* (Pittsburgh: Pittsburgh University Press, 1987); and Monica Hirst and Roberto Russell, *Democracia y Política Exterior: Los Casos de Argentina y Brasil*

(Buenos Aires: FLACSO, Programa Buenos Aires, vol. 4, no. 12, April-June 1987).

20. Institute for European–Latin American Relations (IRELA), *A New Phase in Latin American Integration? The 1986 Agreements between Argentina and Brazil* (Madrid: IRELA, December 1986).

2

South American Domestic Politics and Foreign Policy

Howard J. Wiarda

This chapter explores the domestic bases for foreign policy changes in South America and their implications for U.S. policy. It focuses on the following areas: the transitions to democracy in the region, rising nationalism, strengthened political and economic institutions, European influences, the debt crisis, the drug issue, public opinion, and the search for new social and political models. In all of these areas, South American and U.S. priorities and agendas are becoming so far apart as to be almost irreconcilable. Clearly the changes that have been occurring in South America call for a major rethinking and reassessment of U.S. strategies in the area. Given the crippled U.S. political condition and quasi-paralyzed foreign policy, however, its will and capacity to make these adjustments remains very much open to question.

South American countries have changed enormously in the last twenty-five years. They are no longer weak, underdeveloped countries certain to follow the U.S. lead on most issues. Rather, in the last quarter century, much of South America has emerged from underdevelopment to occupy positions as middle-range powers and Newly Industrialized Countries (NICs). The economies of Argentina and Brazil are major forces to reckon with in the world arena. Moreover, these and other South American countries have become far more modernized and institutionalized in both a political and an economic sense.[1] Greater affluence and development have been accompanied by stronger nationalism and more assertiveness in international affairs. While Argentina, Brazil, Chile, and Peru, and even Bolivia, Ecuador, Paraguay, and Uruguay, are still dependent on the United States in some ways, they have become increasingly independent in others. Independence has been indicated by reestablishing relations with Cuba, staking out increasingly

nonaligned positions, and generally becoming more and more inclined
to "go it alone" in international affairs. These more independent positions are widely accepted and applauded by South American populations. The U.S. presence and position have undergone slippage, and
a certain estrangement has set in with a growing separation and dist-
ancing from the United States.[2] Especially given their new-found economic power and the role of a number of the South American states
as middle-level actors on the world's stage, these changes carry immense
implications for U.S. foreign policy.

U.S. policy in Latin America has always been crisis-oriented. Rather
than paying serious and sustained attention to the area and thus
anticipating new developments with a coherent, informed, rational, and
long-term policy, the United States instead has reacted to crises only
after they occur and in an ad hoc, often ill-informed, and usually fickle
way. Once the crisis-of-the-moment passes, the United States again
tends to ignore the area, turn to issues and areas it presumes to be
more important, and resurrect the older policy (or non-policy) of benign
neglect—until some new crisis again forces its way onto the front pages.
These attitudes and reactive strategies also help explain the neglect,
indifference, and inattention to the critical changes that have been
occurring on the South American continent, changes that will also,
inevitably, carry major implications for U.S. foreign policy.[3]

Democratization

The general trend toward democracy in Latin America in recent
years has been heartening.[4] The corporatist and bureaucratic-authori-
tarian regimes that prevailed in the 1970s have now, for the most part,
been replaced. Whereas a decade ago, two-thirds of the Latin American
countries were under one or another form of military and authoritarian
control, that proportion has now been reversed: over two-thirds of the
countries (if one includes Mexico) representing more than 90 percent
of the Latin American population are now governed democratically. In
the South American continent, Argentina, Bolivia, Brazil, Ecuador, Peru,
and Uruguay have all made dramatic returns to democratic rule. Bolivia, Ecuador, and Peru are perhaps shaky democracies, but democracies nonetheless. Within this region, only Chile and Paraguay are not
democracies.[5]

The United States has been strongly supportive of these democratic
transitions, bolstering democracy at the rhetorical level, assisting it to
flower, and even putting pressures on nondemocratic regimes to move
toward democracy. It is true that most of the impetus to democracy in
South America in recent years has come from South Americans them-

selves and not directly from the United States; but the United States has been a vocal and active supporter of democracy in the region and has tried to assist in the consolidation of democratic regimes once they are in place.[6]

U.S. motives in supporting these thrusts have been both ethical and strategic. As a democracy itself with a certain missionary tradition of trying to bring the benefits of democracy to other countries, the United States is naturally pleased that Latin America is now also, finally, achieving democracy. The strategic reasons are at least as important. Democratic regimes, the United States has found, tend to be less bellicose, less involved in their neighbors' internal affairs, less inclined to conflict, and in general cause fewer problems for the United States than other kinds of regimes. Strong democracies are the best guards against communism and Marxism-Leninism on the one hand and repressive authoritarians on the other—both of which cause the United States no end of trouble. In addition, although it took the Reagan administration some time to learn these lessons, standing for democracy is the best and surest way to get the Congress, the bureaucracy, the media, church and human rights groups, and public opinion—to say nothing of U.S. allies—to support the goals of U.S. policy. For the United States, then, a properly-conceived democratic posture is not just the moral and right thing to proclaim; it also serves important strategic interests.[7]

It should not be thought, however, that having a larger number of democracies in South America represents a cure-all for U.S. foreign policy problems there. Unfortunately that is the conclusion that too many analysts, inside and outside the government, have reached: that once Latin America achieves democracy, then all the issues that separate them will also be resolved. It is true that Presidents Alfonsín (Argentina), Febres (Ecuador), García (Peru), Paz (Bolivia), Sanguinetti (Uruguay), and Sarney (Brazil) are probably the most moderate and most democratic collection of leaders we are likely to see for a long time. That is by no means to say, however, that differences have been ameliorated. Furthermore, there seems to be no serious and coordinated effort within the U.S. government to deal with the continuing disagreements between the United States and these governments—however democratic they may be or, in one or two cases, precisely because they are democratic. At least six major areas of concern command our attention.

First, important countries like Argentina and Brazil have some fundamental disagreements with the United States over basic national interests. These differences will not be ameliorated by any change of regimes in Buenos Aires or Brasilia.[8]

Second, the very process of democratization has opened up new vistas, new promises, and also new fads to the South Americans. By no means should it be assumed that all of these new perspectives will be favorable to U.S. interests; indeed quite the contrary is likely to result—in the form of greater sentiment for nonalignment, stronger anti-Americanism, and more articulate, widespread, and more publicly-expressed opposition to specific U.S. policies.

Third, the form that Latin American democracy has taken (in Argentina, for example) is far closer to European-style democracy (as in France, Spain, or Italy) than it is to the U.S. system. That is not necessarily a barrier to good relations, but it does complicate the issue (and the lives of many U.S. administrators abroad and their programs) and it does not provide the common political-cultural basis of agreement that the United States enjoys with some other countries.

Fourth, Latin American democracy may be inclined to take some radical directions. Among South American intellectuals and church people particularly, the insistence is often strong that the transition to democracy in their countries has so far been only partial and incomplete. They will concede that "some" progress has been made, but only "bourgeois democracy" has been achieved. Now, they believe, it is necessary to take an additional step, which in the Marxian lexicon they use is inevitable, toward a more "advanced" and "progressive" form. They wish to be on the "cutting edge" of a new kind of democracy. By this they often mean socialism and perhaps even Marxism-Leninism, but of an "independent" sort. None of these postures would seemingly bode well for U.S. policy.[9]

Fifth, the democratic regimes that have come to power in South America are not at all in agreement with U.S. policies on a host of issues: trade, debt, Central America, strategic policy, the Falklands/Malvinas controversy (in the Argentine case), nuclear weapons, and so on. Argentine President Alfonsín, for example, emphasized that while his country was Western in geographic location, culture, and political institutions, it would be even-handed, almost neutralist and non-aligned, in its foreign policy. He was prepared to admit no legitimate strategic interests to the United States in all of Latin America.[10] Clearly this will not do from a U.S. perspective, because the United States does perceive legitimate strategic interests even in the Southern Cone. Alfonsín was not alone in these sentiments, however; the foreign ministries of Brazil, Peru, and Uruguay have pushed in many of the same directions.

Sixth, U.S. contingency planning has made no provision for dealing with a reversal of the current democratic trends. The United States has allowed its hopes and wishes for the area to get ahead of serious analysis. Some academic literature tends to see democracy as the inevitable end product of an historical evolution that, once achieved, is unlikely (except by a full-scale fascist regime) to be reversed.[11] Democracy in Bolivia, Ecuador, and Peru is very fragile, however, and could be overthrown at any time; and in Argentina, Brazil, and Uruguay democracy is not as well consolidated, let alone institutionalized, as North Americans would like to think. The United States needs to be prepared in a policy sense if democracy were to be overthrown—especially, as has usually been the case in the past, if several overthrows occur at about the same time.

This is not to say that the United States should not warmly applaud and support the several transitions to democracy in South America. It should and does. But the United States also needs to recognize that not all the outcomes of those transitions will be benevolent toward the United States. Furthermore, the United States needs to develop contingency planning should the democratic trends be reversed.[12]

Nationalism

The new democracy in South America has helped unleash new forms of nationalism as potent political forces. Nationalism existed under the previous military regimes in their national security state forms.[13] The new nationalism, however, is more widespread and reaches to the popular level, and, consequently, is more explosive.

The rising new nationalism in South America takes several different forms. One is a new sense of pride in things Latin American and a corresponding insistence on doing things in a Latin American way. This includes pride in the new political institutions and a desire to develop indigenous democratic institutions and models. We may yet see significant experimentation with new institutions in South America, with indigenous and particularly Latin American ways of doing things (although there may be violent disagreements over what precisely that implies), or with particular and (it will be argued) uniquely Latin American combinations of Western and indigenous models.[14] In particular, with the simultaneous transition to democracy in Spain and Portugal and in South America, we are likely to see a new sense of pride in Iberian-Latin institutions and an effort to set them in marked contrast to Anglo-Saxon ones.

A second manifestation of the new nationalism is a growing resentment of U.S. officials operating in the South American countries and increased difficulties on their part in working with their South American counterparts. Unlike the early 1960s, when U.S. personnel, know-how, and the Alliance for Progress money that went with them were, for the most part, warmly welcomed, the jobs performed by U.S. agencies are now much more difficult. Relations are seldom easy and often strained.

Polls and survey data are quite mixed in their conclusions about South American public opinion. Many South Americans still admire the United States and its accomplishments, affluence, and technology. The degree of admiration for U.S. political institutions, however, has declined. Most South Americans prefer their own cultural and social institutions: The family, strong interpersonal relations, and informal and relaxed lifestyles. They do not view U.S. cities, crime and violence, government and its leadership, or military institutions as something to aspire to or imitate. Admiration for U.S. institutions is much stronger among the older and fading generation than it is among the younger and rising generations.[15]

A third aspect of nationalism is generational in a broader sense than indicated above. The older generation of South American democratic leaders—including the likes of Eduardo Frei, Rómulo Betancourt, Galo Plaza, Fernando Belaúnde Terry, and Felipe Herrera—understood and admired the United States or knew how to function as if they did. In contrast, the newer generation now coming to power as agency heads, as cabinet officers, and even (in Peru) as presidents, grew up intellectually in the 1970s with Marxism and dependency theory, with the U.S. efforts directed against Salvador Allende in Chile, with U.S. aid to and close relations with the military-authoritarians of that era, with a United States that had ended the Alliance for Progress and viewed Latin America through the prism of "benign neglect," and with the twin U.S. traumas of Vietnam and Watergate. For this generation the United States is no longer the model to emulate, and an underlying hostility lurks beneath the surface.

A combination of nationalist resentments have come together over the debt issue. While most South American governments have acted responsibly on the matter of debt, their people are becoming increasingly impatient. They blame the foreign commercial banks, the International Monetary Fund (IMF), and most of all the U.S. government for their economic woes. Moreover, even in educated circles the assumption is strong that the IMF, the commercial banks, and other international lenders operate at the behest of the U.S. government. The stagnation, high unemployment, poverty, underdevelopment, and inability to accommodate the massive debt are blamed on the United States, not on their own corrupt or inefficient governments. Waiting in the wings to take political advantage of these bitter sentiments are populist and demagogic politicians, such as Luiz "Lula" da Silva in Brazil. Unlike the present leadership, these demagogues would repudiate the debt entirely and garner immense political backing in the process—regardless of the dire consequences for their nations' economies.[16]

International bankers and U.S. government officials find it difficult to understand the emotional depth of these nationalist sentiments. They cannot comprehend how South American leaders could sacrifice their nations' future credit worthiness, realizing that assets would surely be seized and all foreign credits would immediately be cancelled if such an "emotional" step as repudiation of debts were taken. These analysts, however (as I have written elsewhere),[17] underestimate the strength of Latin American sentiment on this issue. This is not to predict that all of South America is about to repudiate its debts tomorrow. It is to say, however, that one should not miscalculate the Latin American willingness to suffer heroic sacrifice for some glorious (however futile) cause. Those who are inclined toward such underestimation should read again the Ernest Hemingway novels about Spain—or perhaps García Marquez![18]

It should also be said that right-wing Latin American nationalism and anti-Americanism are as prevalent as the left-wing varieties. Moreover, it is difficult to detect when some fine lines have been passed. In Peru, for example, a logical policy for the United States might be to extend economic aid despite President García's anti-American rhetoric and wait for his term to end. But García may have already crossed the line that separates rhetorical anti-Americanism for domestic political purposes from the real thing. He has been anti-American in private as well as in public; he needlessly (and perhaps foolishly) antagonized Secretary of State George Shultz and thereby hurt Peru's interests. In Chile, it is the right-wing anti-Americanism that is virulent, particularly as a result of U.S. pressures on strongman Augusto Pinochet. The Southern Cone has a long history of right-wing anti-Americanism and one should not underestimate its xenophobic manifestations.[19]

Institutionalization

It is probably fair to say that South American institutions now are stronger than they were the last time democracy prevailed in the region in the early 1960s. The point has general theoretical interest as well as relevance to the analysis of foreign policy. Most students of Third World development, especially those of Latin America, have been highly critical of the influential writings of W. W. Rostow and their incorporation into U.S. foreign assistance programs (Rostow was influential as head of policy planning at the State Department). Rostow, and numerous other early scholars of development, seemed to argue that development followed an inevitable, automatic, and universal path that led to a socially just, pluralist, affluent, democratic, moderate, and middle-class society that looked like an idealized version of the United States itself. The Latin American experience in the late 1960s and early 1970s, however, seemed to invalidate the Rostow formulations; a wave of military coups occurred, democracy was halted, the middle class often proved to be reactionary rather than progressive, and pluralism and social justice were attacked. All of Rostow's assumptions seemed wrong.[20]

The return to democracy in South American countries may force us to reassess Rostow's formulations. Rostow was clearly wrong in the short term, but in the long run he may yet prove to have been correct (here the discussion at the theoretical level has relevance for the South American countries). There is more affluence in South America now than in 1960 when Rostow wrote, the middle class is considerably larger and more secure, the lower classes are often better off, there is a stronger sense of social justice, literacy is more widespread, pluralism is better established, the associational life (business groups, labor unions, political parties, civic associations of all sorts) is far stronger, and there has been a gradual evolution toward democratic rule. In short, the social base is now far stronger and more solidly supportive of democracy than it was a quarter century ago when the Alliance for Progress, in consonance with Rostow's ideas, was launched.[21] It may be, therefore, that the era of dictatorship and bureaucratic-authoritarianism of the 1960s and 1970s was only an aberration or temporary interruption, and that the "inevitable" and "universal" effects of modernization have in fact worked their inexorable effects toward moderate, middle-of-the-road democracy. That Rostow may be correct is something that most scholars of development are not ready to admit, but we should be prepared to acknowledge that he may have been prescient.

All this implies that democracy in South America has a considerably stronger base than previously, that South America's historic associational and institutional vacuum has begun to be filled, and that the chances of consolidating and sustaining democracy are now better. One should not overstate this point, however; it remains necessary to make some sharp distinctions about the type and degree of institutionalization with regards to the individual countries of the region.

It is useful to distinguish first between social, economic, and political institutionalization. In South America, it seems clear that in the last twenty-five years considerably more social and economic growth has occurred than political development. Urbanization, social change, rising literacy, economic modernization, and rising living standards have all gone forward at rapid rates; but political development—democratization, institutionalization, associational life—while improving, has lagged behind. We now know that social change, economic growth, and political development are not automatically correlated; indeed, socioeconomic change may even undermine and disrupt political development.[22]

Second, we must distinguish between democratic and authoritarian institutionalization. While attention has generally been focused on the transitions to democracy in many countries, in Chile and Paraguay institutionalized authoritarianism has been very difficult to overcome. Furthermore, one should not forget the strong authoritarian tendencies still present in the countries that have made the transition to democracy, which could reassert themselves under certain conditions.

The distinction between countries needs to be made. The situation and conditions in each country are different; no single transcendental process is at work in South America. Argentina under President Alfonsín was more democratic than at any time in the last sixty years; but there were also signs of the old fragmentation, and the strength of the nondemocratic and antidemocratic forces should not be underestimated. Brazil's President Sarney consolidated his position, but he was still looked upon by all sides as a weakly legitimated and transitional president. (The question is "transitional" to what?) Bolivia is economically bankrupt and politically chaotic; it is a miracle that Bolivian democracy has lasted as long as it has. Ecuador has a "tempered democracy": An elected government, but one where the familiar disintegrative processes continue—*pronunciamentos* by military leaders, a congress in the hands of the opposition, efforts to impeach the president, threats by the army to dissolve the congress, and other rumblings from the barracks.[23] Uruguay has not solved its pressing economic problems and, like Argentina, the polity remains fragmented.

Hence, while it is probably accurate to argue that the developmental theories of Rostow and others deserve a close reexamination based on the longer-range trends in Latin America toward democratization, in the short term it is clear there is nothing automatic, universal, or inevitable about the process.

New Models

All of the older models of development in Latin America are dead. None of them have worked as anticipated. The dysfunctionality of the development models ranges across the political spectrum from left to right. The general discrediting (for different reasons) includes Cuba under Fidel Castro as well as Chile under Pinochet, the Nicaraguan Revolution as well as the earlier revolution of the Brazilian generals. In between stand a variety of other "models" that also have not operated very well: the "Nasserism" of the Peruvian military from

1968–1975, the "socialism" of Michael Manley in Jamaica, the "corporatism" and bureaucratic-authoritarianism of a number of military regimes in the 1960s and 1970s, and "populism," Peronism, and the various other "isms" tried earlier.[24]

Nor is the United States regarded any longer as the premier political and economic model to emulate. This stands in marked contrast to the situation 125 years ago when, as the report of a commission to rewrite the Argentine constitution put it, "the democratic government of the United States represents the last word of human logic"; and again, "the committee has been guided . . . by the provisions of a similar constitution recognized as the most perfect, viz., that of the United States."[25] One cannot conceive of a South American politician saying anything similar today.

The current situation also stands in sharp contrast to that of twenty-five years ago when the United States stood as the political, economic, and moral exemplar. Then came the assassination of John F. Kennedy, racial conflict, Vietnam, student protests, urban violence, Watergate, Jimmy Carter's national "malaise," economic downturn, Ronald Reagan's conservative free-market ideology, the decline of American competitiveness, and so on. None of these events, persons, or processes enhanced U.S. prestige in South America. In fact, over the past quarter century, the elements in American society that Latin Americans most admired have steadily eroded. The size and strength of the U.S. economy and its technology evoke a grudging and perhaps jealous admiration, but this is based on pragmatic needs rather than any emotionally positive response. In this and other ways, U.S. relations with South America have become more a marriage of convenience than anything resembling a love match. South America knows that it needs U.S. capital, investment, technology, and access to markets, but little sentiment exists to be like the United States in very many particulars.[26]

Curiously, while the United States has declined as a model, South American efforts to fashion indigenous models have not worked out very well either.[27] In the 1960s and 1970s, there was a considerable fascination in various countries with fashioning an indigenous model of development, or one that combined local features with the best of imported institutions. The feature that would have to be accommodated in such a model, however, included corporatism, organic-statism, patrimonialism, and authoritarianism.[28] For some countries, it also implied bringing the Indian civilizations into the political process as full participants, and erecting a social, cultural, and political system based on significant Indian input. While many intellectuals were sympathetic to the idea of a genuinely Latin American model of development, they were divided over the specific ingredients that would be included. They much preferred, it turned out, a model that blamed the continent's problems on outside (especially U.S.) influence, and the move to fashion a Latin American model of development declined.

Little remains with regard to an appropriate and desirable developmental model. The older Latin American designs are dead, the newer ones are moribund, and the U.S. is of diminished attractiveness. Consequently, many South Americans have tended to look toward Europe and to find certain "advanced" or "progressive" manifestations to be admired. It is not Margaret Thatcher's United Kingdom or Helmut Kohl's Federal Republic of Germany toward which South Americans look. They are more attracted to Mitterrand's vision of a socialist France (while Jacques Lang and Régis Debray were seen as defining the regime, before Mitterrand began following a more conservative course) or to the Spanish socialism of Felipe González (while he, too, was taking an anti-American and pro-Nicaraguan stance and before reality set in there as well). In these ways South Americans are searching for a model that is not only an alternative to the U.S. example, but that stands as critical of it.

Other South Americans are not any more sure that "progressive" Europe (West or East) is any more an appropriate model for them than is the United States. They argue that neither the United States nor Europe provide models for South America.[29] More and more South Americans are concluding that only a pragmatic, eclectic, pluralist, and reasonable regime that is neither too far to the right nor too far to the left will serve them well. This helps account for the current presence in South America of more centrist, moderate, middle-of-the-road governments than ever before in hemispheric history.

The Debt Crisis

Latin America has been going through the worst economic crisis since the 1930s. In country after country, the economy has turned stagnant or shrunk, living standards have fallen, and the gross national product has been set back to 1960s' levels.[30] The burden of the decline has fallen heaviest on the shoulders of the poor.

The causes of the recent downturn are several. They include quadrupling oil prices during the 1970s, declining global markets for Latin America's primary exports, diminished U.S. aid during the 1970s era of "benign neglect," and extravagant and often wasteful spending by Latin American governments and state agencies. To help maintain existing economic levels in the face of these long-term downward trends, the Latin American governments and public sector enterprises borrowed heavily at high interest rates from commercial banks that were flush with petrodollars, with the encouragement of the U.S. government seeking to substitute private loans for public foreign aid. As long as the world economy was expanding, the loans did not appear to be onerous; once the global recession hit in 1979–80, however, it became impossible for the debtor countries to meet their obligations. Interest payments continue to be paid to the banks but virtually no principal. Meanwhile, the total debt for the continent has soared to over $400 billion—enough to threaten not only the Latin American economies but the commercial banks and perhaps the international financial system as well.

Although the U.S. government has proved willing to step in during genuine emergencies, such as in the Mexican bankruptcy of 1982 and with the Baker Plan to stimulate U.S. investment in Latin America and replenish the international lending banks, it generally prefers to let the parties to the problem—the commercial banks and the Latin American governments—work out solutions by themselves. The U.S. position is that these are regular commercial debts and the Latin American countries must honor their obligations. In practice, this has meant that the IMF imposes conditions on the Latin American countries, pronouncing them "credit-worthy" and therefore eligible for more loans provided they put their internal economic houses in order. The conditions have generally included cutbacks in public services, reduced subsidies of such items as food and oil products, diminished social programs for the poor, decreased imports, wage freezes for or firings of employees in the public services, general belt-tightening, and increases in exports which are usually achieved at the cost of domestic consumption. None of these programs help increase the popularity of the government that carries them out; austerity has in fact proved to be unpopular at a time of rising expectations and more combustible nationalism throughout the hemisphere. Those most often blamed are the local governments, the banks, the IMF, and, especially, the United States. "Outside forces" are viewed as most responsible and as collectively serving as the handmaiden of U.S. interests.[31]

South Americans tend to see the debt as part of the northern nations' obligations to the southern ones. The massive transfer of wealth from the United States to South America that has occurred as a result of the unpaid debt is the main agenda item of the North-South "negotiations." Besides, some South Americans reason, this is money owed them for past decades or centuries of exploitation of their resources. The U.S. banks were in it for their own profit, the argument goes, and therefore the risks involved are the banks' responsibility. In any case, it is now the obligation of the banks and the U.S. government to help debtors out of the crisis. Rather than seeing unemployment and hunger spread and living standards decline, the United States and its banks (one and the same, in this way of thinking) have an obligation to come to their rescue and forgive the debt.

South American governments have so far rejected this popular notion concerning the debt. In the new climate of democracy and the necessity of government to respond to popular demands, however, this cannot last forever. Most governments of the area continue to pay lip service to their obligations to repay their debts. Everyone knows that they cannot pay in full but that the fiction must be maintained. By making some attempts at repayment, they can continue to qualify for more loans and avoid the ostracism and severe financial costs that an outright repudiation would bring. But demagogic politicians are waiting for the next round of elections; for nationalist reasons and to garner popular acclaim they would be willing to remove the oppressive debt in one fell swoop. They reason—perhaps accurately—that even if they repudiate their debts, the United States would eventually bail them out in order to serve the strategic interests at stake.

Distinctions must again be made among individual countries. Bolivia is in de facto default of the debt, although creditors do not publicly acknowledge the fact out of fear of spreading the possibility of repudiation to the larger debtors. Peru is, like Bolivia, nearly broke, so that President Alan García's gratuitous statement that Peru would pay 10 percent of its earnings to service the debt was actually that much more than Peru had been paying. Chile's economy has gone through boom-and-bust cycles and is currently in a boom of indeterminable length, which also had the effect of again propping up the regime of Augusto Pinochet. Paraguay, a traditional economy now embarking on rapid growth, followed a conservative fiscal policy and did not borrow so heavily abroad. Argentina and Brazil are the key countries: they both have massive debt and have so far followed "responsible" policies of paying lip service to their obligations and obeying IMF conditions of imposing austerity in return for a continuing flow of new loans. But in both countries there are powerful opposition movements that may come to power who are calling for outright repudiation and an end to the debt burden.

The debt issue is complicated because it is not just a financial one (the obligation to pay back the loans), but involves political, nationalist, and strategic issues of major importance as well. So far, the debt problem has been managed relatively successfully, but at any moment the proverbial child is liable to call out, "But the Emperor has no clothes on."

The Drug Issue

U.S. attitudes and policy toward drugs have gone through various permutations in recent years. First came a limited and lackadaisical effort to discourage drug use directed at the audience of U.S. consumers. That attempt failed in part because drug use was at that time widely thought to be a "lifestyle" issue on which persons could exercise "choices," and in part because the warnings coming from the Reagan administration fell on deaf ears. When it proved impossible to change American consumer habits, the focus shifted to the source of the drugs. Numerous efforts failed to persuade, cajole, or pressure South American (and other) governments into cutting off production. Since it most directly affected U.S.–Latin American relations, it is this second strategy that is the focus of the following remarks. The failure of this second strategy led to a third strategy, a much more sophisticated effort aimed at the U.S. public via television and other media, featuring prominent athletes and other cult and opinion leaders. It was much more successful, partly because by then the medical evidence of the permanent damage done by drugs to the mind and body was overwhelming.

But let us return to the second stage of the anti-drug campaign, which most affected U.S.–South American relations. We concentrate here on the international dimensions of the problem and its potential to wreak havoc on U.S.–Latin American ties, leaving aside for now any moral considerations. We present a listing of why the issue is so complex and difficult and why the potential for severe damage to U.S.–South American relations arising out of it is so alarming.[32]

1. Drug use in a mild form is habitual and traditional among many Latin American indigenous elements, who chew coca leaves as a means of warding off hunger and pain. Unlike the United States, there is in Latin America no Calvinistic sense of sin or moral outrage at such widespread popular use of the drug.

2. Drugs (marijuana, poppies, coca) are a profitable cash crop for many Latin American farmers. They do not use the products themselves, there is no moral stigma attached to growing them, and their incomes are augmented four or five times as compared with growing more traditional crops. It is unreasonable to suggest that poor farmers give up this new income for the sake of a U.S. anti-drug campaign.

3. Most Latin Americans of the upper and middle classes do not use drugs, nor do their children. They therefore do not see the drug problem with the same urgency as do persons, especially parents, in the United States. Nor is the limited drug use in Latin America related to a rising incidence of crime and violence as it is in the United States. Drugs are not a major police problem for most South American coun-

tries. Until this changes—and there are signs that drug use by Latin American teens and others is spreading and thereby becoming a moral and a police problem—North Americans cannot expect Latin Americans to view the drug issue in the same scary way that they do.

4. Efforts to eradicate drug production do not cause the producers to disappear. Instead, they simply move on to another country. For example, Colombians turn to drug production as a major export crop (now surpassing coffee!) developed only after the eradication campaign in Mexico forced the producers to move to another country.

5. Drug production by now is so widespread that it cannot be eradicated. Many areas of South America are seas of drug plants, rather like wheat in the American midwest. It is inconceivable that all this production can be eliminated.

6. The highly publicized campaigns to wipe out the production have not been effective. Production is carried out not in factories that are visible to helicopters and patrolling police, but in small, isolated, pots-and-pans processes located in dense jungles. No sooner is one of these primitive "factories" found and destroyed than more spring up in the same locale. The problem is so immense as to be unsolvable.

7. Large government operations, like the U.S.-run Operation Blast Furnace in Bolivia designed to drive the price of drugs down by eliminating markets and production, does not work very effectively. The Bolivian operation was very costly and cannot be often repeated; it was only a small drop in a very large bucket, and in the long run had almost no effect on prices or production. Nor does spraying of the drug crops work. It contaminates the environment, ruins nearby non-drug crops, and causes long-term disease and cancer in the population; hence, democratically-elected governments cannot permit it.

8. Many Latin American governments are not opposed to drug production as long as the producers do not threaten the government itself. It adds immensely to the GNP, keeps farmers happy, and enables the government to get away with fewer subsidies for its people and lower salaries to public employees.

9. The last point is an especially sticky one. The fact is that many local and even national officials in Latin America, as well as military and police officials, are in the pay of the narcotics traffickers. Neither the national governments nor these officials are prepared to cooperate with a drug eradication program that cuts into their own incomes.

10. The U.S. Drug Enforcement Agency (DEA) officials whom the United States sends to Latin America, unlike their State Department counterparts, often do not have strong backgrounds in the culture, languages, politics, or sociology of the area. They tend sometimes to ride roughshod over Latin American sensitivities and to ignore the

conditions that make the issue so complex and difficult. Nor do the DEA officials always endear themselves to the State Department itself or to U.S. embassies abroad. Not only are there bureaucratic rivalries, administrative overlaps, and personal animosities involved, but their functions are entirely at odds. The job of the U.S. embassy mission is, by and large, to get along with, accommodate, and maintain good relations with the host government; that of the DEA in the same country is to provoke change and sometimes confrontation. The actions of DEA officials in South America in carrying out their mission has not always been welcomed by the rest of the embassy team.

It is unlikely, therefore, that the solution to the U.S. drug problem will come from Latin America. Realistically, it can only come from the United States itself through interdiction (which raises another set of problems), education, and ultimately changed mores and consumer habits. Efforts to solve a U.S. problem by putting pressure on or intervening in Latin American internal affairs will produce backlashes, generate ill will, and prove counterproductive. If the markets can be made to dry up on the U.S. side, which will certainly be a long-term process, then production will surely dry up on the South American side. The reverse is not true, however, because the unlikely reduction of Latin America production would only move it to Asia, the Middle East, or Africa. In the meantime, an insensitive and heavy-handed U.S. approach has the potential to wreak enormous damage upon our relations with South America.

Public Opinion

United States foreign policy in South America, and in Latin America in general, has had as one of its basic aims the promotion of democracy. Democracy as a goal of foreign policy has been pursued for both ethical and strategic purposes. The question remains, however, of whether Latin America wants democracy, or wants it all that much, or wants it in the same form that U.S. citizens envision, and whether—in the last analysis—the pursuit of democracy is a valid basis for foreign policy.[33]

The answer as to whether Latin America wants democracy is a resounding yes—but with important qualifications. In poll after poll in country after country, South Americans favor democracy and representative government. The surveys that exist indicate that when given their choice of alternative political systems, 80, 85, or 90 percent (depending on time and place) prefer representative rule.[34]

These same surveys also indicate that this is an abstract choice of preferences conceived in a vacuum. Although overwhelming majorities of South Americans prefer representative government, they are not certain that U.S.-style representative government will work in their countries. Democracy is good in the abstract, but their own countries, they believe, are too fragmented, too uninstitutionalized, or even too "uncivilized" for democracy to work. Based on their own national histories, they believe democracy leads to chaos, libertinage, and national breakdowns. Democracy is good and workable in the "Anglo-Saxon countries," but South Americans remain skeptical as to whether it works for them. Hence, if one asks South Americans the question that USIA pollsters seldom do—what they mean by democracy—the answer is almost always "strong" or "firm" government. About the same percentage that prefer representative government also favor strong government. This represents the two options that have always been open to South America: Representative government versus strong or authoritarian government, democracy versus Caesarism. The surveys thus indicate that while representative government is the South Americans' first choice, if it does not work they may easily opt for the substitute of strong government.[35] This also means that the U.S. strategy of putting so many of its eggs in the one democracy basket may be an imprudent one.

Moreover, these same surveys show very little support for what we think of as democracy's supporting institutions. While 85 percent and more of South Americans prefer representative government, only about 30 percent favor political parties of any kind. They view political parties like George Washington viewed "factions," as divisive agencies detracting from the national purpose. An even lower percentage of South Americans—about 27 percent—view trade unions in a favorable light.[36] If the elementary civics and political science textbooks are correct that political parties and trade unions are essential to democracy and necessary for the pluralism that undergirds democratic life, then it is clear that South American democracy has a very weak institutional base. It may be that South Americans believe they can have democracy without a strong institutional life—perhaps not an invalid assumption if the model of democracy for South America is the direct democracy of Rousseau and the notion of an intuitively known "general will," and not Locke or Madison.[37] The third explanation arising from this data is that South Americans, when one probes beneath the surface, are actually not much in favor of democracy at all. Whatever alternative is chosen, democracy—and with it U.S. foreign policy—seems shakier in South America than we may have thought.

This conclusion regarding the tenuousness of democracy in South America is reinforced by survey data on political attitudes among the lower classes. Representative democracy as the United States knows it is often supported by the South American upper and middle classes—

but not necessarily the lower classes. These classes, like others in their societies, often support "democracy" in the abstract; but in practice they generally prefer a strong, nationalistic, paternalistic, populist, authoritative (if not downright authoritarian) regime, rather like Perón in Argentina. Between 40 and 60 percent of the population may support a Peronist-like system of statist nationalism that may verge on populist socialism. Once again, the portents for democracy and for U.S. foreign policy are not propitious if such attitudes prevail.[38]

South American attitudes toward the United States are similarly divided. On the one hand, a large majority of South Americans consider the United States to be a friend and admire its economy, technology, and national wealth. They tend to be envious of the strong democracy and representative government found in the United States and they admire the free speech, system of justice, and relative lack of corruption in American life. About half of the South Americans surveyed have a generally favorable impression of the United States while only about a quarter have an unfavorable impression. At the same time, South Americans make it clear that they are appalled by certain features (or what they perceive as features) of American life—the drug use, impersonality, lack of strong moral and religious values, erosion of the family structure—and believe their own moral and cultural values to be superior. Similarly, while most South Americans admire and respect the United States, they are strongly opposed to some aspects that have particular relevance for foreign policy. They are opposed to what is seen as U.S. militarism, interventionism (in Central America and the Caribbean), and heavy-handedness. Many South Americans were particularly opposed to the government of Ronald Reagan, which they saw as confirming all their worst prejudices about the United States as an uncivilized, gunslinging, lawless, dangerous, wild west country that shoots first and asks questions later.[39] (This attitude is largely based on movies rather than first-hand experience of the United States, and is often fomented and augmented by inaccurate or unrepresentative media coverage or by intellectuals with a political interest in presenting a distorted view.)

Complicating these relations is the fact that some South Americans are intensely jealous and envious of the United States. The hate stems not so much from what the United States does—its occasional gaffes and mistakes—but because of what it is and stands for: Success and modernity compared to South American failure and backwardness. To the extent this attitude is widespread, as it is in Argentina, the United States is certain to be envied and disliked regardless of what it says or does. There is certain to be a high degree of anti-Americanism, given these attitudes, no matter who is in power in Washington or in

Buenos Aires. In that sense, U.S. relations with some of the South American countries may range from correct to frosty, but they are never likely to be "good."[40]

Overall, South American public opinion is probably more independent, less favorably disposed toward the United States, even more manifestly anti-American than it was twenty-five years ago. Then the U.S. image was overwhelmingly favorable in South America; but now the region is both more nationalistic and less pro-American. One suspects that this change has more to do with South America's greater development, independence, and assertiveness, combined with a perceived U.S. decline, than it does with any specific U.S. action or even set of actions over this period.

The Agenda of Issues

Not only are the United States and South America diverging on the range of issues discussed above, but increasingly even the respective agendas of issues no longer contain the same items.

What are the basic or bedrock U.S. interests in South America? Essentially they may be summarized in a series of items.[41]

1. Security interests: Preventing "more Cubas," protecting the "southern flank," helping protect U.S. interests in the South Atlantic and the South Pacific, guaranteeing the sea lanes, maintaining bases or listening posts, preventing "foreign powers" (viz., the Soviet Union) from securing a foothold or establishing bases, securing the borders, containing communism, assuring that in the event of a general conflict U.S. forces are not held up by having to deal with some local Soviet satellite in South America (the "economy of force" doctrine).
2. Economic interests: Maintaining access to the markets, raw materials, and labor supplies of the area; being able to invest and remit profits; opening up South American markets to U.S. products.
3. Political interests: Maintaining stability in ways that protect interests #1 and #2, allowing for change that is not radical.
4. Economic development and social progress: Assisting modernization that leads to these ends, both as a good in itself and because it contributes to interests #1, #2, and #3.
5. Democracy and human rights: Emphasizing these goals again both as ends in themselves (thus satisfying U.S. requirements for an ethical foreign policy) and because they also contribute to #1, #2, and #3.

What are the priorities of the South American countries? Not only are their priorities different from those of the United States, but the two lists converge hardly at all.

1. Regime survivability: This is the highest priority of any South American government. In a context of weak legitimacy and an uncertain tenure in office, where stability cannot be taken for granted, a regime must protect its own interests first and by almost any means. North Americans, who take stability for granted, seldom understand this need or the policies to which it often leads.

2. Sovereignty and territorial integrity: These doctrines are alive and well in South America where *realpolitik,* border issues, and irredentism are prevalent. Argentina's claims to the Falklands/ Malvinas Islands are just the tip of the iceberg of the potential for inter-state conflict in South America.[42]

3. Economic development and social progress: This is a very high-order priority in South America, far higher than the U.S. preoccupation that is almost exclusively strategic.

4. Trade, commerce, investments, and markets: While the U.S. preoccupation is strategic, the South American one could be summed up in three words: trade, trade, trade. South America particularly wishes continued free access to U.S. markets, including especially capital markets, and is very much concerned with the protectionist thrust in the United States Congress that would limit the entry of Latin American products.

5. Democracy and human rights (in their more advanced forms): Unless there is evidence to the contrary, it may be surmised that South America strongly favors democracy and human rights not necessarily for their own sake but in large part to qualify for U.S. and international aid and so they can show to the world that they are as "civilized" as anyone else. These may not be noble or elevated reasons for favoring democracy, but perhaps such cynicism is warranted given South America's previous track record of loyalty to democratic precepts.

6. Security, stability, and order: These are concerns for internal order, what Jeane Kirkpatrick once called the "Hobbes problem" in Latin America,[43] not concerns for Cuban or Soviet-inspired insurrection—which is the U.S. preoccupation. In fact, with the exception of the *Sendero Luminoso* movement in Peru and a potential security problem in Chile, the South American subsystem is currently freer of leftist insurrectionary threats than at any time since the 1950s. The very absence of such threats enables

South America to flaunt the United States in ways it would not have done before and to stake out more independent foreign policy positions.

7. A place in the sun: South America wishes, perhaps even above the other priorities listed, to be afforded a sense of dignity, worth, and respect, and to be included among the "civilized" nations. They do not wish to be treated as "banana republics" or to be of interest only to U.S. vice presidents who must attend funerals there.

8. Independence: Most South American countries recognize their continuing dependence on the United States for economic, trade, and security reasons. But they also wish to diversify that dependence, to become more independent, and to open up relations with a broader spectrum of nations. The United States will have to adjust, probably painfully, to some of these transformations.

9. Alternative routes to development: While a major U.S. preoccupation in South America is regime stability, many South Americans are still casting about for an appropriate and innovative development formula. Such experimentation on their part is likely to produce ruptures of instability; many South Americans are willing to run that risk for the sake of achieving an authentic and genuinely indigenous model of development—which they have never really had in their 160-year history as independent nations—and probably to the considerable chagrin of U.S. strategic planners.

One is struck in reviewing these lists how far removed the U.S. priorities are from the South American ones. It is not just that the individual items are sometimes different, but that the entire agendas show very little convergence or complementarity. Moreover, even when there are items present on both lists—such as democracy, for example—it is plain that the parties often mean something quite different by that item or that their reasons for supporting it are quite different. The issue may not be subject to precise empirical verification, but one wonders if ever before have the two main parts of the Americas been so far apart.

Conclusions

Considerable signs of maturity are evident in U.S.-South American relations.[44] With most of the countries of the region, the United States has begun to put its relations on the same normal and regular footing that is the basis of its relations with much of Western Europe. This is not to say that there are no serious issues in U.S.-South American relations—there are, in fact, many of them—but it is to say that policy toward South America has become more routinized and no longer carried out on a crisis basis as was so often the case in the past. The causes of this new maturity in U.S.–South American relations are many, but undoubtedly important among them is the fact that the U.S. preoccupation with Central America has led to indifference and neglect toward South America. Such neglect is rightfully lamented by many scholars,[45] but among the unintended consequences has been a certain maturing of U.S. relations with quite a number of the countries of the area. There are many areas of bilateral and multilateral differences, but for the most part these are dealt with in the normal channels of negotiations and diplomacy rather than through some crash program for the region that is here today and gone tomorrow, or some CIA intervention. Given the previous U.S. track record in the region, I count such boring and even humdrum relations as steps in the right direction.

On the other hand, the range of issues that divide the United States from South America is large and growing larger. The community of interests that the United States and South America commonly shared historically as part of a New World order is dangerously thin. The "Western Hemisphere Idea"[46] of a commonality of experiences, histories, and aspirations shared by all of the Americas as distinct from their Old World forebears, may now finally be laid to rest. On virtually every issue and subject here discussed—democracy, nationalism, institutionalization, models of development, debt, drugs, public opinion, and the agendas of priorities—there are large differences that will not soon or easily be resolved. Not only are the policy and issue differences strong and increasing, there is as well increasingly little shared basis of understanding and mutuality of interests on which a firmer partnership and better relations can be forged.

It would require a major effort on the part of the United States and South America to begin working on these issues in a serious way, to manage ("resolve" would be too strong a word) them in an efficient, mutually satisfactory, and amicable manner, and to lay the basis for better future relations. Unfortunately, little of that is likely to happen, for U.S. foreign policy has been increasingly politicized on all sides and the entire American foreign policy system is increasingly immobilized and fragmented. Hence, we can expect little in the way of positive, concerted, and long-term policy at the highest levels of the United States government. Whatever new policy initiatives we see, therefore, are likely to come not from the top but from lower levels of the U.S. government. Moreover, such initiatives and solutions as are presented at these levels are likely to be partial, tentative, and incremental, as distinct from holistic and grandiose. Given past U.S. experience in the

South American region, that may not be an altogether bad or inappropriate basis for U.S. foreign policy.

Notes

1. Statistics on this growth may be found in the annual *Social and Economic Progress in Latin America* (Washington, D.C.: Inter-American Development Bank, yearly).

2. Sanford J. Ungar, ed., *Estrangement: America and the World* (New York: Oxford University Press, 1985).

3. For an overall perspective on U.S. relations with Latin America, see Howard J. Wiarda, *In Search of Policy: The United States and Latin America* (Washington, D.C.: American Enterprise Institute, 1984); see also Frederick B. Pike, *The United States and the Andean Republics* (Cambridge: Harvard University Press, 1977). Good reviews of the foreign policies of the South American states may be found in Harold E. Davis and Larman C. Wilson, eds., *Latin American Foreign Policies* (Baltimore: Johns Hopkins University Press, 1975); and Elizabeth G. Ferris and Jennie K. Lincoln, eds., *Latin American Foreign Policies: Global and Regional Dimensions* (Boulder: Westview Press, 1981).

4. The author is completing a book on the subject for the Twentieth Century Fund, tentatively titled *The Democratic Revolution in Latin America: Implications for United States Policy*; see also Paul W. Drake and Eduardo Silva, eds., *Elections and Democratization in Latin America, 1980–1985* (La Jolla: University of California at San Diego, 1986).

5. Guillermo O'Donnell, Philippe C. Schmitter, and Laurence Whitehead, eds., *Transitions from Authoritarian Rule: Prospects for Democracy* (Baltimore: Johns Hopkins University Press, 1986); an earlier survey is Howard J. Wiarda, ed., *Continuing Struggle for Democracy in Latin America* (Boulder: Westview Press, 1980).

6. See Kevin J. Middlebrook and Carlos Rico, eds., *The United States and Latin America in the 1980s* (Pittsburgh: University of Pittsburgh Press, 1986).

7. For further elaboration, see the forthcoming book by the author, *Finding Our Way? Toward Maturity in U.S.–Latin American Relations* (in preparation).

8. See, for example, Wayne A. Selcher, *Brazil's Multilateral Relations: Between First and Third Worlds* (Boulder: Westview Press, 1978); also Teixiera Soares, *O Brasil no Conflito Ideológico Global* (Rio de Janeiro: Cívilizaçao Brasileira, 1980).

9. The materials in this section are based on observations made during extended research trips by the author to Latin America in 1985 and 1987.

10. Raúl Alfonsín, "Address by the President of Argentina, Dr. Raul Alfonsín" (Amherst: University of Massachusetts, Mimeo., November 20, 1986).

11. The apostle of this point of view is W. W. Rostow, *The Stages of Economic Growth* (Cambridge: Cambridge University Press, 1960).

12. The analysis here reflects the conclusions of a major research project being carried out at the American Enterprise Institute under the author's direction entitled "Updating U.S. Strategic Policy in Latin America."

13. Jack Child, *Geopolitics and Conflict in South America* (New York: Praeger, 1985).

14. See the author's paper, "Interpreting Iberian–Latin American Interrelations: Paradigm Consensus and Conflict," Occasional Paper No. 10 (Washington, D.C.: Center for Hemispheric Studies, American Enterprise Institute, 1985); published also in Howard J. Wiarda, ed., *The Iberian–Latin American Connection: Implications for U.S. Foreign Policy* (Boulder: Westview Press and American Enterprise Institute, 1986).

15. The information here is based on numerous United States Information Agency (USIA) surveys of various South American countries. See also *New York Times* (November 17, 1986), which reports on a major survey of Mexico; and Enrique J. Baloyra and John Martz, *Political Attitudes in Venezuela: Societal Cleavages and Political Opinion* (Austin: University of Texas Press, 1979).

16. See, by the author, *Latin America at the Crossroads: Debt, Development, and the Future* (Boulder: Westview Press and American Enterprise Institute, 1987); also Christine A. Bogdanowicz-Dindert, "The Debt Crisis—The Baker Plan Revisited," *Journal of Inter-American Studies and World Affairs* 28 (Fall 1986), pp. 33–46.

17. Howard J. Wiarda, "United States Relations with South America: Painful Readjustments," *Current History* (January 1987), pp. 1ff.

18. The Hemingway writings are *Death in the Afternoon, The Sun Also Rises,* and *The Fifth Column and Four Stories of the Spanish Civil War;* by García Marquez, see *One Hundred Years of Solitude.*

19. See Frederick Pike, *Hispanismo, 1898–1936: Spanish Conservatives and Liberals and Their Relations with Latin America* (Notre Dame: University of Notre Dame Press, 1971); also Mark Falcoff, "Spain and the Southern Cone" in Wiarda, ed., *Iberian–Latin American Connection.*

20. The author's own critiques of the Rostow thesis may be found in the essays "Misreading Latin America—Again," *Foreign Policy*, No. 65 (Winter 1986-87), pp. 135–153; and "Alternative Paradigms: The 'Conflict' and 'Consensus' Models," Chapter 5 in Howard J. Wiarda, *Corporatism and National Development in Latin America* (Boulder: Westview Press, 1981).

21. See the four-volume study by Larry Diamond, Juan Linz, and Seymour Martin Lipset, eds., *Democracy in Developing Nations* (Boulder: Lynne Rienner Publishers, forthcoming); one volume is devoted to Latin America.

22. Samuel P. Huntington, *Political Order in Changing Societies* (New Haven: Yale University Press, 1968).

23. John S. Fitch, *The Coup d'Etat as a Political Process: Ecuador, 1948–66* (Baltimore: Johns Hopkins University Press, 1977); see also the series of articles in the *Washington Post* (January 1987) reporting on the most recent Ecuadorian confrontations in this long process.

24. See Chapter 1 of *Latin America at the Crossroads*; also Howard J. Wiarda, "The Latin American Development Process and the New Developmental Alternatives: Military 'Nasserism' and 'Dictatorship with Popular Support,'" *Western Political Quarterly* 25 (September 1972), pp. 464–490.

25. Quoted in L. S. Rowe, *The Federal System of the Argentine Republic* (Washington, D.C.: The Carnegie Institution, 1921).

26. See the survey results reported in *New York Times* (November 17, 1986), p. 1.

27. By the author, "Interpreting Iberian–Latin American Relations."

28. See the discussion in Riordan Roett, *Brazil: Politics in a Patrimonialist Society* (Boston: Allyn and Bacon, 1984); also Wayne Selcher, ed., *Political Liberalization in Brazil: Dynamics, Dilemmas, and Future Prospects* (Boulder: Westview Press, 1986).

29. An excellent discussion of the issues is in Edward G. McGrath, ed., *Is American Democracy Exportable?* (Beverly Hills: Glencoe Press, 1968).

30. William R. Cline, *International Debt* (Washington, D.C.: Institute for International Economics, 1984); John H. Makin, *The Global Debt Crisis* (New York: Basic Books, 1984); M. S. Mendelsohn, *The Debt of Nations* (New York: Priority Press, 1984); Alfred J. Watkins, *Till Debt Do Us Part* (Washington, D.C.: University Press of America for the Roosevelt Center for American Policy Studies, 1986); and Thomas Scheetz, *Peru and the International Monetary Fund* (Pittsburgh: University of Pittsburgh Press, 1986).

31. *Latin America at the Crossroads;* based on the author's extensive research trip around South America, July-August 1985.

32. The analysis here is used on field research in South America in 1985 and 1987; see also John Mills, *The Underground Empire* (New York: Doubleday, 1986).

33. McGrath, *Is American Democracy Exportable?*

34. The analysis here is based on a variety of USIA surveys of Latin American democracy.

35. Natalio Botano, "New Trends in Argentine Politics," paper presented at the Seminar on the Southern Cone, The Argentine-American Forum, Washington, D.C., June 5-6, 1983; also Claudio Velez, *The Centralist Tradition in Latin America* (Princeton: Princeton University Press, 1980).

36. Botana, "New Trends in Argentine Politics."

37. Richard M. Morse, "The Challenge of Ideology in Latin America," *Foreign Policy and Defense Review*, vol. 5, no. 3 (Winter 1985), pp. 14–23.

38. See especially Baloyra and Martz, *Political Attitudes.*

39. Based on USIA surveys; also *New York Times* (November 17, 1986), p. 1.

40. Falcoff, "Spain and the Southern Cone"; also Carlos Rangel, *The Latin Americans.*

41. For a more extended discussion of these differences, see Howard J. Wiarda, "Changing Realities and U.S. Policy in the Caribbean Basin: An Overview" in James R. Green and Brent Scowcroft, eds., *Western Interests and U.S. Policy Options in the Caribbean Basin* (Boston: Oelgeschlager, Gunn and Hain, 1984), pp. 55–98.

42. Mark Falcoff, "Arms and Politics Revisited: Latin America as a Military and Strategic Theater," in Howard J. Wiarda, ed., *The Crisis in Latin America* (Washington, D.C.: American Enterprise Institute, 1984), pp. 1–9.

43. Jeane Kirkpatrick, "The Hobbes Problem: Order, Authority, and Legitimacy in Central America," paper presented at the 1980 Public Policy Week

of the American Enterprise Institute, Washington, D.C., December 1980; published in AEI's Public Policy Week *Proceedings* (1981).

44. See the analysis presented in *Finding Our Way*.

45. For example, Riordan Roett, "Democracy and Debt in South America," *Foreign Affairs*, vol. 62, no. 3 (1984), pp. 695–720.

46. Arthur P. Whitaker, *The Western Hemisphere Idea: Its Rise and Decline* (Ithaca: Cornell University Press, 1954).

3

The Status of South American Geopolitical Thinking

Jack Child

Geopolitical thinking has been a common feature of several author-itarian military dictatorships in South America in the period from the 1960s to the early 1980s. It formed the intellectual base for the "National Security State" and influenced a series of internal and inter-state policies and development programs in this period. The principal argument made in this chapter is that this geopolitical thinking in South America is an important phenomenon but one that is little known or understood in academic, policymaking, or strategic circles outside of the region. Although closely associated with the Latin American military, such forms of thought are not exclusively the property of the military, and do not necessarily disappear when military regimes give way to elected democratic governments. Geopolitical thinking is closely tied to deep currents of nationalism and patriotism, and thus it has a tendency to endure regardless of the type of regime.

In addition, there are close ties between South American geopolitical thinking and certain potential or existing conflict situations. These situations in turn stimulate geopolitical modes of analysis and insure that there is a popular and policymaking audience for arguments that base national irredentist claims on geopolitical rationales. Thus, in Argentina one of the common explanations for the deeply felt need to recover the Malvinas Islands is that they are geopolitically vital for Argentine interests in the South Atlantic and beyond. In a similar vein, the Antarctic programs of several South American nations (among them Argentina, Brazil, Chile, and Peru) are frequently explained and justified in geopolitical terms. Several longstanding inter-state strains in the subcontinent (such as Argentine-Brazilian rivalry, Bolivia's quest to regain an outlet to the sea, and Peruvian-Ecuadorian tensions) also can be explained, at least partially, in terms of geopolitical thinking in these countries.

At the same time, one must take note of the fact that there is a current in South American geopolitical thinking that sets aside these nationalistic quarrels and stresses the need for South American integration and the common bonds of the Latin American roots of these nations. Recent bilateral agreements between the two key countries of Argentina and Brazil also have geopolitical roots and have been applauded in the prolific literature that reflects geopolitical thinking in these countries. The increasing association of these more positive aspects of geopolitical thinking with redemocratizing currents in South America suggests that democracy may be strengthened in the region if the more enlightened forms of geopolitical thinking prevail over the more aggressive and chauvinistic ones.

Geopolitical Thinking: The Conceptual Framework

Semantics of "Geopolitics"

The conceptual framework of South American geopolitical thinking begins with the semantic problem of defining the term "geopolitics."[1] At a simplistic level, the term is sometimes used as synonymous with "political geography" in that it stresses the relationship between geography and politics. This approach focuses on the various ways in which the geographic environment provides opportunities and challenges to the political, social, cultural, and economic activities of people and states.

This first-level definition of geopolitics as political geography does not capture the flavor or impact that geopolitical thinking has had in South America, especially over the past three decades. Geopolitical thinking in South America in this period goes beyond simple relationships between geography and politics to include a certain aggressive and nationalistic, even chauvinistic, tone, which in turn led in some cases to a confusion of means and ends and to the well-known excesses of the national security states in the region.

To appreciate the full significance of the concept of geopolitics in the Southern Cone, it is necessary to broaden the definition from the simple relation between geography and politics to that between geography and power politics. Geopolitics becomes one of the principal instruments by which the nation-state defends itself and achieves certain goals by using geography to enhance the projection of its national power. The nation-state is seen as a living organism, threatened by a variety of internal and external enemies that challenge its survival in a cruel and hostile Darwinian world. The environment is not only hostile, but is also dynamic and ruled by a series of "geopolitical laws" that govern the birth, growth, survival, and death of states. To insure the survival and prosperity of their nation, the geopolitical thinkers, and especially the military ones, devised the national security state to protect their country in this hostile environment.

Regional and national variants further shape these currents of geopolitical thinking. Generally speaking, the more aggressive and nationalistic forms of geopolitical thinking are to be found in the military institutions of the three key Southern Cone states—Argentina, Brazil, and Chile; while the integrationist current of geopolitical thinking is most strongly evidenced in Uruguay and Peru. In contrast, in Central America and the Caribbean there are few indications of such independent geopolitical thinking, largely because the influence of the United States is heavily felt in strategic and military matters, which tends to preclude the full development of autonomous geopolitical thinking.

The Roots: The Organic Theory of the State

Southern Cone geopolitical thinking is deeply rooted in classical European geopolitical thinking, and especially in the various schools that focused on the biological parallel between the nation-state and living organisms. These nineteenth- and twentieth-century European geopoliticians devoted much of their time and attention to establishing links between geography, political science, and international relations. They were seeking to prove the existence and validity of scientific laws that would govern these links and provide guidelines for the statesman. Even in the early stages of this quest, there were sharp divisions between the "determinists," who argued that geography pre-ordained human fate, and the "possibilists," who believed that geography merely increased possibilities or obstacles.

The discipline of geopolitics had not yet acquired academic respectability when one current of European geopolitical thinking was captured by fascism and used by Adolf Hitler as a pseudo-scientific justification for Nazi Germany's expansionism and theories of racial superiority. This negative legacy thereafter haunted geopolitics, making it almost a taboo word (except in a pejorative sense) in Europe and the United States. To this day the critics of Southern Cone geopolitical thinking refer back to the Hitlerian perversion of geopolitics when they call geopolitics "the geography of fascism" and draw certain parallels between European fascist regimes and the authoritarian National Security States established by the military in the Southern Cone.[2]

The conceptual starting point of South American geopolitical thinking is the same as the organicist predecessor in Europe: the nation-state as a living organism which is born, grows, reaches a peek, declines, and dies. In this process people as individuals are conceived as replaceable cells within the larger organic structure, and thus the interests of the state are placed above those of the expendable individual. The degree of a state's growth is a function of the space and natural and human resources it can acquire. States do not live in isolation, however; they frequently must struggle against other states in order to defend their resources and acquire the space and resources they must have in order to expand. The basic task of the geopolitician is to study this process in order to discover the scientific laws that govern it and advise the political leadership on how to proceed.

Five Geopolitical World Visions

The framework of South American geopolitical thinking can also be stated in terms of five conceptual visions of the relationship between geography and power politics.

The *maritime* geopolitical perception argues that the most effective means for a nation to project its power is by controlling key choke-points where sea lanes of communication are constricted by land masses. The emphasis is on getting possession or influence in a relatively small number of straits, canals, peninsulas, islands, and passages. The maritime geopolitical perception is closely associated with U.S. Admiral Alfred Thayer Mahan (1840–1914), who is frequently credited for the strong U.S. interest in the Caribbean and a trans-isthmian canal. As might be expected, the maritime geopolitical concept is especially prevalent in naval circles. In South America the maritime theories have focused on defense of the South Atlantic, possession of key islands, and control of the Drake Passage and Antarctica. The Argentine Navy has its own counterpart to Admiral Mahan: Almirante Segundo Storni, who lived about the same time and stressed the importance of the sea in Argentine geopolitics.

The *continental* geopolitical vision parallels the maritime one. It stresses that the nation-state is a land animal, which competes with other states as they try to dominate key continental "heartlands." The key proponent of this approach was the British geographer Sir Halford Mackinder (1861–1947), who argued that the state that controlled the heartland of Central Europe would command the Eurasian "world island" and, ultimately, the world. In terms of South American geopolitical thinking the continental vision has emphasized the need to fill the basically empty inner core of South America (especially the

Amazon Basin) and to break away from the coastal cities that are the legacy of the colonial period. This vision has found outlet in programs to move national capitals (in Brazil and Argentina) and in the building of ambitious road and communication networks to open up the interior of the continent. In addition, the two landlocked nations of South America (Bolivia and Paraguay) have been the focus of attention of continental geopoliticians, who note the key role these nations could play as the center of the continent is finally developed.

With the Second World War and the coming of the strategic bomber, and subsequent development of nuclear weapons and ballistic missiles, a third geopolitical vision emerged: The *aerospace* one. The aerospace geopolitician argues that these new weapons and transportation vehicles require that attention shift from control of land and sea to domination of the third dimension (aerospace). Its principal focus of analysis, however, has been the relationship between the two superpowers; it has not had great impact in South American geopolitical thinking except in some air force circles.

The fourth geopolitical vision, the *revolutionary* one, began to emerge during the Cold War as the massive destructive power of nuclear weapons made their use in warfare less credible. Although guerrilla warfare has always existed at a tactical level, the revolutionary geopolitical vision goes beyond tactics to link them to radical political ideologies that argue that the key "space" is not land, sea, or air, but the "interior space" of the hearts and minds of men. To the South American geopolitical thinker who firmly believes in the organic concept of the state, the revolutionary threat is an extremely serious one, since it comes from within the organism itself, even though it has outside inspiration and support. The triumph of the Cuban Revolution in 1959 and the subsequent attempts to export it jolted the South American armed forces, who feared they might suffer a fate similar to that of Batista's military. As will be shown in subsequent sections, this perceived threat to the organic state by its own cells turned malignant was one of the fundamental justifications for the National Security States of the 1960s and 1970s, and for the violations of human rights that were rationalized as necessary to defend the state itself.[3]

The fifth geopolitical vision is the *resource* one. It argues that a series of demographic, ecological and economic factors have brought humanity to a point where competition for key resources will be more important than competition for geographic space. The energy crisis of the 1970s produced a strong impulse to develop this geopolitical vision, although demographic pressures have also emphasized the political power of food resources. The oil-producing Latin American nations fully understand the geopolitics of petroleum, and the need to defend their resources from those who desperately need them. By the same token, the energy-poor nations of South America have focused their attention on areas where these resources can be exploited.

South American Geopolitical Thinking
Through the 1970s

Historical Background

The ideas of the nineteenth century European geopolitical schools made their impact on the South American military establishments, especially those such as Chile and Argentina that professionalized their doctrine and organization under Prussian tutelage beginning in the late nineteenth century. This helps explain why geopolitical ideas were not rejected by Southern Cone military establishments after World War II when they were in the United States and Europe because of their association with Nazi Germany. Although geopolitical writers in South America did not necessarily accept the Hitlerian concept of geopolitics, they did not reject geopolitical thinking; indeed, several authors took note of the unfair way in which all of geopolitics was being attacked because of this association with Nazism.[4]

For about two decades after World War II, South American geopolitical writers circulated their ideas among a narrow circle of peers. Geopolitical books and journals did not have wide circulation or much of a civilian audience, and geopolitical ideas had little salience in the media and educational systems. Contributing to this situation was the overwhelming U.S. predominance in hemisphere strategic matters, and the patronizing attitude on the part of the United States toward any idea emerging from the Southern Hemisphere. The Inter-American Military System was dominated by the United States in these years after World War II, and there was little room for ideas emanating from other nations of the hemisphere.[5]

The 1960s and 1970s

The situation began to change in the mid-1960s, when the larger and more sophisticated military establishments of the Southern Cone began to become more independent of the U.S. strategic tutelage. The militaries in several of these nations strongly perceived a severe threat from guerrilla warfare, and did not feel that the old Inter-American Military System under U.S. control had the ability to respond to the new threat. A series of military regimes took power in the Southern Cone in these years, and some of them created National Security States in response to the perceived guerrilla threat. In particular, the Brazilian military revolution (1964), the Peruvian military revolution (1968), the Chilean military regime (from 1973), and a series of military regimes in Argentina and Uruguay (1976 on) came to power at least partly as a response to the threat of subversion. Military leaders felt they had in geopolitical thinking and the National Security State an answer to the threat. Their strategic independence from Washington increased as they intensified their anti-guerrilla struggles and as the United States, especially under the Carter administration, responded with a strong emphasis on punishing the violators of human rights. With the parallel decline of U.S. strategic influence and the growing independence of the South American military establishments, the previously ignored geopolitical literature began to acquire a larger audience. Especially in Chile, Argentina, and Brazil, the late 1960s and 1970s saw a spate of geopolitical books, journals, and articles that circulated in the popular press and educational curricula as well as in military circles. Geopolitics became popularized.

The revitalization of geopolitical thinking had two dimensions. The first argued that the organic state was being attacked from within by the "cancerous cells" of subversion that had to be "extirpated" by "surgical" means, violently if necessary. The second dimension of geopolitical thinking dealt with external affairs. It rested on the need for the organic state to project its influence outward and obtain access to more resources and "living space" (*lebensraum*). Geopolitical thinking consequently exacerbated a series of old border and territorial disputes, such as the War of the Pacific (Chile-Peru-Bolivia), the Beagle Channel controversy (Argentine-Chile), the historic Argentine-Brazilian rivalry, the Malvinas/Falklands Islands dispute, and control of Antarctica and the South Atlantic.

Geopolitics and the National Security State

The common point of departure of both geopolitical thinking and the National Security State is the organic theory of the state and the biological metaphor that presents the nation-state as a vulnerable entity struggling to survive in a hostile world. Internal security was to be guaranteed by educating, repressing, or eliminating the individual replaceable cell. External security was to be achieved by increasing the power of the state in all its fields: Military, economic, political, and psycho-social.[6] The end product of this line of analysis was a coherent doctrine of national security, which some authors have called the "ideology of the Southern Cone military" in the 1960s and 1970s.[7]

The role of the United States in this process is controversial. Some authors argue that the Southern Cone National Security State was deliberately established by the United States as a means of controlling the South American states through "intermediate exploiters" (that is, the Latin American military establishments).[8] There is little evidence to support this argument, however, and it does not take into account the strong contribution made by Southern Cone geopolitical thinking. What appears to have happened is that the Southern Cone military establishments copied some of the institutions of the U.S. National Security System (the NSC, CIA, and the senior war colleges) and applied them to the very different South American environment. In this process they were strongly influenced by latent geopolitical thinking, the organic concept of the state, the authoritarian tendencies of the Latin American military officer corps, and the strong perception of threat posed by Marxist guerrillas. These elements combined in powerful and unexpected ways, and, in the absence of effective democratic checks and balances, produced the National Security States and their well-documented excesses that typified the South American subsystem in the late 1960s, the 1970s, and into the 1980s.

Some National Variants

The generalizations made above have a number of national variants. Geopolitical thinking was most fully developed and made its biggest impact in the ABC countries (Argentina, Brazil, and Chile), and even there different priorities were given to different objectives. The remaining nations tended to imitate and react to the geopolitics of the ABC states, with some original thought in Uruguay and Peru.

Brazil

Brazilian geopolitical schools have profoundly impacted both internal affairs and the rest of South America. Geopolitical thinking provided many of the domestic ideas that sustained the military revolution of 1964–1985. Geopolitical analysts in other South American countries carefully studied their Brazilian counterparts, copying some and strongly criticizing others. This phenomenon was especially evident in Argentina; it fed strong currents of Argentine-Brazilian rivalry.

The key aspect of Brazilian geopolitical thinking is the way it supports the concept of "greatness," that moment when Brazil will have fulfilled its destiny of becoming the first world power to emerge from the Southern Hemisphere. Geopoliticians explicitly trace the path to Brazil's destiny of greatness in several steps. They begin with Brazil looking inward, moving the capital, developing an interior communications network, and effectively employing territory and resources. This is followed by projections of power toward Brazil's neighbors as it becomes a regional power. Finally, Brazil will move on to acquiring status as a first order power on the world scene.[9] Brazilian geopolitical arguments that support this line of reasoning are closely followed by its neighbors; they sometimes give rise to accusations that the Brazilians who are embarked on fulfilling an expansionist "manifest destiny" are "imperialists" (or worse yet "subimperialists" at the service of the United States), an accusation that deeply offends Brazilian geopoliticians.

The Hispanic American geopoliticians who use the term "subimperialist" with regard to Brazil take note of the fact that for many years Brazil's progress was nurtured by an informal alliance with the United States. This alliance was especially close during World War II, when Brazil was the only Latin American nation to provide ground troops to the Allied forces and to receive large quantities of military and economic aid in the process. Several Argentine geopoliticians who dwelt on this theme argued that Brazil must break the unnaturally close alliance with the United States before Brazil could return to being a true Latin American nation.[10] This in fact occurred during the Carter administration when relations between the United States and Brazil became strained over a number of issues. To many Argentine geopoliticians, this loosening of traditional U.S.-Brazilian ties permitted the unprecedented strengthening of Argentine-Brazilian links that followed.

Traditional Brazilian geopolitical thinking has been basically continental in nature, and has focused on such topics as the need to move inland from the coast and develop the Amazonic "heartland" (which also happens to be the heartland of South America). The suspicions of Brazil's Spanish-speaking Amazonic neighbors have been aroused by this geopolitical thrust, which has certain parallels with the manifest destiny of the United States in the nineteenth century when the U.S. drive to become a bioceanic continental nation was fulfilled at the expense of Mexico.[11] But Brazilian geopolitical thinking also has a maritime thrust focused on the need to project power into the South Atlantic sea lanes of communication ranging from the "Atlantic narrows" (Recife to Dakar), to the South Atlantic, and beyond to Antarctica. Brazilian naval geopoliticians in particular have argued that the South Atlantic is a strategic vacuum, and that there should be a South Atlantic Treaty Organization (SATO) as a counterpart to NATO, in which Brazil would play a key role.

The 1973 energy crisis provided a strong impetus to currents of resource geopolitics in Brazil because of its lack of adequate energy resources and dependency on outside sources to achieve developmental goals. Important energy projects were launched in these years, to include the massive hydroelectric complex at Itaipú and the attempt to obtain nuclear energy technology transferred from West Germany. These initiatives caused difficulties in Brazil's relationships with Argentina (because of the downriver effect of the Itaipú dam) and the United States (because of the Carter administration's non-proliferation policies).

Argentina

The Argentine geopolitical school is almost as important as the Brazilian and is certainly as prolific. It also shows certain limitations and idiosyncracies that reflect some basic differences. Argentina's geopoliticians seem less confident of their ideas than their Brazilian counterparts, and they waste creative energy in internecine squabbles and disputes between fragmented groups and different sub-schools.[12] There is a sense of frustration among Argentine geopoliticians, a feeling that Argentine "greatness" has been denied to the nation by some conspiracy of enemies that must be found and dealt with. They see the nation as victim of numerous past geopolitical aggressions, and suggest that Argentina is a geopolitically unsatisfied nation that cannot rest until past wrongs are righted. Further energies are expended on the usually futile search for a great unifying "Argentine National Project" that will bind together all patriotic Argentines in a grand scheme for development and movement toward the country's rightful destiny.

Another debilitating feature of Argentine geopolitical thinking is its reactive nature, especially toward the ideas and writings of Brazilian (and to a lesser extent Chilean) geopoliticians. Historically, the theme of Portuguese-Brazilian expansion at the expense of the Spanish-speaking world was a fundamental one.[13] The Brazilian geopolitical path to greatness is seen as a distinct threat by most Argentine geopoliticians. This perception, which was quite strong up to the late 1960s, diminished somewhat with the weakening of U.S.-Brazilian ties.

Chile also absorbs much of the Argentine geopolitician's attention. Historical rivalries are paramount, based on territorial disputes and problems in establishing the boundaries between the two nations. In the 1960s and 1970s these had a specific focus in the Beagle Channel and the issue of sovereignty of three key islands at the eastern mouth of the Channel (Lennox, Picton, and Nueva), which almost led to war in 1978. The larger geopolitical issue, however, had to do with Argentine perceptions of Chilean penetration of Patagonia and the South Atlantic, and of Argentina's Antarctic claim.

The Argentine geopolitical parallel to Brazil's theme of filling the Amazonic heartland is the deeply felt desire to recover the islands of the South Atlantic (Malvinas/Falklands, South Georgia, South Sandwich, and South Orkneys) and consolidate its sovereignty in the region. Two related themes are to keep both Chile and Brazil out of the "Argentine" South Atlantic as well as to make good Argentina's Antarctic claim. In a larger sense this Argentine geopolitical thrust southward is a continuation of the nineteenth century drive to bring first the Pampas and then Patagonia under effective control of Buenos Aires. However, unlike Brazil's push inward, the Argentine thrust to the south is maritime and not continental-heartland in nature. This gives a strong naval tone to much of Argentine geopolitical writing.[14] A unifying theme is that of the "Argentine Sea," which ties together the three basic parts of "Tri-Continental Argentina": Mainland Argentina, Antarctic Argentina, and Insular Argentina (i.e., the South Atlantic islands). Thus, effective control of this "Argentine Sea" means expelling the historic usurper (Great Britain), keeping out the old rivals (Brazil and Chile), and making sure that new potential adversaries do not consolidate their position in Argentine Antarctica.

Argentine geopoliticians are not as deeply concerned with resource geopolitics as their Brazilian counterparts, since Argentina is basically self-sufficient in energy. However, there is strong interest in potential oil reserves in the Malvinas Basin, as well as in Antarctic oil, for the time when Argentina's current reserves run out. Argentina's privileged status as a major exporter of foodstuffs (mainly grains and meat) has had a geopolitical impact in terms of the political implications of these exports in a hungry world.[15]

Chile

The most significant aspect of geopolitical thinking in Chile in the 1970s is that the military regime of General-President Augusto Pinochet created the first true Chilean geopolitical school at the same time it set up the Chilean National Security State based on geopolitical principles and the theory of the organic state. Before 1973 (the date when Pinochet assumed power in the bloody coup against Salvador Allende), a loosely connected group of Chilean geopolitical writers existed but with no coherent doctrine or set of geopolitical projects as in Argentina and especially Brazil. What geopolitical thinking that did exist was largely confined to military circles. Pinochet's own Senior War College thesis (written when he was a colonel) dealt with geopolitics, but it was not generally known outside of the officer corps. The Pinochet regime in the 1970s set about giving structure and support to his geopolitical thinking by increasing the role of geopolitical ideas in government, the media, and the educational system. It is significant that shortly after Pinochet came to power his old War College thesis was published (this time for a much broader audience) by the prestigious Editorial Andrés Bello. It was later translated into English as *Introduction to Geopolitics*. The creation of a Chilean Geopolitical Institute followed, along with an impressive production of geopolitical journals, books, and projects. This was accompanied by a systematic search for "geopolitical laws" that would guide the statesman in the process of governing the National Security State.[16]

Some Chilean geopoliticians have advanced their own version of Chile's manifest destiny towards greatness. In part this rests on the belief among certain members of the military regime that they are among the very last defenders of Christian western values against a decisive onslaught by Marxist-Leninists and the internal corruption of the West. But there is also an arcane geopolitical theory that holds that the core of human civilization has been historically shifting westward, following the sun. Thus, the cradle of human culture began in the Middle East, shifted to the Mediterranean, then to Northern Europe and to the United States, and now is about to move again to the Pacific. Chilean geopoliticians see their country as one of the key Pacific Basin nations that will share in this new center of human civilization and power.

Chile's unique geography imposes severe restraints on geopolitical projects to increase its *lebensraum* and influence. The common metaphor is that Chile is like a tube that can only expand out the ends since it is constrained by the Andes to the East and the Pacific Ocean to the West. The expansion north was achieved in the War of the Pacific (1879–1883), and Chile need be concerned only with preserving the gains made in that conflict at the expense of Peru and Bolivia. The major focus of the geopolitician's attention is therefore south, to the control of the inter-oceanic passages (Beagle Channel, Strait of Magellan, and the Drake Passage), and the protection of Chile's Antarctic interests.

A Chilean parallel exists to Argentine geopoliticians' ideas regarding a "Tri-Continental Argentina" welded together by an "Argentine Sea." "Tri-Continental Chile" consists of mainland Chile, Chilean Antarctica, and Insular Chile, which includes the Pacific Ocean islands (Easter, Robinson Crusoe), the Magellanic and Beagle Channel islands, the Cape Horn Group, and the Diego Ramirez group that lies between South America and Antarctica. The geopolitical concept of a "Chilean Sea" has roots going back to the last century, when the victorious Chilean fleet during the War of the Pacific made a "Chilean Lake" of the waters west of Chile.[17]

Despite the clear nationalistic and aggressive tone of much of Chilean geopolitical writing, there is also a current of cooperation with Argentina, especially in keeping newcomers out of the Antarctic sectors where Argentina and Chile have overlapping claims.[18] This raises the intriguing possibility of combined Argentine-Chilean (or Southern Cone) activities in what could be called their "Antarctic condominium" (discussed below).

Uruguay

Geopolitical thinking in Uruguay usually reflects the reality that this small nation plays a secondary role in South American international relations as a buffer between larger states. Uruguayan geopoliticians generally acknowledge that this situation severely limits the nation's geopolitical possibilities, although some optimistically speak of Uruguay's key role as a "hinge" or bridge between larger nations, which could increase its importance if handled with skill.

A related idea in Uruguayan geopolitical thinking in the 1970s was the integrationist theme proposed by Quagliotti de Bellis when he argued that the three smaller states of the Southern Cone should join their resources to form URUPABOL (Uruguay, Paraguay, and Bolivia), which would in turn be the core for South American and eventually Latin American economic and political integration.[19] Uruguayan Antarctic interest in this period was stimulated by some geopolitical writings that stressed its historical role as a port of departure for Spanish South Atlantic activity, and the need for Uruguay to have an Antarctic presence.

The Uruguayan National Security State set up in the 1970s seems to have little relation to explicitly geopolitical thinking. Rather, it was based more on copying Brazilian and Argentine models in response to the threat of the Tupumaro urban guerrillas. There was much coordination and cooperation between Uruguay's military leaders and those of Argentina and Brazil, especially on intelligence and counterinsurgency matters, and this factor seems to have a greater role in shaping the Uruguayan National Security State than geopolitical thinking as such.

Peru

Peruvian geopolitical thinking presents some unique features. Although there was no geopolitical "school" or National Security State based on organic principles (in the sense of the Brazilian, Argentine, and Chilean ones), there was an evident interest in geopolitical thinking by key individuals in the reformist military regime that governed Peru from 1968 to 1980. Chief among these figures was General Edgardo Mercado Jarrín, who held key posts in the military regime. After retiring, he founded the *Instituto Peruano de Estudios Geopolíticos y Estratégicos* (IPEGE). General Mercado Jarrín and IPEGE, with its journal, publications, and seminars, stressed the geopolitical factors in Peru's development projects and international relations.[20] The Institute was founded around the date of the centennial of the War of the Pacific (1979), and indeed the first journal issues focused on this theme with a strongly anti-Chilean tone. Attention later shifted to the border difficulties with Ecuador and other issues, such as opening up the Amazon, the future of the Pacific Basin, the Law of the Sea, and Peruvian interests in the Antarctic.[21]

Other South American Nations

Geopolitical ideas are much less evident in the remaining nations of South America. Paraguay and Bolivia have small institutes devoted to geopolitical studies, but their production is sporadic and their ideas are generally based on the geopolitical literature of the larger Southern Cone countries. In Ecuador, the Army's Military Geographic Institute has published some geopolitical material, but on a small scale.

South American Geopolitical Thinking in the 1980s

General Considerations

The decade of the 1980s saw a brief but significant war in South America, one that was rooted in geopolitical thinking, and which had important political and geopolitical consequences. Ironically, one of the repercussions of the Anglo-Argentine conflict over the Malvinas/Falkland Islands was to shift South American geopolitical thinking away from aggressive themes to ones that stress South American cooperation and integration. Whereas the geopolitical literature of the 1960s and 1970s commonly stressed narrow nationalism and chauvinistic calls to redress past geopolitical injustices, in the post-Malvinas period the prevailing themes have often been South American integration, cooperation for development, peaceful solution of disputes, and the need to support the delicate path to democracy. This trend has not, however, wholly eliminated the prior aggressive tone in substantial segments of South American geopolitical literature, which still devotes much of its attention to possible conflicts, and indeed tends to make their peaceful resolution more difficult. Finally, there is in South American geopolitical thinking a growing focus on Antarctica as an area and an unresolved resource and sovereignty problem that clearly lends itself to geopolitical analysis.

The Malvinas/Falklands Conflict and Its Aftermath

The Malvinas/Falklands conflict emerged as a watershed event, not only in Argentine political and military history, but also in the broader framework of South American geopolitical thinking.[22] The conflict was explicitly foreshadowed by a number of Argentine geopolitical writers, who in the early 1980s laid out in detail the scenario that eventually was launched by the Argentine military junta in April 1982. While this is easier to see in hindsight, it raises the intriguing possibility that a more sensitive reading of the geopolitical literature in this period might have given some warning to leaders and analysts of other nations. The foreshadowing of the conflict also raises the possibility that other South American conflict situations with geopolitical roots (such as South Atlantic tensions or competition over Antarctica) might be similarly presaged in the literature. The foreshadowing of the conflict was especially notable in Argentine geopolitical and military journals, although in the early months of 1982 strong hints also appeared in the major newspapers.[23]

The conflict produced a large body of narrative, history, and analysis to the point of a genre of "Malvinas literature" in Argentina. Much of this was at the personal and tactical level and contained little material that was geopolitical in nature. Geopolitical and senior military institutes, however, especially those in Argentina, produced numerous articles and works on the conflict and its geopolitical implications. The material written during the heat of the fighting and the immediate aftermath was uneven and frequently full of bitter rhetoric, directed especially against the United States.[24] With time, however, Argentine geopolitical writers produced perceptive and balanced analyses, even when cast from a nationalistic Argentine position.[25]

The postwar geopolitical literature in other South American countries followed predictable patterns. The nations most interested in the conflict, as indicated by their attention in geopolitical publications and journals, were Peru, Brazil, and Chile (as well as Venezuela). The geopolitical literature of Peru, a strong Argentine supporter, emphasized how the war fundamentally changed basic patterns of international and strategic relations in the hemisphere. General Mercado Jarrín was especially mordant in his criticism of the United States. He argued that the Malvinas conflict represented an historic turning point as Latin America finally abandoned the old dependency on the United States and took responsibility for its own defenses and strategic thinking.[26]

Chilean geopolitical analysis was much more cautious, and early post-war writings stressed the interrelationship of the Malvinas/Falklands issue with the Beagle Channel dispute and conflicting Argentine-Chilean claims in Antarctica. The Chilean literature frequently referred to the islands as "Falklands" or "Malvinas/Falklands."[27] A similar pattern shows up in the Brazilian geopolitical literature, which also frequently included the not-too-subtle point that the disastrous outcome of the war for Argentina meant that Brazil should be prepared to take a more active role in South Atlantic defense.[28]

An observable trend in the post-Malvinas South American geopolitical literature is an acceleration of the move away from U.S. strategic doctrine and towards indigenous South American geopolitical ideas. This trend paralleled the theme that the old institutions of the inter-American peace and security system, created under U.S. leadership, had been seriously undermined in the Malvinas/Falklands crisis, and that the time had come for Latin America to put its own security system into being.[29] Although the intensity of this feeling subsided along with the bitterness over the U.S. "betrayal" of Argentina and the Inter-American System, its insertion into regional geopolitical thinking has been one of the enduring legacies of the conflict.

The South Atlantic

As suggested above, a by-product of the Malvinas/Falklands conflict was renewed geopolitical interest in the South Atlantic, the inter-oceanic passages, and Antarctica. Many Latin American geopolitical analysts, who had long complained that outsiders had rarely taken the Southern Cone seriously, now saw themselves embroiled in an issue involving important strategic matters such as power projection over petroleum resources, sealines of communications, alternate inter-oceanic routes in case of closure of the Panama Canal, and control of important access routes to the Antarctic Peninsula (where numerous nations have interests and scientific installations).[30] One geopolitical writer coined a new term for the broad South Atlantic–Antarctic area stressing this linkage: *Atlantártida*, translated as "Atlantarctic."[31]

The revived interest in the South Atlantic–Antarctic region was especially serendipitous for many Brazilian maritime geopoliticians, who were seeking a balance to the traditionally continental thrust of Brazilian geopolitical thinking. In terms of the three phases of Brazil's path to becoming a great power, this emphasis on the South Atlantic and Antarctica meant moving from the first step (effectively occupying its own boundaries) to the key second step of pushing outward and projecting power into new areas. The post-Malvinas Brazilian geopolitical literature has included many articles and monographs stressing how this theater of operations is a natural region for Brazil to move into as it fulfills its broad responsibilities under the Rio Treaty, especially in light of Argentina's disastrous attempt to impose its own geopolitical control on the islands and oceanic expanses of the region.[32] It should be noted that the Rio Treaty boundaries extend to the South Pole.

To some extent the renewed geopolitical emphasis on the South Atlantic in the 1980s built on two ideas that had been developed in previous decades. The first of these was a narrow Argentine concept of the South Atlantic as the "Argentine Sea" tieing together Tri-Continental Argentina.[33] The second concept was that of a South Atlantic Treaty Organization (SATO), which would form a parallel to NATO and fill the strategic void in the South Atlantic. The idea of a SATO had first made its appearance in the early 1970s and included association with the United States; in the post-Malvinas atmosphere, proposals for SATO excluded the United States and served as a vehicle for Latin military cooperation.[34]

Redemocratization and Geopolitical Thinking

A particularly sensitive topic in the 1980s is the relationship of geopolitical thinking to the move towards democratic governments. The earlier association between geopolitical thinking and the National Security State suggested to many observers that geopolitical thinking was a potential threat to the redemocratization process, and had to be brought under control at the same time as the National Security States were being dismantled and the militaries increasingly subjected to civilian control. However, as several analysts have noted, the military leadership of the National Security States had insured that geopolitical ideas, linked to patriotic and nationalistic themes, were inserted into the media and educational systems and thus generally survived their departure.[35]

There are indications that the attempt to include influential civilians in the student bodies of the key senior war colleges during the period of the National Security States has had an impact on this group of elites. Although the influence of these individuals may not be as great in a democratic regime as in a military one, they do represent an important segment of Southern Cone leadership that has been exposed to, and in many cases accepted, the tenets of geopolitical thinking as presented in the senior service schools.[36]

The case of Chile, with its long period of military rule under an explicitly geopolitical leadership cadre, has attracted much attention.[37] As several of the Southern Cone nations returned to democracy in the 1980s, South American geopolitical literature began to include articles critical of Chile and President Pinochet; one biting commentary in an Argentine military journal in 1984 specifically labelled him "the South American Fuhrer."[38]

In the decade of the 1980s, significant segments of the Southern Cone armed forces and their civilian leadership are embarked on the difficult and delicate task of redefining the role of the military in a democracy. In this process there is a recognized need to shift the focus of geopolitical thinking away from the aggressive and highly jingoistic trends of the past and thus reduce the use of geopolitical arguments to buttress a higher role, profile, and budget for the military.[39]

Solution of the Beagle Channel Islands Issue

A dramatic example of the contrast between Southern Cone geopolitical thinking in the 1980s and the previous period can be seen in the treatment of the issue of the Beagle Channel Islands. In the late 1970s geopolitical writings in both Argentina and Chile were a strong stimulus to nationalistic rhetoric and even war fever. The geopolitical literature on both sides went beyond juridical or political analysis to accuse the other side of deceit, expansionism, and treacherous preparations for war. The geopolitical institutes and senior war colleges produced much of the inflammatory geopolitical literature; numerous active and retired officers were involved in efforts to keep the issue alive in the public's imagination in case the war mobilization preceded to its ultimate conclusion.[40]

President Raúl Alfonsín made the solution of the Beagle Channel issue one of his foreign policy priorities, in part because of the military's use of the issue to justify its role, size, and budget, Even after the Holy See's declaration of peace and friendship was signed between Chilean and Argentine representatives, Argentine nationalists and military officers lobbied hard against ratification. It was approved only after Alfonsín's personal involvement.

The effect of the settlement has been salutary for relations between the two countries as well as for the broader process of shifting Southern Cone geopolitical thinking away from conflictual themes and towards greater cooperation and integration.[41] The prior jingoistic geopolitical writings on the Beagle Channel issue have given way to more objectively analytical themes, although some Argentine geopolitical authors continue to complain about the way the settlement favored Chile.[42]

South American Conflict and Geopolitical Thinking

In a manner similar to the Beagle Channel situation, there is a contrast between the continental geopolitical conflict situation in the 1980s compared with that of the previous decades. In the 1960s and 1970s it was possible to speak of a set of "perpendicular tensions and diagonal alliances" between the major actors in the Southern Cone of South America.[43] The perpendicular tensions were between Brazil-Argentina; Argentina-Chile; Chile-Peru; Peru-Brazil; and Ecuador-Peru. The diagonal alliances (more realistically "understandings") were between Argentina and Peru, and Brazil and Chile. This balance-of-power arrangement responded to a set of geopolitical laws, especially the "law of discontinuous borders." It argues that when two nations have a touching (contiguous) border their relations will tend to be difficult, while if they are close but not touching they are more likely to get along. The balance-of-power system was generally viewed as stable, but there was also a realization that if conflict broke out between any two antagonists, there might be a tendency for the remaining actors to also get involved in the conflict.[44] Toward the end of the 1970s the Beagle Channel problem and the Centennial of the War of the Pacific heightened these tensions, to the point that the geopolitical literature of these years included a number of destabilizing war hypotheses between various actors in the geopolitical balance of power scheme.[45]

In considerable contrast, there are few such scenarios seen in the geopolitical literature of the late 1980s. Events in the late 1970s and early 1980s have combined to reduce the emphasis on the aggressive side of geopolitics: The peaceful passing of the Centennial of the War of the Pacific, the reaction to the Malvinas/Falklands conflict, the solution of the Beagle Channel problem, and the return to elected civilian regimes in most of the South American countries.

The more optimistic analysts argue that the old alliances and antagonisms have in fact faded away and have been replaced by the new geopolitics of Latin American integration, solidarity, and cooperation. General Mercado Jarrín's views, published in 1986, are representative of this opinion: "The Malvinas and the recent Beagle award changed the traditional realignment of South American forces and the old geopolitical scheme graphed on two axes: Lima-Buenos Aires and Santiago-Brasilia. Any Southern Cone foreign ministry that continues to act on the basis of these old axes would do so because it had no sensitivity to geopolitical realities and was living under a severely outdated perception of facts. Today there is an opening up to a greater sense of regional cooperation and integration in hemispheric relations, which responds to present-day problems."[46]

The Theme of Latin American Integration

The idea of Latin American integration, although not a new theme in the geopolitical thinking of South America, acquires renewed vigor and new connotations in the 1980s. Whereas in the 1960s and 1970s the concept of integration was limited principally to international economic ties or development schemes, in the 1980s it began to assume an anti-U.S. tone (especially after the Malvinas/Falklands conflict), or at least became associated with schemes for Latin American coordination that excluded the United States. Although integration remained primarily an economic concept, it also began to appear in the geopolitical literature, especially in Peru and Argentina.

In fact, a sub-genre of Southern Cone geopolitical thinking could be labelled "the geopolitics of liberation through integration," with roots in dependency theory, anti-colonialism, and "third positions" ranging from old Peronista ideas to contemporary Third World movements. In the 1980s it received a strong impetus during the Malvinas/Falklands war with Latin American resentment at U.S. policies in that conflict. The problem of crushing foreign debts and the rebellion against the traditional institutions of the Inter-American System all supported the idea that Latin America's salvation was through integration, and that geopolitics might play a role in this process. Some of the earlier writings in this vein stem from the prolific pen of General Juan Guglialmelli.[47] Perhaps the more vocal contemporary spokesman for this geopolitical theme was General Edgardo Mercado Jarrín of Peru, who had long advocated a basic revision of the Inter-American System, especially its security arrangements, to serve Latin American interests as opposed to U.S. interests.[48]

Within the security sphere, the proponents of a "geopolitics of liberation through integration" speak of the concept of "integral security."[49] They mean that Latin American security can no longer be defined by the traditionally narrow strategic-military dimension held by the United States. Rather, contemporary security now must include many fields of human concern: Political, economic, social, and cultural, as well as the more strictly military ones. To cite an example, the debt problem is seen as having fundamental security implications under the concept of Latin American "integral security," because it mortgages national independence and because repayment of the debt seemingly requires socially explosive austerity measures.

Joining their colleagues in the fields of economics and political science, many geopolitical thinkers have advocated integration as the way out of Latin America's multifaceted crises. Some geopolitical thinkers warn, however, that integration must be approached cautiously lest it be used to hide yet another facet of domination by the colonial powers that have plagued Latin America. Thus, a common theme in the geopolitical writing of the 1980s is whether there is to be "integration for liberation or integration for dependency."[50]

The integration theme, while mainly multilateral in nature, also concerns itself with key bilateral ties. Chief among them is the Argentine-Brazilian relationship, which many geopolitical analysts see as the historical driving force in Southern Cone international relations. The improvement in Argentine-Brazilian relations through the 1980s did in fact mark a change in basic patterns of South American relations.[51] Other improved bilateral ties that have had considerable geopolitical impact because of the way they weaken old conflictural geopolitical relationships have been Argentina-Chile (by means of settlement of the Beagle Channel dispute and projects for possible Antarctic cooperation) and Brazil-Peru (through joint development of the Amazon Basin).[52]

A corollary of the geopolitical integration theme has been the improvement of ties between institutions and people involved in these matters. In part this is a function of the technology of communications, which has greatly facilitated the process of consultation among key South America leaders.[53] But formal cooperation agreements have also been signed between various geopolitical institutes to increase their contacts and joint projects, a phenomenon that was markedly absent in the more chauvinistic period of the 1960s and 1970s.[54] It would be unrealistic to assume, however, that the old geopolitical suspicions and antagonisms have totally disappeared. The geopolitical literature of the 1980s still contains conflictual themes and accusations of aggressive nationalism rooted in past conflicts.[55]

Heartland Geopolitical Themes

The old heartland thrust of South American geopolitical thinking of past decades shows up in the 1980s in continuing efforts to develop the Amazon Basin as well as in other ways. Works by Meira Mattos and Mercado Jarrín are representative of this current.[56] But, in contrast to prior geopolitical writings on the South American heartland, which concentrated on Brazil's unilateral development efforts, contemporary works tend to support multilateral or bilateral efforts. Thus, there is an emphasis on the Amazon Basin Pact as a major structure for international cooperation (although there is also some suspicion that the pact represents a Brazilian ploy to dominate its neighbors).

The old heartland theme of moving capital cities away from their original coastal locations also shows up in President Alfonsín's proposal to move the Argentine Federal Capital from Buenos Aires to the small remote city of Viedma.[57] Although the proposal was motivated primarily by a desire to get away from the congested capital of Buenos Aires with one-third of the nation's population, geopolitical reasons are also behind the proposals. These lie in the Argentine geopolitical thrust to the South, away from the Rio de la Plata area toward Patagonia, the Southern Islands, and Antarctica.

Heartland geopolitical themes also show up in Bolivia's perennial complaint about being a "mediterranean" (i.e., landlocked) country. A recent argument in this connection is that Bolivia is the natural heartland of the South American continent, and that South America's development will be stunted and its integration thwarted unless Bolivia has the chance to link this natural heartland to the outside world via the sea outlet.[58] The argument has a historical basis in that the colonial Charcas region (today Bolivia) was a key transportation nexus for land routes within the Spanish empire. Bolivia is where two major South American river basins (Amazon and Pilcomayo-Parana-Plata) come together and where portage or canals could be used to link them.

To a significant extent heartland geopolitical thinking is linked to transportation routes,[59] and the development of these heartlands is a function of major construction efforts in road or canal building. Recent years have seen the initiation of numerous such projects, to include the Brazilian Trans-Amazonic road network and the Peruvian "Marginal Highway" on the eastern slope of the Andes. However, these projects, as well as a number of others, have not reached their planned potential due to high costs, the limited value of the areas they opened up, other priorities, and the concern over ecological damage.

Pacific Basin Geopolitics

Many of the Chilean geopolitical ideas of superiority in the Pacific Basin have been challenged in the 1980s. This is due in part to Chile's relative isolation under the Pinochet regime, an isolation that increased in the 1980s when more and more of the Southern Cone governments reverted to elected civilian regimes. One strong challenge to Chilean assumptions of geopolitical control of the Pacific area came from Peru, especially in the form of the ideas of Mercado Jarrín.[60] Peru has recently been in the forefront of Law of the Sea issues, and for a time based a significant portion of its economy on a short-lived Pacific fishing boom.

To some extent Ecuador has also challenged the Chilean pre-eminence in Pacific Basin geopolitics. Speaking somewhat poetically, Ecuadorean geopolitical writers argue that Ecuador was "Janus-like" because, like the Roman god of two faces, it had to look geopolitically in two directions.[61] One of these was to the Atlantic via the recovery of Amazonic territories lost to Peru, and the other was to the Pacific in terms of both her Galapagos Island possessions and south to a possible Antarctic interest.

Geopolitical Interest in Central America

A new theme in South American geopolitical thinking in the 1980s has been the attention paid to developments in Central America and, to a lesser extent, the rest of the Caribbean. This is a region that has historically held little interest for South American geopoliticians, who tended to ignore it or look upon the smaller nations of the region with patronizing disdain.

This view changed with the triumph of the FSLN revolution in Nicaragua, the stepping up of insurgency in El Salvador in 1980 and 1981, and the Argentine involvement in training the *contras* in Honduras, all of which drew the attention of South American geopolitical thinking to Central America. The creation of the South American Contadora Support Group (Argentina, Brazil, Peru, and Uruguay) further accelerated this process, raising the possibility that South American military personnel or units might be involved in some sort of conflict resolution procedures.

Resource Geopolitical Issues

The old, somewhat exaggerated geopolitical concerns (mostly Argentine) regarding the joint Brazilian-Paraguayan hydroelectric projects along the Parana River have subsided as patterns of Brazilian-Argentine cooperation in the 1980s began to replace mutual suspicion. The Argentine-Brazilian understandings and agreements also included important ones dealing with nuclear programs, further contributing to the general improvement of relations between the key nations of the Southern Cone.[62]

Argentine emphasis on foodstuffs as instruments for geopolitical leverage continued in this period and were indeed heightened as a result of the Malvinas/Falklands conflict, when it became clear that grain and wheat sales to the Soviet Union were an important tool in Argentine foreign policy. The war also revived the old Argentine geopolitical theme of autarky (self-sufficiency) in which Argentina, more than any other Latin American nation, could fall back on its own food and energy resources and cut itself off from the United States and Europe.

The Malvinas/Falklands War also brought renewed attention to the potential hydrocarbon reserves in the basin formed by the islands and the surrounding waters. There was much suspicion in Argentina that one reason for British stubbornness in hanging on to the islands was that they contained vast oil and gas reserves that had been secretly discovered by the British, working perhaps with their U.S. allies.[63] Whether a valid perception or not, the belief that these large fields exist also helped focus South American geopolitical attention on the South Atlantic islands, the Southern Ocean Basin in general, and on the Antarctic Continent that forms the southern limit of the Southern Ocean.

Antarctica

In the 1980s Antarctica began to loom as a region for major South American geopolitical cooperation or confrontation (even conflict).[64] The reasons are a complex mix of issues, actors, problems, and opportunities. They include the belief that Antarctica contains vast amounts of valuable resources (fish, krill, and perhaps oil and precious metals). Antarctica unquestionably offers the geopolitician the possibility of space in which to expand, although one could question whether this "frozen *lebensraum*" has much utility for human habitation or exploitation, leaving aside the environmental damage such human intrusion might cause in delicate Antarctic ecosystems. Further, Antarctica has not only been the focus of many years of geopolitical attention (especially in Argentina and Chile), but in the 1980s has come under new geopolitical scrutiny as many of the old areas of the geopolitical tension on the South American mainland are now of less interest due to resolution of historical problems. Lastly, there is the time pressure exerted by the belief that something may happen in Antarctica in the next few years as the Antarctic Treaty comes up for possible review in 1991.

The renewed interest in Antarctic geopolitics is also linked to the broader issues of South Atlantic geopolitics, to include the Falklands/ Malvinas Islands, other key islands, and the inter-oceanic passages and straits. The geopolitically interrelated nature of these issues, and the presence of a large number of other nations (including the two superpowers and many of their NATO and Warsaw Pact allies, and the largest Third World states) suggests that any conflictual or confrontational outcomes may involve a great deal more than local or subregional players.

It is also significant that the Antarctic activities of the South American nations are basically in the hands of their military establishments, sometimes exclusively. These military-oriented Antarctic institutions and activities are tightly linked to geopolitical institutes and writers, so that it is not surprising that the Antarctic policies of these nations contain much geopolitical thinking.

Antarctic activities and themes have a long historical root in the geopolitical writings of Argentina and Chile,[65] and it can be asserted that the Antarctic consciousness of elites and masses in these two countries is closely linked to geopolitical writings and ideas that circulate in the media, the educational systems, and decision-making bodies. In Brazil this phenomenon is less pronounced, but the influence of major geopolitical writers, such as Therezinha de Castro and General Meira Mattos, has been striking as Brazil began to mount her first Antarctic expeditions in the early 1980s.[66] One Antarctic geopolitical theory in particular has had major impact: De Castro's "frontage" theory, under which the "South American Antarctic Quadrant" should be divided among the six South American nations that have a "frontage" (i.e., a wedge-shaped Antarctic sector defined by open meridians to the South Pole). This has the net effect of reducing the sectors claimed by Argentina and Chile, and granting sectors to Brazil (the largest), as well as Uruguay, Peru, and Ecuador, along with Argentina and Chile. As might be expected, this theory is bitterly opposed by Argentine and Chilean geopolitical writers, while it is viewed with great interest by those in Uruguay, Peru, and Ecuador, where Antarctic geopoliticians have been in the forefront of the move to raise the Antarctic consciousness of both their people and their governments.[67]

A Look Ahead: Geopolitical
Trends into the 1990s

Predictions about the nature and strength of regional geopolitical trends will depend to a considerable degree on the role of the military in the next decade. If the trend towards redemocratization of the 1980s continues and is consolidated, then traditional geopolitical thinking is likely to have relatively less impact and the new modes will aim to strengthen the bonds of integration and cooperation between the South American nations.

On the other hand, should democratic regimes in the Southern Cone fail and permit the return of unelected military regimes and the reestablishment of National Security States, then geopolitical thinking is likely to have a much greater impact, one dominated by some of the more aggressive and nationalistic variants of geopolitical thinking that were evident in the 1960s and 1970s. Moves toward integration and cooperation would be overshadowed by the more chauvinistic and jingoistic arguments of geopolitical thinking at the service of the National Security State.

The above comments are not intended to reduce the sophisticated and complex currents of Southern Cone geopolitical thinking to a Manichean vision of "good civilian geopolitical thinking" versus "bad military geopolitical thinking." However, they do reflect the experience of the past three decades in the sense that when the Southern Cone armed forces took power they tended to establish National Security States based on the organic theory of the state that relied on geopolitical thinking to provide the pseudo-intellectual underpinnings of their ideology. The nature of the geopolitical thinking used in this process tended to view internal opposition as Marxist subversion, and tended to see neighbors as adversaries in a hostile Darwinian world. It is no coincidence that the passing of the National Security States in much of the Southern Cone in the late 1970s and 1980 saw a decline in this aggressive variant of geopolitical thinking and its replacement by more positive forms.

Assuming that most of the democracies of the Southern Cone will consolidate their roots and endure into the 1990s, we can tentatively identify some geopolitical trends that are likely to project into this period.

In general, the old inter-state conflicts in South America will lose their relevance and will have a tendency to recede into the mists of history, or will be the subject of renewed attempts at solution. Many of the geopolitically-based old bilateral strains (Argentina-Brazil, Chile-Argentina, Peru-Chile) have diminished in the 1980s and this trend is likely to continue. On the other hand, tensions with certain outside nations will remain unabated and may be exacerbated by increased emphasis on resource geopolitics (especially energy). Thus, Argentine-British strains over the Malvinas/Falklands and South Atlantic–Antarctic claims will not disappear and will continue to have important geopolitical foundations. To the extent that Argentina can capitalize on South American and Latin American integration, it will be able to muster considerable hemisphere support (at least at the rhetorical and diplomatic levels) in the struggle to obtain the Malvinas/Falklands and other southern islands.

Success in this endeavor is contingent on the basic success of South American integration efforts. Although these will focus fundamentally on economic, developmental, and political issues, geopolitics can also make a contribution if the positive aspects of geopolitical thinking predominate. Thus, the struggle between "integration for liberation" and "integration for dependency" will tilt toward the "liberation" side as South America (and the rest of Latin America) continues its trends toward greater independence, self-sufficiency, and links to the world beyond the hemisphere and the United States. One corollary of this process may well be a much greater South American role in helping to solve Central American problems, either through the Contadora process or some successor. Geopolitical analysis may contribute to this process, which could include verification, monitoring, and peace-observing efforts by the larger South American nations in Central America.

Heartland geopolitical concerns (i.e., development of the Amazon Basin, Argentina's thrust southward, and Bolivia's attempt to regain her outlet to the sea) will continue, but with a lower profile as the rhetoric subsides and as there is a growing realization that many of these heartland geopolitical ideas have limited practicality, and that any payoffs will be modest and very far in the future.

A major arena of geopolitical cooperation or confrontation in the 1990s will likely be Antarctica, the sub-Antarctic islands, and the South Atlantic. The multiple reasons for this, explored in the prior section, have to do with maritime and resource geopolitics, the perception of vast exploitable energy and food bonanzas in the region, the time pressures on the Antarctic Treaty, the link to the Malvinas/Falklands problem, and the use of the region as an arena for Brazilian power projection. It should be noted in passing that the false perception that the Antarctic Treaty "expires" in 1991 must somehow be corrected to avoid a peaking of tension around that year. There are distinct possibilities of inter-South American national confrontations in Antarctica and the Southern Ocean if one nation decides to exploit resources unilaterally or try to make good a sovereignty claim in an irresponsible manner. However, if the integrative geopolitics discussed above continue to bear fruit, then a more likely outcome is a cooperative "South American condominium" approach to Antarctica that will leave aside the national sovereignty claims of Chile and Argentina, as well as the destabilizing implications of the Brazilian "frontage" approach. Should this trend continue, then non-South American powers in the American Antarctic quadrant and the corresponding segment of the Southern Ocean may have to face the opposition of a unified Southern Cone.

Notes

1. This section and the following draw on the author's prior work on South American geopolitical thinking, especially *Geopolitics and Conflict in South America: Quarrels Among Neighbors* (New York: Praeger, 1985), and *Antarctic and South American Geopolitics: Frozen Lebensraum* (New York: Praeger, 1988).

2. Oscar Caviedes, *The Southern Cone: Realities of the Authoritarian State in South America* (Totowa, N.J.: Rowman and Allenheld, 1984); Colonel Luis A. Leoni Housay, "Pinochet: El Fuhrer Sudamericano," *Revista de Temas*

Militares (Argentina), no. 11 (September 1984), pp. 5–20; Joseph Comblin, *A Ideología da Sequranca Nacional* (Rio de Janeiro: Editorial Civilizacao Brasileira, 1978); and José Alfredo Amaral Gurgel, *Sequranca e Democracia* (Rio de Janeiro: Livraria José Olympio, 1978).

3. General Augusto Pinochet Ugarte, *Geopolítica* (Santiago: Andrés Bello, 1973); and Coronel Julio von Chrismar, "Geopolitica y Seguridad Nacional," *Seguridad Nacional* (Chile), no. 21 (1981), pp. 36–43.

4. General Pinochet, *Geopolítica* (1973), pp. 60–61; and Colonel Jorge E. Atencio, *¿Que es la Geopolítica?* (Buenos Aires: Pleamar, 1965), pp. 122–125, 360.

5. Jack Child, *Unequal Alliance: The Inter-American Military System, 1938–1978* (Boulder: Westview Press, 1980).

6. Coronel von Chrismar, "Geopolítica y Seguridad Nacional" (1981), pp. 36–43.

7. Jorge A. Tapia Valdés, *El Terrorismo del Estado: La Doctrina de la Sequridad Nacional en el Cono Sur* (Mexico: Editorial Nueva Imagen, 1980); Joseph Comblin, *A Ideología de Segurança Nacional* (Rio de Janeiro: Editorial Civilizaçao Brasileira, 1978); Genaro Arriagado, *Sequridad Nacional y Bien Común* (Santiago: Talleres Gráficos Corporación, 1976); and Julio J. Chiavenato, *Geopolítica, Arma do Fascismo* (São Paulo: Global Editora, 1981).

8. Jorge A. Tapia Valdés, op. cit.

9. Lewis Tambs, "Como o Brasil Joge o Xadrez Geopolítico," *A Defesa Nacional*, no. 686 (November 1979), pp. 135–149; Oliveiros S. Ferreire, "A Geopolítica do Brasil Revisitada," *Política e Estrategia*, vol. II, no. 4 (October 1984); and Octavio Tosta, "Geopolítica do Brasil," *A Defesa Nacional*, no. 71 (January 1984), pp. 107–122.

10. General Juan E. Guglialmelli, "Argentina-Brazil: Enfrentamiento o Alianza para la Liberacion," *Estrategia*, no. 26 (September 1975), pp. 1–29; and Florentino Díaz Loza, "Geopolítica del Brasil," *Estrategia*, no. 29 (July 1974), pp. 30–40.

11. César José Marini, *La Crisis en el Cono Sur* (Buenos Aires: SACI, 1984).

12. Among the major writers are General Juan E. Guglialmelli, Colonel Jorge Atencio, and Almirante Jorge Fraga; the major journals are *Estrategia* and *Geopolítica*; and the principal publishing house is Pleamar.

13. General Juan E. Guglialmelli, "El Destino Manifiesto Brasileño y el Atlántico Sur," *Estrategia*, no. 39 (March 1976), pp. 5–24.

14. Osiria G. Villegas, "Imperium Jurisdiccional," *Geopolítica*, no. 21 (March 1981), p. 7; Almirante Segundo Storni, *Intereses Argentinos en el Mar* (Buenos Aires: A. Moen, 1916); and César José Marini, op. cit.

15. Osiria G. Villegas, "El Petroleo como Arma en el Campo Económico," *Geosur*, no. 13 (September 1980), p. 27.

16. Juan Carlos Stack, "Filosofía y biología: Fundamentos de la Geopolitica Contemporánea," *Revista Chilena de Geopolítica*, no. 3 (1985), pp. 7–13; Mario Arnello Romo, "Principios Fundamentales para un Proyecto Nacional de Chile Futuro," *Revista Chilena de Geopolítica*, no. 2 (1985), pp. 7–16; Colonel Luis A. Leoni Houssay, "Pinochet: El Fuhrer Sudamericano," *Revista de Temas*

Militares, no. 11 (September 1984), pp. 5–20; and Mario Barros van Buren, "La Geopolítica en los Postulados Internacionales de Chile," *Revista Chilena de Geopolítica*, no. 1 (1984), pp. 33–39.

17. Federico Marull Bermúdez, *Mar de Chile y Mar Andino* (Santiago: Universidad de Chile, 1975).

18. Francisco Orrego Vicuña, *Política Antártica de Chile* (Santiago: Universidad de Chile, 1984).

19. Bernardo Quagliotti de Bellis, *Constantes Geopolíticas en Iberoamérica* (Montevideo: Geosur, 1979); "Bases para una Geopolítica del Uruguay," *Geosur*, no. 36 (August 1982), entire issue; and *Uruguay en el Cono Sur: Destino Geopolítico* (Buenos Aires: Tierra Nueva, 1976).

20. General Edgardo Mercado Jarrín, *La Política Exterior del Gobierno Revolucionario Peruano* (Lima: Ministerio de Relaciones Exteriores, 1972); *Sequrided, Política, Estrategia* (Lima: Imprenta del Ministerio de Guerra, 1974); "La Seguridad Integral," *Revista de la Escuela Superior de Guerra*, no. 75 (July 1972), pp. 17–30; and "Bases para una Geopolítica Peruana," *Geosur*, no. 19 (March 1981), pp. 3–35. See also Walter Reinfarje Bazan, "El Porque y para que del IPEGE," *Estudios Geopolíticos y Estratégicos* (Peru), no. 1 (January 1979).

21. General Edgardo Mercado Jarrín contributed the following articles on these themes to *Estudios Geopolíticos y Estratégicos*: "Proyeciones del Brasil," no. 3 (December 1979), pp. 5–33; "Pacto Amazónico: Nuevo Esquema Geopolítico," no. 4 (May 1980); and "Coyuntura Geopolitica Latino Americana," no. 9 (December 1983), pp. 5–26.

22. Wayne A. Selcher, "Recent Strategic Developments in South America's Southern Cone," in Heraldo Muñoz and Joseph Tulchin (eds.), *Latin American Nations in World Politics* (Boulder: Westview Press, 1984), pp. 101–117.

23. General Juan E. Guglialmelli, "Islas Malvinas: Exigir Definiciones a Gran Bretaña," *Estrategia*, no. 67-68 (November 1980-February 1981); "Estrategia Nacional: Juego de Simulación—Islas Malvinas," *Revista Militar*, no. 704 (April 1981); and Alberto E. Asseff, *Proyección Continental de la Argentina* (Buenos Aires: Pleamar, 1980), p. 232. See also *La Prensa* (Buenos Aires), January 24, 1982.

24. "Editorial," *Revista Militar*, no. 708 (April-June 1982); General Osiria G. Villegas, "Guerra de las Malvinas," *Revista de la Escuela de Defensa Nacional* (Argentina), no. 30 (August 1982), pp. 100–110.

25. General Juan E. Guglialmelli, "La Guerra de las Malvinas," *Estrategia*, no. 71-72 (April-September 1982), pp. 19–90; Carlos J. Moneta, "El Conflicto de las Malvinas," *Estudios Internacionales* (Chile), no. 60 (October 1982), pp. 361–409; Captain José E. Cortines, "El Conflicto de las Malvinas: Implicancias de una Crisis," *Revista de la Escuela de Guerra Naval*, no 19 (November 1983), pp. 75–83; María del Carmen Liaver, "La Incidencia del Conflicto Malvinas en el Subsistema del Atlántico," *Geopolítica* (Argentina), no. 28 (1984); and Comodoro Ruben O. Moro, *La Guerra Insudite: Historia del Conflicto de Atlantico Sur* (Buenos Aires: Pleamar, 1985). For an extensive bibliography of the conflict, see Roberto Etcheparaborda, "La Bibliografía Reciente Sobre la

Cuestión Malvinas," *Revista Interamericana de Bibliografía*, 24 (1984), nos. 1 and 2.

26. General Edgardo Mercado Jarrín, "Coyuntura Geopolítica Latinoamericana," *Estudios Geopolíticos y Estratégicos*, no. 9 (December 1983), pp. 5–20; and "Malvinas: Un Cambio Geopolitico en América Latina," *Estudios Geopolíticos y Estratégicos*, no. 8 (October 1982).

27. Admiral Francisco Ghisolfo Arays, "Conflicto Atlántico Sur: Reflexiones," *Revista de Marina* (Chile), no. 751 (November 1982), pp. 717–721.

28. See the writings by Therezinha de Castro in *A Defesa Nacional*: "O Atlántico Sur: Contexto Regional," no. 714 (July 1984), pp. 91–108; "Geopolítica do Confronto," no. 716 (November 1984), pp. 85–94; and "O Cono Sul e a Conjuntura Internacional," no. 712 (March 1984), pp. 17–34.

29. Jack Child, "Present Trends in the Inter-American Security System and the Rio Treaty," *Anuario Jurídico 1983* (Washington, D.C.: Organization of American States, 1984); Cesar Arias Quincot, "La Administración Reagan y el Conflicto de las Malvinas," *Estudios Geopolíticos y Estratégicos*, no. 8 (October 1982), pp. 24–29; and Bernardo Quagliotti de Bellis, "Inglaterra, Estados Unidos y las Malvinas," *Geosur*, no. 34 (1982), pp. 3–23.

30. General Genaro Diaz Bessone, "Atlántico Sur: Su Importancia Estratégica," *Futurable*, no. 3 (September 1979), pp. 11–23; Inter-American Defense College, *Importancia Estratégica del Pacífico Sur, Atlántico Sur, y la Antártida* (Washington, D.C., 1984); General Carlos de Meira Mattos, "Atlántico Sur y su Importancia Histórica," *Estudios Geopolíticos y Estratégicos*, no. 8 (October 1982); General Carlos de Meira Mattos, "South Atlantic: Strategic Importance and Caribbean Link," *Free World Security* (Washington, D.C.: CIS, 1979).

31. Admiral Fernando A. Milia, "¿Hay un Futuro en el Atlántico Sur?" *Futurable*, no. 14 (2d Trimestre 1982), pp. 58–63.

32. See footnote 29 supra.; also Admiral Joao Goncalves Caminhe, "Visao Geostratégica do Atlántico Sul," *Cuadernos de Estudos Estratégicos*, no. 6 (February 1985); Luiz Paulo Macedo Carvalho, "Interesses e Responsabilidades do Brazil no Atlántico Sul," *A Defesa Nacional*, no. 711 (January 1984), pp. 75–80; and Francisco Russ Santos, "O Brazil nes Betalhas do Atlantico," *A Defesa Nacional*, no. 722 (November 1985), pp. 5–22.

33. See the discussion of Argentine geopolitical thinking in the previous section; also Primavera Acuna de Mones Ruiz, *Antártida Argentina* (Buenos Aires: Librería del Colegio, 1984); Admiral Jorge A. Fraga, *La Argentine y el Atlantico Sur* (Buenos Aires: Pleamar, 1983); and César José Marini, *La Crisis en el Cono Sur* (Buenos Aires: SACI, 1984).

34. Armando Alonso Pineiro, "Hacia el Tratado Militar del Atlántico Sur," *Revista de Temas Militares*, no. 1 (January 1982), pp. 44–55; Major Ernesto Fernández Maguer, "¿Es Viable la OTAS?" *Revista de la Escuela Superior de Guerra*, no. 456 (September 1981), pp. 61–70; and Carlos J. Moneta, *Geopolítica y Política del Poder en el Atlántico Sur* (Buenos Aires: Pleamar, 1983), p. 133.

35. Howard T. Pittman, "The Impact of Democratization on Geopolitics and Conflict in the Southern Cone," paper presented at Latin American Studies Association, Boston, 1986; Council on Hemispheric Affairs, *Washington Report on the Hemisphere*, May 3, 1983, pp. 4–5.

36. General Antonio Jorge Correa, "A Influencia da ESG no Pensamento Político . . . das Elites Brasileires," *Sequranca e Desenvolvimento*, no. 19 (1975), pp. 19–25; Colonel Florentino Díaz Loza, *Geopolítico para la Patria Grande* (Buenos Aires: Ediciones Temática SRL, 1983); and Oliveiros S. Ferreira, "A Geopolítica do Brasil Revisitada," *Política e Estrategia*, vol. 2, no. 4 (October 1984).

37. "Creación del Instituto Geopolítico de Chile," *Sequridad Nacional*, no. 21 (1981), pp. 7–18; and Mario Arnello Romo, "Principios Fundamentales para un Proyecto Nacional de Chile Futuro," *Revista Chilena de Geopolitica*, no. 2 (1985), pp. 7–16.

38. Colonel Luis A. Leoni Houssay. "Pinochet: El Fuhrer Sudamericano," *Revista de Temas Militares*, no. 11 (September 1984), pp. 5–20.

39. Rogelio García Lupo, "El Rol de los Militares," *Estudios Geopoliticos y Estratégicos*, no. 9 (December 1983), pp. 57–60; and discussions by the author with Virginia Gamba in Washington, D.C., in January 1987.

40. "La Región Austral y el Conflicto con Chile," *Geopolítica* (Argentina), no. 11/12 (September 1962), pp. 3–5; Admiral Francisco Ghisolfo Arays, "Chile, País Atlantico," *Revista de Marina* (Chile), no. 757 (1982), pp. 712–715; Colonel Luis A. Leoni Houssay, "Problemática Austral Argentina," *Revista Militar* (Argentina), no. 704 (April 1981); and General Osiris Villegas, *El Conflicto con Chile en la Región Austral* (Buenos Aires: Pleamar, 1978).

41. María Teresa Infante, "Argentina y Chile: Percepciones del Conflicto en la Zona del Beagle," *Estudios Internacionales* (Chile), no. 67 (July 1984), pp. 337–358; José Rodríguez Elizondo, "Geopolítica Jarrín, Relaciones del Perú con Brasil," in Eduardo Ferrero Castro (ed.), *Relaciones Internacionaies del Perú* (Lima: CEPEI, 1986), p. 71.

42. Antonio Raúl Mantel, "Las Malvinas y el Beagle en el Contexto Estratégico: Que Pasó," *Revista de Temas Militares*, no. 9 (1984), pp. 33–44; General Roberto M. Levingston, "Antecedentes, Negociaciones y Consecuencies del Tratado de Paz y Amistad Argentino-Chileno," *Revista Argentina de Estudios Estratégicos*, vol. 2, no. 3 (January 1985), pp. 9–13.

43. Jack Child, *Geopolitics and Conflict in South America: Quarrels Among Neighbors* (New York: Praeger, 1985), pp. 175–179.

44. Salvador Reyes, *Fuego en la Frontera* (Santiago: Aranciba Hermanos, 1968), pp. 152–153.

45. Antonio Cavalla Rojas, "¿Guerra en el Cono Sur?" *Cuadernos Semestraies*, no. 4 (1978), pp. 227–244; Martín Congrains, *Guerra en el Cono Sur* (Lima: Editorial Ecoma, 1979); and Fernando Garcia Della Corta, *El Juez me Robó Dos Isles* (Buenos Aires: Almafuerte, 1970).

46. General Edgardo Mercado Jarrín, "Relaciones del Perú con Brasil," in Eduardo Ferrero Castro (ed.), *Relaciones Internacionales del Perú* (Lima: CEPEI, 1986), p. 72.

47. General Juan E. Guglialmelli, *Geopolítica del Cono Sur* (Buenos Aires: El Cid, 1979).

48. Instituto Latinoamericano de Estudios Económicos y Sociales, *El Imperativo de la Integración Latinoamericana* (Lima: Instituto Latinoamericano

de Estudios Económicos y Sociales, 1982); Julián Licastro, "Unión Latinoamericana de la Teoría a la Practica," *Estudios Geopoliticos y Estratégicos*, no. 9 (December 1983), pp. 73–77; General Edgardo Mercado Jarrin, "Relaciones del Peru con Brasil," in Eduardo Ferrero Castro (ed.), *Relaciones Internacionales del Peru* (Lima: CEPEI, 1986,) pp. 61–88; and General Edgardo Mercado Jarrín, "Coyuntura Geopolítica Latinoamericana," *Estudios Geopoliticos y Estrategicos*, no. 9 (December 1983), pp. 5–20.

49. Capitán Raúl Parra Maza, "La Geopolítica en Latinoamérica," *Estudios Geopoliticos y Estratégicos*, no. 2 (April 1979), pp. 60–68.

50. Colonel Florentino Díaz Loza, *Geopolítica para la Patria Grande* (Buenos Aires: Ediciones Tematica SRL, 1983), especially Part 5.

51. General Juan E. Guglialmelli, "Argentina-Brasil: Enfrentamiento o Alianza para la Liberación," *Estrategia*, no. 36, (1975), pp. 1–29; General Genaro Díaz Bessone, "La Entente Argentina-Brasil y su Proyección," *Futurable*, no. 6 (1980), p. 8; Wayne A. Selcher, "As Relacoes Brasileño-Argentinas," *Politica e Estrategia*, vol. 3, no. 1 (January 1985); and Selcher, "Recent Strategic Developments in South America's Southern Cone," in Heraldo Muñoz and Joseph Tulchin (eds.), *Latin American Nations in World Politics* (Boulder: Westview Press, 1984), pp. 101–118.

52. General Carlos de Meira Mattos, *Uma Geopolítica Pan-Amazónica* (Rio de Janeiro: Livraria Jose Olympio, 1980); and General Edgardo Mercado Jarrín, "Relaciones del Peru con Brasil," in Eduardo Ferrero Castro (ed.), *Relaciones Internacionales del Perú* (Lima: CEPEI, 1986), pp. 61–88.

53. "Top Leaders Consult on Problems," *Washington Post*, October 5, 1985, p. A-21.

54. Instituto Geopolítico y Estratégico, Perú, "Declaración Conjunta IPEGE-EVEGE," *Estudios Geopolíticos y Estratégicos*, no. 9 (December 1983), pp. 103–4.

55. Ricardo Alagia, "Las Ideas Fuerza Argentinas," *Geopolítica*, no. 29 (1984), pp. 50–60; and Arthur Cezar Ferreira Reis, "Imperialistas ou Subimperialistas," *A Defesa Nacional*, no. 71 (September 1984), 133–138.

56. See Footnote 53 supra.; also General Edgardo Mercado Jarrín, "Pacto Amazónico: Nuevo Esquema Geopolítico." *Estudios Geopolíticos y Estratégicos* (Peru), no. 4 (May 1980), pp. 54–60.

57. "Tierra del Fuego: Microchips and Sheep," *Wall Street Journal*, October 17, 1986.

58. Discussions by the author with Bolivian foreign ministry official, Lima, Peru, October 1986.

59. For the geopolitics of transportation routes, see Salvador Alaimo, "Geopolitica de los Vuelos Transpolares," *Antártida* no. 12 (May 1982), pp. 50–58; and Bernardo Arboleya, "Cuenca del Plata, Geopolítica y Transporte," *Futurable*, no. 4 (December 1979), pp. 69–75.

60. See, for example, General Edgardo Mercado Jarrín, "Geopolítica de la Cuenca del Pacifico," in his *El Perú y la Antártida* (Lima: IPEGA, 1984), pp. 195–218.

61. Colonel Jorge G. Negrete, "Geopolítica, Primera Parte," *Revista Geográfica* (Ecuador, Instituto Geográfica Militar), no. 3 (July 1967), pp. 11–36;

Colonel Jaime Barberis Romero, "Geopolítica: Ciencia Moderna y Dinamica," *Revista de Ciencias Internacionales* (Ecuador), no. 15 (1982–1983); and Colonel Jaime Barberis Romer, "Geografía y Geopolítica," *Revista Geográfica* (Ecuador), no. 17 (December 1982), pp. 53–55.

62. Wayne A. Selcher, "Recent Strategic Developments in South America's Southern Cone," in Heraldo Muñoz and Joseph Tulchin (eds.), *Latin American Nations in World Politics* (Boulder: Westview Press, 1984), pp. 108–110.

63. Adolfo Silenzi de Stagni, *Las Malvinas y el Petróleo* (Buenos Aires: El Cid, 1982); also *Buenos Aires Herald*, January 6, 1985, p. 3.

64. For a more extensive analysis of South American Antarctic geopolitics, see the author's *Antarctica and South American Geopolitics: Frozen Lebensraum* (New York: Praeger, 1988); and "South American Geopolitical Thinking and Antarctica," *ISA Notes*, vol 11, no. 3 (Spring 1985), pp. 22–28.

65. Among some of the principal geopolitical writers in Chile and Argentina who have addressed Antarctic themes are Juan Carlos Beltramino, Captain Alberto Casellas, Admiral Jorge A. Fraga, Admiral Fernando Milis, Francisco Orrego Vicuña, Vicente Palermo, and Bernardo N. Rodríguez.

66. Brazilian Antarctic geopolitical writers include Pericles Azambuja, Therezinha de Castro, General Carlos de Meira Mattos, and Aristides Pinto Coelho.

67. Among the authors in Uruguay, Peru, and Ecuador who have included Antarctic geopolitical themes are Leslie Crawford, General Edgardo Mercado Jarrín, Julio Musso, and Beatriz Ramacciotti de Cubas.

4

Brazil and the Southern Cone Subsystem

Wayne A. Selcher

From Conflict to Cooperation

The 1970s produced a pattern of international politics in South America that was much more conflictual and troublesome than the current essentially cooperative tone.[1] There were intermittent tensions between leftist and rightist regimes, several active border disputes (principally Argentina-Chile, Ecuador-Peru, and Bolivia-Chile), and on-going rivalries between Argentina and Brazil during the period of nationalistic Peronist governments in Buenos Aires (1972–1976) and beyond. The geopolitical and national security models in vogue in the Southern Cone military establishments tended to describe international politics as a zero-sum game, with emphasis on conflict, competition, expansionism, "flash points," and a balance of power paradigm rather than on cooperation or solidarity. Even Argentine and Chilean interest in Antarctica took on a more contentious and exclusivistic style than that of the non–South American countries present there. Human rights violations under military regimes made several countries targets of general Western censure.

Economic integration efforts through the Latin American Free Trade Association (LAFTA) and the Andean Pact ground to a halt over differences in relative national advantage, especially between larger and smaller members. Chile withdrew from the Andean Pact in 1976 over foreign investment policies and a common external tariff, and pursued a vague "Pacific Basin" strategy. Toward the end of the decade Argentina turned toward the USSR as a major trading partner, and Brazil found interesting markets in Black Africa and the Middle East. In the continent as a whole, the surge of foreign borrowing reinforced a trend toward independent national development strategies.

In the Southern Cone, Argentina posed a factor of instability, with erratic foreign policies varying as a function of personal idiosyncrasies and the perennial internal power disputes among groups, including the 1976–1983 military governments.[2] Its relationship with the rest of South America was hindered by a revival of its traditional sense of uniqueness and separateness in Latin America, compounded by the resurgence during the 1970s of long rivalries with its two largest neighbors, Chile and Brazil. At the same time, an apparent decline in American influence on the continent during the Carter administration promised to give more play to local actors and possibly to more discordant local tendencies. The 1982 Falklands/Malvinas War, to many observers, just appeared a logical (albeit unexpected) outgrowth of the quarrelsome tendencies of the previous decade, bolstered by a Galtieri government with an overblown sense of Argentina's power and strategic significance, special relationship with the Reagan government, and support within the continent.

The effects of this war, in reality, marked an abatement of the threat of force, because of the embarrassment suffered by the Argentine military, the negative effects of the war losses, and the concomitant replacement in several countries of military regimes by more representative civilian governments with more cooperative agendas in foreign policy and concern about the maintenance of democracy and human rights. (The obdurate exceptions through the 1980s remained Chile and Paraguay.) The Falklands War demonstrated the obvious breakdown of the traditional Inter-American System, just as the issues of politicization of the foreign debt, trade difficulties, Central American conflict, and American attempts under Reagan to reincorporate Latin America as a sphere of influence became more pressing and highlighted mutual Latin American interests.

The 1984 settlement of the Chilean-Argentine border controversy in the Beagle Channel[3] and the slackening (but not cessation) of Bolivia's coastal territory claims against Chile with the passage of the 1979 centennial of the start of the War of the Pacific allowed common developmental concerns to come to the fore rather than the divisive national security matters previously raised. Argentina and Chile followed up on the Beagle Channel settlement with 1984 treaties on physical integration and economic complementarity and a 1985 treaty on cross-border cooperation in the centrally-located Pino Hachado Pass area of the Andean frontier.

A general acceleration of inter-Latin American consultations has facilitated a more cooperative continental subsystem, first with an unusual level of intermittent consultations among presidents and then, in November 1987, with the meeting in Acapulco of eight Latin American presidents, all from South America except Mexico's President de la Madrid. A broader acceptance of the integrationist ideas of the Latin

American Economic System (SELA) policy research group now gives credibility to alternatives to the current system of relationships within Latin America and vis-à-vis the North, without stridency toward the U.S. or Western Europe. At the same time, although precise indicators are lacking, transnational relationships among professional and labor classes and political parties (as well as smugglers) appear to be on a decided increase, a new integrationist phenomenon over the more accustomed forms of state-to-state relations dominating the region.

Country Profiles

Argentina

The foreign policy results of the Falklands War for Argentina were definitely not, as some had initially feared, of a sort to cause brash vengefulness or a choice for the nuclear option to try once again to prove superior status, prestige, and regional leadership. Under the civilian government of Raúl Alfonsín, inaugurated in December 1983, Argentina began to address more objectively and constructively, and in a conciliatory and coherent way, its Latin American (rather than its would-be European) identity, its disadvantageous influence position in South America, and its failures in erratic power-oriented policies and nationalistic rhetoric during the military regime.

The common theme of Alfonsín's moderate continental policies and activist initiatives has been to "normalize" the situation and to bring Argentina to the position of a reliable, reasonable, and trustworthy partner, most notably with establishment of a South American subgroup (the Lima Group) to support the Contadora negotiating forum, settlement of the Beagle Channel controversy, and continuation of economic integration with Brazil.[4] The national preoccupation with gaining sovereignty over the Falklands through negotiations continues as a chief priority, but with reduced vehemence and general Latin American support that is only verbal. Buenos Aires has developed no concrete political alliances or strategies to counter the British insistence on maintaining control and a military presence, the 1986 British declaration of a 150-mile exclusionary fishing zone there, or Margaret Thatcher's unprecedented 1987 electoral victory for a third term as prime minister.

Reintegration with Latin America received high priority, with a strategy to promote economic integration and political coordination, support democratic government, revive regional multilateral institutions, discourage arms races and regional disputes, and keep the region clear of the East-West conflict.[5] The theme has been reconciliation and cooperation rather than continental leadership. Alfonsín has frequently used democratic justifications for his activist multilateral foreign policy stances, in issues such as the foreign debt and Central America, as well as an external expression of internal policy.

The military governments were characterized by the presence of combative and authoritarian nationalists with a narrow, parochial, and heavily anti-Communist view of foreign affairs oriented to the Cold War. The government of the Radical Civic Union (UCR), in contrast, has many classic liberal members with cosmopolitan and integrationist leanings conducive to cooperative solutions at the continental level, although less helpful in North-South issues such as the restrictive foreign debt, sovereignty over the Falkland Islands, and agricultural disputes with the European Common Market.[6] The continental popularity of the figure of President Alfonsín himself, the chief architect of national foreign policy, has improved the country's image among its regional partners.

As always, it is difficult to postulate the current directions as a longer-term trend in the country's continental relations. Should the UCR's present classic liberal style of governance be replaced by a statist-nationalist group, either the Peronists or the military, Argentine foreign policy could take more conflictful or disruptive courses.

Chile

The second major Southern Cone actor and the most introverted, Chile continues to suffer a decided disadvantage in its continental position because of the negative human rights reputation of the Pinochet dictatorship among the civilian-ruled South American countries and foreign approval of the democratization movement against Pinochet. Regime differences have, for example, impeded the progress of cooperation with Argentina under the 1984 treaties because the Alfonsín government does not want to cooperate closely with a dictatorship.

Unlike its neighbors, Chile practices a diplomatic style characterized by Muñoz as "praetorian-ideological"—dogmatic, confrontational, anti-Communist, and dominated by military officers instead of diplomats.[7] General Pinochet, a geopolitical theorist, places his imprint clearly on the country's foreign policy. Chile's foreign policy efforts aim to assure continuing power for the military government and to overcome the effects of political isolation. So while Chile is not a disruptive force on the continent, neither is it an active participant or initiator in South American international trends. Its political future represents one of the major question marks in Southern Cone international politics.

The Three Buffers

As a group, Bolivia, Paraguay, and Uruguay have traditionally been regarded either as buffer states or as zones of competition between Argentina and Brazil. Recent trends, and the rise of Argentine-Brazilian cooperation in the 1980s, have affected each one's international position differently. All three, however, suffer size disadvantages relative to their larger neighbors, and all three will be pulled into the ongoing process of transnational economic integration in the Rio de la Plata Basin, South America's largest international population cluster.

Bolivia's weaknesses of high foreign dependency, chronic instability, and the cocaine trade hinder its ability to exercise an effective and coherent foreign policy and also make it an object of concern for its neighbors. The main objective of its foreign policy has been to recover a way to the sea, lost to Chile in the War of the Pacific. This has occasioned a long-running dispute with Santiago, subject to periods of greater or lesser fervor on Bolivia's part. Bolivia regularly takes the issue to regional organizations. Regime compatibility or incompatibility with neighboring states has had a major impact on the tone of the relations with local states. Because of its continentally-centered position, Bolivia's foreign policy options have taken several courses over recent time: Tilting toward either Argentina or Brazil, maintaining an equilibrium between those two influences, or following a proclivity toward any of three regional groupings to which Bolivia belongs—the Andean Pact, Cuenca del Plata Accord, and Amazon Pact.[8]

Paraguay, under the Alfredo Stroessner dictatorship from 1954 to 1989, was the most stable of the three buffers. When Stroessner came to power, his country was heavily dependent on Argentina. The growth of Brazilian influence there in the 1970s gave rise to a "pendular policy" between Argentina and Brazil, Paraguay's chief continental partners. By the late 1980s, Paraguay had developed such close transnational economic relationships with Brazil that a future Paraguayan government would probably be unlikely to repudiate them. Argentina, with many Paraguayan exiles, was critical of the Stroessner dictatorship after Alfonsín came to power, but maintained several important projects of binational cooperation. Brazil has sufficient presence in the country (particularly in the Itaipú hydroelectric complex) that there is concern in Brasília about the nature of Stroessner's successor. Yet, in consonance with its general policies, Brazil considers Paraguayan politics an internal matter. Toward the rest of the continent, Stroessner followed a low-profile policy in order to minimize overt criticism of his dictatorship and of its role in contraband and drug smuggling.[9]

Uruguay, "the quintessential buffer state," in the phrase of Tulchin,[10] has lately become more of a bridge than a fence in light of its bilateral

TABLE 4.1

Brazil's Growing Predominance on the South American Continent, 1960–1986

		Population (millions)			
		1960	1970	1980	1986
A.	Brazil	72.6	95.8	121.3	138.5
B.	Rest of South America	74.2	94.7	118.5	134.8
	RATIO of A:B	0.98	1.01	1.02	1.03

		Gross Domestic Product (billions of 1986 dollars)			
		1960	1970	1980	1986
A.	Brazil	68.3	123.8	284.8	333.8
B.	Rest of South America	124.1	197.9	286.0	292.0
	RATIO of A:B	0.55	0.63	0.99	1.14

		Value Added to Economy by Mfg. (billions of 1986 dollars)			
		1960	1970	1980	1986
A.	Brazil	17.7	34.4	81.1	86.9
B.	Rest of South America	24.1	41.4	58.4	60.1
	RATIO of A:B	0.73	0.83	1.39	1.45

Source: Inter-American Development Bank, Economic and Social Progress in Latin America, 1988 Report (Washington, DC: IADB, 1988), Statistical Appendix.

participation as third party in Argentine-Brazilian economic integration. With few resources other than agricultural, and a chronically stagnated economy, a framework of economic complementarity worked out with its two principal foreign partners is welcome. President Julio Sanguinetti's government has been enthusiastic in its support for Argentine-Brazilian cooperation, and the immediate prospect is for greater Uruguayan reliance on both nations. Cultural factors and the proximity of Montevideo to Buenos Aires favor Argentine influence, while economic factors tend to favor that of Brazil. Uruguay has been affected by trends toward democracy or dictatorship in its larger neighbors, yet has not seen it necessary to perform a conscious balancing act. The Sanguinetti government characteristically assumes a conciliatory position on regional political issues and emphasizes economic concerns and regional cooperation.

Brazil

Of the three major Southern Cone actors, the largest single national factor in the future of South American international relations is the role of Brazil on the continent.[11] One of the major determinants of Brazil's relationship to South America has been its growing economic primacy on the continent, particularly in industry, in which it is a Third World leader. (See Table 4.1.) Southern Cone economies over the longer haul have been weaker and more sluggish than Brazil's, even though the area is the most developed region of Latin America. The most probable outcome is a continued widening of this gap, although the speed of change may vary over time. Such superiority will provide Brazil with both greater relative capabilities and potential problems arising from intended or unintended political influence effects, economic penetration, and other entanglements.

Brazil's Lusophone culture, the immensity of the country, the geographical distance of much of its population from Spanish South American population centers, and middle and upper class fascination for things American or European led historically to a sense of separateness and distinctness that hindered serious Brazilian self-identification, beyond rhetoric, as a South American nation. In this decade, however, the question of how Brazil should relate to the rest of South America has been a subject of domestic and continental debate, with increasingly practical consequences and an expanding range of possibilities.

Brazil's Political Relations in South America

Current Political Characteristics

From 1970 through 1987 the political bases of Brazil's relationship with the rest of South America experienced major changes that made Brazil more predominant in South America, but also facilitated the emergence of the present pattern of expanding bilateral cooperative ties. Brazil has adroitly managed contradictions of disparity in any size and interests that in other regions of the world could well have occasioned major disagreements and long-term animosities.

Brazilian relations with the rest of South America during most of the 1970s were troubled by ideological differences, Brazil's unusually rapid economic growth, and neighbors' concerns that it was an American surrogate or an expansionist power. Brazil under the military regime in the early and mid-1970s was optimistic about years of strong economic growth, and in its "emerging world power" orientation turned away from hemispheric affairs and toward a global view of its economic interests. Signs of accommodation were visible in the latter years of the Ernesto Geisel government (1974–1979), however, including the 1976 proposal to create an Amazon Pact (formalized in 1978) for coordinated development in the river basin. The 1977 breaking of the military assistance agreement with the United States, over the Carter administration's human rights linkages, made Brazil seem less a U.S. proxy to its neighbors.

The clearest change in the nature of the relationship came during the government of President Joao Figueiredo (1979–1985), with his emphasis on improving relations and avoiding frictions in South America. The economic boom had passed, and thoroughly faded dreams of imminent major power status belied the earlier hope that Brazil's interests would soon be similar to those of the developed states. The consensus grew in Brazil, in and out of government, that its national development could not be planned or achieved separately from that of the rest of Latin America.[12] The government began several years of emphasizing South-South economic and political relationships, a position that logically required a credible improvement in relations with neighboring states and acceptance of many types of political regimes. A now more economically vulnerable and less euphoric Brazil also seemed less threatening to its neighbors.

The Figueiredo government designed an expansion of treaty ties with most South American nations and carried out an unusual pace of exchanges of official visits at the presidential and ministerial levels. (President Figueiredo was the first Brazilian president to visit Bogota, Lima, and Caracas, and the first to visit Buenos Aires in forty-five years.) The Itaipú-Corpus hydroelectric power controversy with Argentina over joint waterways rights, of several years' duration, was settled to mutual satisfaction (and to that of Paraguay) in a matter of months. Above all, the evolution of Brazilian-Argentine relations away from the rivalry of the 1970s to their present state of cooperation, through changes of government from military to civilian rule in both countries, has been one of the most positive features of recent South American international relations.[13]

The relaxation of many Argentine-Brazilian tensions was, of itself, a major aid to Brazil's unprecedented overall rapprochement with Spanish South America. So was Brazil's cautious tendency to continue to tilt away from the United States with a mild Third World position sufficient to establish a claim to independence, but not enough to alienate Washington. Undergoing political liberalization itself, Brazil was able to take advantage of what became a continental shift toward democratic rule by frequently injecting principles of freedom and democratic rhetoric into diplomatic speeches and joint declarations with neighboring governments.[14] The March 1985 inauguration of an indirectly elected civilian government, under President José Sarney, made that parallelism much easier, above all with the government of Raúl Alfonsín in Buenos Aires.

Determinants of the Current Situation

Brazil's political relations with all South American governments are now good to excellent, and commercial negotiation problems are treated as technical matters rather than as causes for political recrimination. Although Brazil customarily prefers bilateral relations to multilateral, it has been active in the Cartagena group on Latin debt and the Lima subgroup to the Contadora process on Central American tensions. Brazil's role in both of these has been one of information and dialogue rather than one of promotion and innovation, but these groups are useful to Brazil in that they set out moderate guidelines to resolve the issues at hand. Brazil has also encouraged the cooperative tone and functional usefulness of the Amazon Pact, the River Plate Basin group, and the Latin American Association for Integration (ALADI). Activity in multilateral groups puts Brazil more in line with Spanish American interest in such forums, but Brazil still pursues a notably less prominent role than its size might suggest.

Brazil has not taken on a hegemonic "responsibility" for South American events, nor has it carried out covert interventions or stated preferences about the internal affairs of neighboring states. South America continues to receive consistent high-level attention and summit diplomacy appropriate to a gradualist policy of long-term cooperation without domination.

Brazil's role as a regional actor has been shaped by its cautious diplomatic style resulting from a decision not to exercise fully its capabilities for influence in order to protect its positive image in the region. It has been very selective as well about the type and quantity of its military equipment sales in South America, and maintains locally significant but small military supply and training programs only in Paraguay and Suriname, the former as a gradual process of evolution and the latter begun in 1983 as a counterweight to Cuban influence. These are the only South American states in which Brazil could be considered to have a sizable foreign aid program. Brazil has shown neither embarrassment with such ties to military regimes nor has it shown any interest in urging domestic political reforms. The Foreign Ministry maintains only "proper" relations with Chile's Pinochet regime, and its pronouncements in favor of strengthening democracy on the continent have been couched in very general terms. Any degree of specificity would be a major departure from long-standing non-interventionist practice.

Brazil has clearly rejected the roles of (1) continental hegemon ("Colossus of the South"), (2) assertive Third World champion, and (3) American regional surrogate or ally. Brazil is an essentially moderate and nonthreatened status-quo power on political issues, so it tends to emphasize economic payoffs, avoid entanglements, stay out of others' conflicts, encourage peaceful settlement of disputes, keep diplomatic dialogue open, and cultivate the reputation of a trustworthy partner. Brazilian diplomats and military officers are much more likely to

TABLE 4.2
South American Public Opinion on Brazil Regarding International Cooperation and Conflict, March 1981

The following questions were included in the survey:

1. "Our country as a nation has certain interests. With which countries of the world should we work most closely to advance and improve ourselves?"

2. "Which are the South American countries which work the most for peace?" (First choice only.)[a]

3. "Which, in your judgment, are the most conflictive countries of South America?" (First choice only.)

	Chile	Uruguay	Ecuador	Argentina	Venezuela	Colombia	Peru
Question 1:	64%	51%	36%	27%	19%	15%	5%
Question 2:	35	37	13	1	4	15	14
Question 3:	2	5	3	6	2	2	1

[a]Brazil was the second most cited country in five cases, after only the country of the respondent. Brazil was the most cited country in Uruguay; in Argentina 65 percent of the respondents cited their own country, and no other country received over 1 percent mention.

Source: Gallup Sud (Montevideo) Survey #5 (March 1981) done for the United States Information Agency and partially reported in USIA's Foreign Opinion Note of June 26, 1981.

express concern, usually in a carefully worded way, than to contemplate action to handle a political problem in South America. The usual explanation given by officials is that, learning from frustrations experienced by major powers, Brazil finds interventionist efforts counterproductive and unlikely to yield lasting positive results for the intervening power. Further, Brazilian diplomacy has a tendency to avoid taking an unambiguous stand and to postpone acting on a problem that might disappear of its own accord.[15]

The extent to which this strategy has been successful in a public relations sense is demonstrated, among other ways, by the favorable image Brazil now has in the public opinion of neighboring countries. Based on a March 1981 poll done by Gallup Sud for the United States Information Agency, Table 4.2 shows a willingness in most neighboring states polled to consider Brazil a valuable partner in development and a force for peace on the continent. Table 4.3, with data on perceptions of Brazil's territorial status and ambitions, shows that only Argentines and Peruvians among five countries polled had significant suspicions about Brazil's expansive designs, yet even they discounted the likelihood of imminent border conflicts. The uniqueness of this survey does not allow any trend analysis, but Brazil's later moderate conduct during the 1982 Falklands War (while supporting Argentine sovereignty over the islands), the continued cooperative nature of relations with its neighbors, and inauguration of a civilian government in March 1985 could only have served to lessen somewhat those suspicions in the interim.

TABLE 4.3
South American Public Opinion Regarding Brazil's Territorial Status and Ambitions, March 1981

1. "There are persons who believe that Brazil is an imperialistic country which wants to expand its territory even more. Others believe Brazil is a peaceful country that does not want conflicts with South American countries. In your opinion, does Brazil wish to expand its territory or does it not wish conflicts with other South American countries?"

Respondents	Wants to Expand Its Territory	Does Not Want Conflicts	No Opinion
Argentina	32%	23%	45%
Peru	31	52	17
Ecuador	21	61	18
Uruguay	7	80	13
Chile	6	62	32
Colombia	Not polled		
Venezuela	Not polled		

2. "In your opinion, what possibilities exist that there may soon be border conflicts between Brazil and other South American countries: very probable, not very probable, improbable, or not probable at all?"

Respondents	Very Probable	Not Very Probable	Improbable	Not Probable at All	No Opinion
Venezuela	15%	15%	19%	29%	22%
Ecuador	12	16	36	25	11
Argentina	8	14	19	16	43
Peru	8	18	39	23	12
Chile	2	7	28	37	26
Uruguay	1	6	32	54	7
Colombia	Not polled				

Source: Gallup Sud (Montevideo) Survey #5 (March 1981) done for the United States Information Agency and partially reported in USIA's Foreign Opinion Note of June 26, 1981.

(Bolivians and Paraguayans were not polled, but concerns about Brazilian influence have often been expressed in those two countries, particularly in the Santa Cruz region of Bolivia and in eastern Paraguay.) The terminology of a comparative study of Third World influence by David Myers can be used to describe Brazil's political position on the continent.[16] Those countries that can be seen as "bargainers," with sufficient capabilities to negotiate effectively with Brazil, in approximate descending order of current intensity of interaction, are Argentina, Colombia, Chile, Peru, and Venezuela. Argentina, the only local contender with Brazil for continental influence, has in effect assumed the role of junior partner. The weaker "peripheral dependents," with insufficient resources to counterbalance foreign influence, in roughly descending order of intensity of interaction with Brazil, are Paraguay, Uruguay, Bolivia, Suriname, Ecuador, and Guyana.

Of these, only Paraguay (population 3.4 million) could accurately be classed as a client state, tied to Brazil by trade, contraband, investments, the Itaipú hydroelectric complex, cross-border interactions of a wide variety, many Brazilian settlers and landowners in Paraguay, and a security assistance program important to Paraguay. Brazil will become increasingly identified with what happens in Paraguay, which could give rise to anti-Brazilian nationalism there and regional political embarrassment for Brasília. The expansive and ebulliently nationalistic spirit of the settlers opening Brazil's center-west, along the border with Paraguay and Bolivia, combined with concerns of those two governments about the number of Brazilian settlers on their territory, could create increasing friction over cross-border migration that varies by season, economic conditions, or surges of local nationalism.

Paraguay has ownership of half of the power generated by the binational Itaipú hydroelectric complex and sells most of its share to Brazil. With its growing dependence on these revenues and a flourishing contraband trade into Brazil, Paraguay will be increasingly incorporated into the diversified and growing economy of southern Brazil, radiating out from São Paulo through the expanded transportation networks into southeastern Paraguay. In turn, center-south Brazil will become more dependent on the electricity from Itaipú.

The Political Outlook

From Brazil's perspective, heavy governmental attention will be focused on the changing domestic political alignments and reforms growing out of the 1987–88 Constituent Assembly and on mounting economic problems. Should this internal front become very hotly contested, as is probable, less effective attention will be devoted to foreign policy as the nation becomes preoccupied with its own problems. The current leadership sees its foreign policy options as limited by the hobbling effects of the debt, and is unlikely to come up with a comprehensive and innovative strategic foreign policy "project." Weakness in the Brazilian economy, another near-term prospect, would further hinder national opportunities for cooperation or influence in South America, but Brazil's economic ills would have to be very serious indeed to constitute a disruptive factor in continental political relations.

Brazilian relations with South America will continue to be cooperative, but their intensity will depend largely on their usefulness in achieving the principal national foreign policy economic goals—alleviation of the burden of the debt, the expansion of exports and constriction of imports, the recuperation of economic growth, and the acquisition of advanced technology. Most of the effort to accomplish these ends will have to be made with partners outside South America, particularly if the regional economy sags. Brazilian concerns about drug traffic and guerrillas are growing, along with a willingness to cooperate with others on those matters. Promotion of democracy and political security are likely to be less pressing goals, unless a clear threat to them arises from extremist activity.

Brazil will probably continue its preference for bilateral dealings rather than multilateral approaches. Even if its extra-hemispheric Third World identification should lessen, its Latin American identification is more fundamental and should persist. The foreign debt will become an increasingly political issue at home, with growing domestic pressure to restructure it in a major way to avoid strict fiscal discipline, which will tend to push Brazil into closer agreement with the Cartagena group. Brazil would prefer to continue unilaterally to ignore IMF guidelines and to renegotiate directly with its creditors. A strategy of playing up the political dimension of the debt while not explicitly tying Brazil's financial fate to those of other debtors is most likely to benefit from the atmosphere of pressure on creditors that intra-Latin consultation achieves.

The South American regional environment in the near term should experience more continuity than change, since democratic sentiments and institutions are still predominant. Yet domestic opposition and economic hardships are trying the effectiveness and legitimacy of the civilian governments. Interstate conflict levels are much lower than several years ago and show little sign of resurfacing soon. Territorial disputes could shift onto Antarctica for Argentina, Brazil, and Chile, but the probability of sharp disagreement there over the treaty revision now seems low relative to other probable concerns. A resurgence of violence in the Falklands dispute is quite unlikely, as is Latin American insistence on the issue of Argentine sovereignty.

A mildly cooperative multilateral climate is developing, but institutionalizing good intentions and treaty provisions into regular practice remains a challenge. The system is one of increased interaction possibly moving toward real interdependence. The chief international issues are likely to be the foreign debt, trade relations, and the illegal drug traffic. The most probable sources of regional instability include the presidential succession in Paraguay, social pressure against Chile's Pinochet regime, Bolivia's economic and political malaise, and guerrilla activity in Peru and Colombia. An optimistic international scenario must depend largely on political stability and economic growth in the region, two conditions that certainly cannot be taken for granted.

Further Argentine-Brazilian cooperation is crucial to setting a positive tone for the Southern Cone subsystem, in the political, economic, and security spheres. The current state of affairs suggests continuation of significant regional integration provided that there is neither a falling out over disagreements or the development of close collaboration with third parties. If local states begin to perceive an entente leading to continental domination or otherwise working to their disadvantage, they might be reluctant to commit to further integration.

The democratic governments are becoming less willing to service the foreign debt in an open-ended way indefinitely, since ultimately the principal in most cases is not repayable in its entirety. The economic drain of being net exporters of capital to creditor countries at the cost of national growth will become less acceptable. Eventually, the creditors will have to bear some of the sacrifices and burdens. The major risk in the meantime is a deterioration of domestic political stability in various countries where the social repercussions of worsening economic problems may be aggravated by an international economic downturn. In such a case, the moderately reformist civilian governments now predominant would be heavily pressured by radical opposition on the left and right to the detriment of regional stability.

To prevent this possibility, the current governments may be able to generate sufficient trade surpluses to cover interest payments on the debt. For the sake of domestic economic growth, however, they may unilaterally limit the amount of payments actually made, as Peru did in 1985 and Brazil in 1987. The extent of this practice, and creditor reaction to it, may be a major factor in inter-American political affairs in the near term.

The main potential political trends in the near future that would promote or hinder a cooperative role on the continent for Brazil are the following, listed in descending order of probability.

Potential Political Trends Encouraging Cooperation

1. Continued democratic trends in the continent.
2. Continued favorable multilateral consultation and negotiating climate.
3. Continued Brazilian identification with Latin America, especially in multilateral diplomacy.
4. Continued prominence for developmental, as contrasted to security, issues.
5. Strong politicization of the debt issue with effective Latin unity.
6. Expansion of Brazilian-Argentine-Uruguayan cooperation into a Southern Cone or River Plate subsystem.

7. Granting of Brazilian concessions or preferences such as debt rescheduling or foreign aid to less-developed countries to encourage partnerships or democratic governments, thus placing Brazil in a donor role.

Potential Political Trends Discouraging Cooperation

1. Greater attractiveness and receptivity of non–South American partners in fulfilling Brazil's goals; e.g., China, USSR, Middle East.
2. Lack of follow-through on regional initiatives Brazil undertakes.
3. Attritions caused by poorly managed border problems, such as drug traffic, guerrilla movements, or movements of settlers (particularly with Colombia, Peru, Paraguay, and Bolivia).
4. Regime incompatibilities or serious domestic instability problems.
5. Deterioration of the current cooperative relationship with Argentina.
6. A surge in Brazilian growth accompanied by nationalistic reactions in Spanish America.
7. Brazilian intervention or interference in a neighboring state.

Brazil's Economic Relations
in South America

Current Economic Characteristics

In the field of trade in the late 1970s, South American markets were among the most successful in the world for Brazilian exports. In the peak years of 1980 and 1981, the whole Latin American region received 18.1 percent and 19.3 percent of Brazil's exports, shares larger than those absorbed by the United States.

The next year, however, saw debt management problems throughout the region, constricted international credit, more non-tariff barriers, IMF guidelines mandating restriction of imports and economic slowdown, and pressure on foreign exchange. Intraregional trade declined further in value, a process actually begun in 1979. Brazil's exports to Latin America suffered greatly; in 1983, only 10.4 percent of Brazil's sales were to that region. Its regional imports contracted less abruptly, but many of its bilateral trading agreements failed to come to full promise.

With its own debt repayment schedule, Brazil turned toward more dynamic developed-country markets where it could more reliably accumulate large trade surpluses in hard currency, particularly with the

United States. Success in the U.S. market from 1983 to 1986 and achievement of major commercial surpluses there tended to reverse the economic and political momentum of the earlier Third World drive, as well as to reverse partially the 1970s trend toward closer economic ties with Western Europe. Yet the Foreign Ministry has not relinquished the goal of gradually expanding trade with South America in order to reduce the recent return to dependency on the United States.

South America's chief economic value for Brazil has been as a major market for manufactured goods (often sold by multinational corporations) and as an alternative source of raw materials (with Brazil's state companies as major purchasers). Brazil, in its continental trade, has characteristically (but not always) run a surplus, which has occasionally led trading partners to suspend imports from Brazil. The continuing problem for Brazil in trade negotiations has thus been to continue to place manufactured products in sluggish local economies, while finding enough to buy in return to maintain a trade balance satisfactory to the regional partner.

Finance has been a serious obstacle. Countertrade has provided some relief in the short term, but has been episodic and pursued chiefly with oil producers outside South America. Brazil's very resource, climatic, and industrial diversity has posed problems for its continental trade. As Brazil becomes more self-sufficient in temperate crops (Argentina), aluminum (Guyana and Suriname), copper and phosphates (Chile), tin (Bolivia), coal (Colombia), natural gas (Bolivia and Argentina), and petroleum (Venezuela and Ecuador), it will face a chronic trade surplus unacceptable to its partners and the counterpart problem will become more severe. Brazil will become competitive with its neighbors in some of these products in the mid-term.

Brazil does not trade disproportionately heavily with South America, nor has its share of intraregional trade surged in recent years. Brazil is the largest intraregional supplier of manufactured goods, especially chemicals, basic manufacturers, machines, and transportation equipment. Yet, overall, the role of South America in absorbing Brazilian manufactured exports relative to markets elsewhere has declined gradually.[17] After 1982, sales of capital goods to the region were seriously curtailed by recession.

The geographical concentration by country of Brazil's South American markets from 1972 to 1982 showed much more dispersion of exports than during the previous decade.[18] Brazil's continental trade is directed heavily toward a major Southern Cone bloc in which the markets of Brazil and Argentina serve as poles of attraction for each other and for Bolivia, Chile, Paraguay, and Uruguay.[19] This network is already the major trading configuration within Latin America, and any

TABLE 4.4
Degree of Concentration in Brazil's Trade with Its Principal Latin American Partners, 1981-1986

	Share of Brazil's Exports to Latin America (percentage)					
Country	1981	1982	1983	1984	1985	1986
Argentina	19.6	20.7	29.1	27.4	22.1	24.6
Venezuela	9.1	15.0	11.9	11.7	11.9	12.6
Paraguay	10.0	10.3	10.3	10.7	12.1	10.5
Chile	14.3	9.2	9.2	9.0	9.6	8.9
Bolivia	5.7	2.5	4.8	4.5	6.9	7.4
Uruguay	8.3	4.4	4.6	4.4	5.6	7.3
Peru	6.3	7.1	3.3	4.0	3.7	5.7
Mexico	14.3	10.3	7.4	9.2	8.9	5.6
Ecuador	1.5	2.1	3.0	4.5	4.8	4.8
Colombia	4.5	8.7	6.4	5.5	4.1	3.9
TOTALS	93.6	90.3	90.0	90.9	89.7	91.3

	Share of Brazil's Imports from Latin America (percentage)					
Country	1981	1982	1983	1984	1985	1986
Argentina	18.1	16.2	15.1	22.4	27.6	37.1
Chile	9.3	9.0	7.1	10.0	12.8	14.3
Uruguay	5.3	4.3	5.4	5.2	8.0	14.6
Mexico	23.8	23.1	30.7	28.3	23.1	8.1
Venezuela	29.9	28.6	29.0	24.4	15.6	5.2
TOTALS	86.4	81.2	87.3	90.3	87.1	79.3

Percentages calculated from figures in International Monetary Fund, *Direction of Trade Statistics Yearbook,* *1988* (Washington, DC: IMF, 1988), p. 112.

current trends in negotiations and complementarity are extensions of pre-existing propensities.

Table 4.4 indicates that Brazil's continental imports are much more concentrated in origin than are its exports, largely because of the value of petroleum purchases from Venezuela (especially since 1981) and limited Brazilian imports beyond those from Argentina, Chile, and Uruguay. The prominence of Brazil for the Southern Cone grouping is seen in Table 4.5, which shows a generally increasing reliance on imports from Brazil in Paraguay, Bolivia, Uruguay, and Argentina. Only Paraguay increased the proportion of its exports going to Brazil. The other Southern Cone countries tended to rely less on the Brazilian market over the 1978-1984 period.

Joint Projects

Most of Brazil's joint projects and technological cooperation with developing countries seem to occur within South America. Statistics are incomplete, but a preliminary compilation by the Brazilian Indus-

TABLE 4.5

Brazil's Share in the Imports and Exports of South American Countries, 1981–1986

Country	Percentage of Imports Coming from Brazil					
	1981	1982	1983	1984	1985	1986
Paraguay	25.9	26.5	28.5	32.6	36.1	31.5
Bolivia	14.1	10.2	13.9	21.8	30.9	35.3
Uruguay	19.8	12.7	11.2	16.4	17.8	24.4
Argentina	9.5	12.9	14.8	18.1	16.0	14.6
Suriname	3.6	3.4	4.3	6.0	6.0	8.9
Chile	9.0	7.3	6.4	8.5	8.9	7.9
Ecuador	3.7	3.9	5.0	12.7	6.5	6.8
Peru	5.6	6.1	2.8	6.2	6.0	6.7
Venezuela	2.1	3.9	4.4	5.2	4.2	4.5
Colombia	3.4	5.2	3.5	4.0	3.1	3.6
Guyana	2.3	2.0	1.3	2.2	2.6	0.7

Country	Percentage of Exports Going to Brazil					
	1981	1982	1983	1984	1985	1986
Paraguay	18.3	25.3	21.0	16.0	19.8	39.6
Uruguay	13.0	14.1	11.4	12.2	16.7	27.3
Argentina	6.5	7.4	4.6	5.9	5.9	10.2
Chile	7.3	8.3	4.3	6.2	5.4	6.9
Peru	1.5	2.0	1.7	1.4	1.8	2.9
Bolivia	1.3	2.0	5.0	1.0	0.7	2.2
Ecuador	2.6	7.3	0.1	0.1	0.1	1.1
Venezuela	4.7	5.7	4.4	3.2	1.8	0.8
Guyana	0.7	0.8	0.0	0.8	0.5	—
Colombia	0.2	0.1	0.1	0.4	0.2	0.2
Suriname	0.7	0.1	0.0	4.2	3.7	7.8

Percentages calculated from figures in International Monetary Fund, *Direction of Trade Statistics Yearbook, 1988* (Washington, DC: IMF, 1988).

trial Engineering Association showed that 59.5 percent of the foreign service contracts of Brazilian engineering firms from 1975 to early 1982 were in that continent.[20] With the continental recession after 1981, the demand for these building and construction projects contracted. Services exports will remain a good indicator of economic integration, however, because they are a relatively recent form of relations and lead to deeper ties than simple merchandise sales. The most promising arena for joint services projects appears to be among Brazil, Argentina, Uruguay, and perhaps Paraguay, as a function of economic integration in the River Plate Basin.

The Argentina-Brazil-Uruguay Triangle

The most important and imaginative Southern Cone initiative by far has been the broad and gradual approach to economic integration undertaken by Argentina, Brazil, and Uruguay in negotiating an expanding series of bilateral complementarity agreements, based on comprehensive technical studies to balance comparative advantages. Building on previous agreements and presidential summits, in December 1986, for example, Presidents Alfonsín and Sarney signed amendments to twelve existing protocols (those signed in July 1986) and signed five new protocols. These seventeen working documents cover capital goods, wheat, food supply, trade expansion, binational enterprises, financial affairs, an investment fund, energy, biotechnology, economic studies, early warning and public safety in nuclear accidents, aeronautical cooperation, steel, land transportation, maritime transportation, communications, and nuclear cooperation. Most notable in these results-oriented procedures are elimination of tariffs on 500 capital goods, a large role for the private sector (including in consultations before setting treaties), acceleration of transnational exchanges, specialization by sector of production or activity, agreement on quantitative objectives, mechanisms to keep the flow of trade balanced, and emphasis on stimulating a two-way flow of manufactured goods, agricultural products, and services.

An early product of industrial cooperation was the July 1987 creation in São Paulo of Autolatina, a joint-production merger of Ford and Volkswagen affiliates in the two countries. In the same month, another semiannual summit, in Buenos Aires, inaugurated a common trade currency (the "Gaucho"), produced a protocol on cultural cooperation and one on public administration, added amendments to existing protocols, and saw Sarney visit the closely guarded Argentine nuclear reactor at Pilcaniyeu (used to produce enriched uranium). Both presidents reiterated at the time the theme that they saw the bilateral effort as a step toward Latin American economic integration.

Most of these agreements and protocols came into effect in 1987, so their effectiveness cannot yet be gauged. Private-sector follow-up to the governmental efforts will be crucial. The existence of the attempt in itself is monumental, and the total volume of Argentine-Brazilian trade has grown greatly since the talks began in principle several years before the signing of the first protocols. (Uruguay has been partially included through bilateral treaties within ALADI "partial scope" provisions and President Sanguinetti's presence at several summits.) The process has been carried on with minimal bureaucracy, mutual responsiveness, and a realistic intent to fulfill commitments.

Problems must be attended to in these most ambitious foreign policy projects. Variations in national economic growth rates or internal adjustments would complicate international adjustments, especially if real interdependence were achieved. So would disagreements about the treatment of the participation of multinational affiliates based in the other country, as such participation would affect national policies toward foreign capital and market reserves. The heavily subsidized Argentine industrial sector was initially quite concerned that Brazil would buy only raw materials and in turn swamp Argentina with tariff-free manufactures, but those fears have been somewhat allayed by the results so far and by President Alfonsín himself. The lower level of efficiency in Argentine industry relative to the Brazilian will nevertheless remain one of the persistent structural inequalities requiring constant attention in order to keep a reasonably balanced exchange of products envisioned by an industrial complementarity list.[21] The relationship receives considerably more public attention and controversy in Argentina, because of Brazil's greater size in the exchange and its confidence in its ability to compete, and because of Argentina's greater stakes in the linkage.

Success of the scheme would make Brazil an even larger commercial player in the Southern Cone, yet without explicitly political motives. Another effect of success would be to focus the effective subregional international transactions on a River Plate Basin area that has for some time represented more of the demographic, transportation, and economic reality of Southern South America than has the largely geographical Southern Cone designation.[22] Such a trend would tend to marginalize Chile, while probably drawing Bolivia toward the Basin rather than toward the less attractive Andean economic grouping.

More hopeful Brazilian trade promotion officials see the recently negotiated bilateral upgrading of trade as a model to be applied to other countries, but, in reality, other countries in the region cannot approximate the economic diversity and size of Argentina. There has been some speculation about Mexico's participation in the scheme, through bilateral deals with Argentina and Brazil, but no progress has been attempted on either trilateralization or multilateralization of the complementarity agreements. Expansion of the concept should be delayed until this first configuration shows dependable progress in conditions more favorable than those of the continent as a whole.

The Economic Outlook

Determining Factors

Over the next several years Brazil's chief concerns in its South American relationships will be economic, involving export promotion, debt issues, sales of services, and technological cooperation. Other markets will continue to be more attractive than regional ones. Brazil will suffer increased local competition from other Newly Industrialized Countries (NICs), particularly those in Asia. Brazil will also find it more challenging to purchase merchandise and raw materials as it becomes more self-sufficient in both. The customary manufactured goods for raw materials exchange will not encourage many partners, so management of the trade flow will become more important, especially regarding complementarity and substitution of sources. Brazil has traditionally concentrated much more on promoting exports through multinationals than on seeking longer-term complementarity that would allow trade to flow more steadily in both directions and avoid fluctuations caused by recurrent sectorial disputes or episodic deals.[23] The recent success with Argentina and Uruguay, however, could encourage more comprehensive trade planning with other partners, even for lower levels of return.

Brazil is now relying heavily on trade with the United States, where it has been able to gain large surpluses helpful in achieving yearly targets for balance of trade surpluses. Should U.S. economic growth decline or protectionism increase, Latin America could appear more attractive, although still resistant to quick gains through marketing. Increases in trade with Peru, Ecuador, and Colombia will be less likely than success in the Southern Cone. Yet South America will be an unsatisfactory substitute for the United States as a trading partner. In the longer run, an even more diversified Brazil may need even less from South America, although Brazil's products remain attractive in the region.

Brazil would benefit from progress in regional integration, especially in the Southern Cone. Brazil would be relatively advantaged, for example, if ALADI promoted Latin American cooperation in import substitution through complementarity agreements. Brazil could play a key role in building multilateral regionally cooperative institutions if it were willing to give sufficient concessions to lessen fears of countries at lower stages of development. Brazil, however, is emphasizing bilateral trade deals more than multilateral integrative ones and is not accustomed to granting such concessions. One possible trend, therefore, is continental integration toward Brazil rather than multilateral integration.

Joint ventures in technology (such as petrochemicals, informatics, and nuclear science) and civil construction (such as hydroelectric complexes and airports) hold more promise, especially if the economies pick up. Only meager Brazilian foreign aid to smaller states can be expected beyond import credits. In short, Brazil is becoming a major alternative for its neighbors, but, with the exception of Paraguay, not a dominant one.

Despite recent progress in trade negotiations and plans for joint projects, a downside scenario for Southern Cone economic integration looms as well. It takes into account persistent negative factors in the subregion as a whole. The Southern Cone economies generally will compete poorly globally with the more dynamic and innovative Asian NICs, because of sluggish statism, debt, social disorganization, slowness to absorb or create technology, and lower levels of efficiency and capital input. The European Community could turn toward Portugal, Spain, Greece, and Turkey for products formerly purchased from the Southern Cone. The populations of the subregion are found in separate clusters with insufficiently developed or undependable transportation routes. There is still a local perception that other South American countries have low-quality goods with undependable delivery and weak competitiveness when contrasted with comparable suppliers elsewhere. Integration in these circumstances could promote a subregional economic provincialism relative to global technological change, even as local national barriers are broken down.

Political rivalries and negative cultural and racial stereotypes have not been completely buried. Governments with weak legitimacy are prone to pay protectionist attention to groups complaining when hurt by freer trade, as many who rely on pervasive government price regulation and subsidies will be. The region's characteristic political-economic instability makes transnational economic planning even more hazardous than the usually frustrated national planning.[24] It is indicative of the nature of the subregion that years of attempted multilateral cooperation through the Rio de la Plata Treaty group yielded very little, and that recent integrative progress has been carefully carried out on a strictly bilateral basis. The current Argentina-Brazil-Uruguay scheme, while technically well-conceived, is the result, at least in the short run, of a specific configuration of presidents, ministers, and interconnected pro-integration colleagues who have come to power in the three countries. It has not yet taken firm root in the societies. It remains to be seen, as always in Southern Cone international relations, whether this new departure is really a trend.

The main potential economic trends in the near future that would promote or hinder a cooperative role on the continent for Brazil are the following, listed in an approximate descending order of probability.

Potential Economic Trends Encouraging Cooperation

1. Greater multinational corporation use of Brazil as an export platform to South America.
2. Economic recuperation of the region.
3. Success of countertrade, clearing house mechanisms, or a revolving fund for finance.

4. Deeper private sector ties, especially joint ventures in services, mining, investment, and industrial and technical cooperation.
5. Great increase in U.S. protectionism.
6. Brazilian decision to favor South America in acquisitions and sales (via realigned or managed trade).
7. Complementarity agreements for two-way trade in manufactured goods or for joint marketing agreements.
8. Advances in multilateral integration arrangements, either at a continental level or through the Amazon Pact or River Plate groupings.

Potential Economic Trends Discouraging Cooperation

1. Brazilian option for concentration on relations with more attractive partners outside the region.
2. Declining Brazilian need for regional products.
3. Serious regional economic deterioration.

Brazil's Security Relations in South America

Current Security Characteristics

Through the 1970s, external security issues were summarized in the chief interest of keeping political relations with neighboring countries good enough to prevent the formation of an anti-Brazilian alliance. The traditional conciliatory Brazilian view has been that skillful diplomacy should be adequate to head off potential crises well before they reach security proportions, and that is still the Foreign Ministry's position.

In the first half of the 1980s, however, a number of events converged to provide a more tangible external security dimension to Brazilian foreign policy. The trend toward improving relations with Argentina, begun in 1979, demonstrated the positive value of reducing tensions with its traditional rival. Expanding effective occupation of the northwest frontiers brought the now "live" borders into official attention as the "buffer zone" of sparse occupation was being closed. Borders already agreed to by treaty must now be set and regulated in actual practice. A growing Brazilian presence in Paraguay and the Itaipú Dam itself gave Brazil a stake in that country's future which is hard to deny. (The last several ambassadors to Paraguay have been generals, contrary to usual Brazilian practice.)

Several events in 1982 and 1983 along with the government's responses to them set off an unprecedented public, governmental, and military debate on regional security issues: The Falklands War, impoundment by Brazil of three Libyan aircraft carrying weapons to Nicaragua, and extension of security and economic aid to Suriname as a counterbalance to Cuban influence.[25] Security concerns are also inherent in Brazil's arms sales and its recent Antarctic exploration activities to keep up negotiating credentials for the 1991 conference.

As the 1980s progressed, Brazilian-Argentine rapprochement, the wave of democratization in South America, and the settlement or subsidence of several border disputes and the Falklands issue lowered the continental prominence of traditional security issues in favor of developmental issues. The trend away from national security diplomacy and regional conflict is likely to continue and is helpful to Brazilian interests and the intensification of its cooperation in South America. This does not negate the fact, however, that Brazil is gaining, almost unawares, an implicit stake in a wider range of events on the continent. The extent of that stake and the degree to which it is interpreted as security-related will influence the evolution of Brazil's future security relations with South America.

The Security Outlook

While not giving up the role of ultimate arbiter of internal order, the Brazilian military is developing an international security perspective as well. They will take an active interest in and may set limits on certain foreign policy topics which they deem to be security-related. Within South America these would include aspects of relations with Paraguay, Bolivia, Suriname, Guyana, and Argentina, Amazon colonization, illegal drug traffic, border matters generally (including guerrilla movements), leftist currents in neighboring states, and the health and international competitiveness of the civilian-run national arms industry. While the navy plays a large role in Brazil's newly begun Antarctic explorations, the government has staked no official claims and its policies are unlikely to be exclusionary and conflictful.

Brazil's regular military forces are the largest in Latin America, but are small relative to the size and population of the country. Few enlisted men are permanent and recruits often have health and literacy problems. An unusually high percentage of expenditures has gone to personnel and construction projects rather than to equipment, much of which is worn and outdated. Military expenditures in recent years have been below one percent of the GNP. The army, garrisoned mainly in and around the cities, has had a heavily internal mission and no real combat experience. The services are very limited in airlift or seaborne reach and logistic capabilities, even to the point of developing a rapid deployment force for border areas distant from present major bases. Despite its South Atlantic ambitions, the navy is heavily coastal and riverine.

The Falklands War made the military establishment very conscious of weaknesses accumulated during the years of military rule. Several years of study gave rise to a long-term modernization effort (Land Forces 1990 or FT-90 Project). It aspires to substantially increased permanent army corps size; professionalization in organization, communication, control, and training; and more and higher quality nationally produced equipment. An Amazon and a western military command have been established, as well as an air defense and traffic control system for the southern part of the country. Roads to and along western and northern borders are to be constructed, and transfers of units from elsewhere in the country to these points made feasible. The army is also to form a light air force unit with infantry transports and helicopter gunships.[26] Force modernization plans for the navy and air force are much less ambitious, in keeping with the larger role the army has always played in size, influence, and doctrine in this century.

Concurrently, the national war materials industry, already the Third World leader, is advancing rapidly in quantity and quality of production, extending from small arms ammunition into light tanks, armored vehicles, guided missiles, corvettes, and subsonic fighter planes. Many of these items, now destined heavily for export, will be incorporated into the military's arsenal. Projects for construction of a rocket to launch satellites, a supersonic fighter, and submarines (including a nuclear model) are also underway, with completion time frames in the early to mid-1990s.

Such improvements, while facing increasing domestic economic constraints, apparently have broad civilian support and fit into the civilian government's need to find further legitimate functions for the military. Without planning explicitly to do so, just by bringing its forces up to national size and development levels, Brazil will become the premier military power of Latin America. The government does not see military force as an instrument of foreign policy, but a greater military presence in border areas could implicitly raise continental tensions in moments of severe political disagreements. Brazil may also ultimately have to face up to the strategic implications of its developments in rocketry and nuclear science.

The trends already underway, if successful, will definitely have an impact on Brazil's capability to use military force and to cooperate with or to rival the military establishments of its neighbors. Brazil could become a significant source of equipment, training, or joint production of regional partners. Regional confidence-building measures in civilian and military sectors and good public relations would lessen the likelihood of political strains later and would facilitate enhanced security relationships around the continent as Brazil upgrades its capabilities. Otherwise, the Brazilian advance could easily generate suspicion and political resistance among its neighbors.

Key Security Issues

Brazil's security interests are served generally by continued attention to, and action on, those elements detrimental to its political position in South America. Encouraging nonintervention, evolutionary change, cooperation, and concentration on economic development issues therefore suits Brazil's security needs. Advancement of cooperation with Argentina is at the center of this agenda, and shows early signs of going beyond the political and economic to include security cooperation with a confidence-building effect as well. Consultations and symposia on strategic issues among upper-level military officers of the two countries have been held and gave evidence of decreasing suspicion and advancing willingness to cooperate.

Few imminent "flash points" in South America can be cited, but a few potential future issues are evident. With military units near formerly remote frontiers and increased cross-border movements of persons, Brazil will be more sensitive to increased drug traffic, guerrilla movements, political disturbances, and treatment of its nationals across the frontiers. Currently, the cross-border labor migration and capital flows are heavily from Brazil outward, most in evidence in Paraguay, French Guiana, Uruguay, and Bolivia, in approximate descending order of magnitude. Binational cooperation rather than confrontation is the most probable result, but some disagreements are likely to occur. Leftist revolutionary violence or internal instability in neighboring states could cause military reinforcement of border regions, most recently with Colombia (because of M-19 guerrilla movements) and potentially with Peru and Bolivia. Otherwise, Brazil is tolerant of more typical levels of local disruption. Its large stake in Paraguay makes Brazil the most interested foreign party in the Stroessner succession and in Paraguayan stability and cooperation, especially if, as is already the case in Bolivia, political factions with pro- and anti-Brazilian biases should emerge and secession to join Brazil becomes an issue.

For Brazil, arms sales are still a commercial matter rather than a foreign policy tool. As Brazil's military equipment industry becomes larger and more diversified, there will be more pressure to sell in South America. The Falklands War convinced South American military establishments of the need to modernize their forces and to increase their

degree of self-reliance.[27] The recent Brazilian-Argentine political understanding and a January 1986 aeronautical treaty between them raise
the possibility of coproduction, local assembly, or joint research and
development, a practice that could conceivably be extended to other
states as well (although there are no immediate signs that this will
occur). Brazil's defense industry will outpace all others in Latin America
and could serve as an alternative or auxiliary source of technology and
supply for more countries by the early 1990s. With expanding Brazilian
influence on the continent by that time, defense supply, training, and
technology arrangements will have domestic and international political
significance or symbolism, even if the primary motives remain economic. Such developments would create an enhanced role in training,
missions, and exchanges for the Brazilian military in the continent,
even though the arms industry is largely a civilian operation.[28] (About
half of Brazil's fifty-four military attachés abroad in 1985 were in South
America.)[29]

Weighing against full realization of Brazil's potential as regional
defense industry hub are local political instability, nationalism, and a
possible reluctance of partners to accept the second or third level of
technology such arrangements would entail. Extracontinental suppliers
will remain more competitive for sophisticated state-of-the-art equipment. From Brazil's perspective, major new extracontinental markets
(such as China, Saudi Arabia, and some Western nations) are certain
to hold more promise than South America in total sales volume. Brazil
may also choose to refrain from being a large supplier to South America
in order to avoid political controversy with its neighbors.

The nuclear technology development rivalry between Brazil and
Argentina was diminished, but not eliminated, by a late 1985 agreement
to discuss mutual inspection of nuclear facilities. It was followed up
by Sarney's visit to Argentina's Pilcaniyeu uranium enrichment plant
in July 1987, resulting in a joint presidential declaration that the two
countries would use nuclear energy only for peaceful purposes. As at
least a start toward confidence-building and presenting a favorable and
peaceful image to the world, the principle was successful. Implementation, however, may be cosmetic and tentative because nuclear research
remains one of the most nationalistic and secretive issues on both sides
and is likely to continue so. For the time being, actual mutual inspection
has been deemed unfeasible, but a permanent working group of diplomats and technical specialists consults on questions raised. Important
segments of the programs of both nations are not under international
safeguards, and neither government is willing to accept such safeguards.
Both countries supply nuclear technology and equipment to other Latin

American nations, and are expanding mutual cooperation in nuclear research and supply, thus opening up second-tier supplier issues.

Argentine advances tend to drive the rivalry, and Brazil feels pressure to "keep up." Brazil became all the more suspicious when its intelligence community was surprised by the November 1983 announcement by Argentina that its scientists had mastered uranium enrichment through a secret program and were moving to complete the fuel cycle. President Alfonsín's transfer of nuclear development to civilian control and reduction of the budget calmed some fears. Yet Brazil is unwilling to accept second place status in enrichment capability and has concerns about Argentina's longer-term political stability. In September 1987, President Sarney announced that Brazil, too, had mastered uranium enrichment, but he reiterated the peaceful purposes of the nuclear research program. (Sarney had informed Alfonsín by telephone two days before the public statement.)[30] Argentine fears, however, are stirred by reports and rumors in the Brazilian press and among intellectuals and scientists about a secret "parallel" nuclear science program in Brazil, under military control, and reports of a supposed highly guarded nuclear test site being prepared in the Amazon in the Serra do Cachimbo.

At this point, further progress in confidence-building measures could lower tensions enough to allow a sub-regional safeguards agreement growing out of Brazilian-Argentine initiatives. Recent political understandings and consultations on nuclear issues give some reason for hope, because the issue deserves and is receiving ongoing high-level attention in both governments. Meanwhile, bilateral cooperation is likely to be limited to more peripheral areas of nuclear science. In a negative scenario, the nuclear issue, if poorly managed, could conceivably find both countries ultimately on the edge of nuclear weapons status, then pushed (perhaps inadvertently) over the threshold into the decision to produce by a quirk event or rumor. Such a chain of events would not augur well for Southern Cone political cooperation.

The main potential security trends in the near future that would promote or hinder a cooperative role on the continent for Brazil are the following, listed in an approximate descending order of probability.

Potential Security Trends Encouraging Cooperation

1. Continued Brazilian-Argentine political understanding.
2. Continued low prominence of border disputes in South America.
3. Continuation of civilian governments on the continent.
4. Greater training of South American military officers in Brazil.
5. Mild increase in Brazilian military assistance programs.

6. Regional confidence-building measures.

Potential Security Trends Discouraging Cooperation

1. Poor management of cross-border traffic and mistreatment of foreign nationals across the borders, with troublesome incidents or incursions.
2. Poor management of Brazil's growth in military capabilities.
3. Radical or anti-Brazilian regimes in neighboring states.
4. Resurgence of Brazilian-Argentine nuclear technology rivalry.
5. Emergence of a Brazilian capability and will to project military power beyond its borders.
6. Brazilian military intervention in a neighboring state.

Implications for U.S. Policy

General Considerations

Through increasing interactions with its neighbors and the growing primacy of its economy on the continent, Brazil is gradually acquiring greater interests and influence in South America, at a pace not matched by other local states. Judging, however, by the extent of its extracontinental priorities, its apparent predispositions to restraint, the record so far, its considerable international dependence, the degree of its attention to internal affairs, and the weight of counterbalancing local and external influences, Brazil is definitely not a hegemonic power in South America. To the contrary, Brazil's policies and actions do not presently appear to constitute major official concerns beyond Argentina, Paraguay, Bolivia, Uruguay, Suriname, Guyana, and perhaps Chile. Colombia and Venezuela are heavily turned toward the United States and the Caribbean Basin. More substantial relations with Peru, Ecuador, Colombia, and Venezuela will be required before Brazilian influence can really be said to be effectively continental in scope.

There appears, however, to be a consensus on the continent that a politically stable, democratic, and economically healthy Brazil is a definite asset to the local well-being. Brazil's steadily growing potential encourages neighbors toward peaceful accommodation, a process aided by Brazil's cooperative style and "good neighbor" role. Brazil will likely continue this cautious diplomatic style, but from time to time may be faced with pressure to turn mere concern into concrete action through the option of using its potential influence in South America, to take a clearer and more committed position than it has done heretofore. The nature of these commitments, how they are carried out, and international and domestic reaction will be important signposts for a more active Brazilian role on the continent. The practical realization by Brazil of the consequences of its continental primacy, in the context of its global policies, then, carries some implications for the United States.

Political Implications of Brazil's Primacy

Brazil's acceptance of a larger South American role will increase the likelihood of coordination of its foreign policy with those of other regional states in issues of foreign debt repayment and Central American conflict, among others. The debt repayment issue will rise in Brazil's regional priorities, and the sense of shared interests with other debtors will grow. Brazil will most likely continue to prefer to work out its own arrangements with creditors, using the Latin consensus for support, unless creditor intransigency or economic collapse make the unilateral approach unworkable.

Domestic stability and continuity in Brazil, particularly under a democratic regime, would be important for continental stability and evolutionary change. Brazil's support for democracy in South America, however, is likely to be more abstract than concrete.

The political understanding with Argentina is likely to continue and serve as a positive tone-setter for South American international politics. It could aid considerably in the building of regional stability and sounder multilateral institutions, with more local autonomy. Closer cooperation between the two states would also free the United States from the temptation to support preferentially either Argentina or Brazil, a questionable "option" that has not proved advantageous in recent administrations. The general economic health of the area, including resolution of the debt dilemma, will be very important (but not sufficient) to keep local international cooperation moving forward.

Close political identification with the United States will be resisted because it would hinder Brazil's emerging role by suggesting dependence on the U.S. or an American-Brazilian coordination in regional affairs. Brazil as a middle power is ultimately restricted in its activities on the South American continent by potentially strong pressure exerted counter to Brazilian interests by the United States when its own security interests are threatened. It is thus to Brazil's advantage to avoid injection of superpower security issues into South American or South Atlantic international politics and to encourage continuation of the current low U.S. political profile on the continent.

Economic Implications of Brazil's Primacy

For Brazil, its South American trade will not substitute in variety, value, or potential surplus for trade lost in the United States through protectionism. A chief disadvantage Brazil suffers relative to the United States in trade with South America is its growing difficulty in finding enough to buy to keep a balanced trade flow. Yet Brazilian manufactures will begin to rival those from the United States in South American markets, especially in the Southern Cone and especially if the River Plate Basin integration continues.

Security Implications of Brazil's Primacy

Brazil's important security interests are heavily in South America. Its chief security interest is to guard regional stability and its own influence in the South American continent by keeping East-West competition out of South America and the South Atlantic. This concern explains its decision against cooperation with the United States in constructing a base on Trindade Island in the South Atlantic, its aid to the Bouterse government in Suriname, and its active role with Argentina in promoting the South Atlantic as a "zone of peace." Even though its continental security interests parallel those of the United States in some cases, it would be politically unacceptable to appear to be acting in concert with Washington.

In practical terms, Brazil accepts the American role as leading extra-regional power in South America, even while seeking to safeguard its own foreign policy independence. The lesson of Brazil's low-key reactions to Central America, Grenada, and the Falklands, in contrast to its actions in the Libyan and Suriname cases, is that Brazil is reluctant to confront or associate itself with a great power in security issues not directly affecting it, but is able to take adequate action to defend its own interests when they are affected. The sense in Brasília that the Suriname security and economic aid effort is taxing, although small by global standards, suggests the current close limits Brazil places on its willingness to set up donative client relationships. Yet, for reasons of nonintervention, Brazil is unlikely to be interested in a regional security system.

Brazilian-Argentine nuclear rivalry will continue at a muted level, but still represents a serious long-term problem. The opportunity now exists to achieve effective bilateral or subregional safeguards. These measures must originate, however, from regional actors rather than from the United States or the larger international community. Although avoiding proliferation of nuclear weapons capability to Argentina and Brazil is probably the chief predictable security issue for the United States in the Southern Cone, there is relatively little the United States can do about it.

Brazil is unlikely to pursue bellicose policies toward its neighbors, but it will have to manage their concerns about Brazil's growing military capabilities and Brazilian migration and economic influence across borders into neighboring countries. Brazil has the potential, through sales, coproduction, training, and military exchange, to be a significant defense supplier to South America. The case of Paraguay will be a demanding entanglement because of the stakes involved for Brazil. Despite these stakes, Brazil has had no interest in joining with the United States to urge democratic evolution in Paraguay.

Brazil will seek greater rights in Antarctica in the probable treaty review beginning in 1991, but will not be a major player or pursue exclusionary principles. Brazil would be in a position to serve as mediator in border disputes that may flare up, such as between Colombia and Venezuela, Guyana and Venezuela, or Ecuador and Peru.

Brazil is unlikely to go out of its way to please the United States. In general, however, U.S. and Brazilian political-security interests in South America will be compatible. A democratic Brazil will quietly and reliably, but on its own, support evolutionary change, regional cooperation, low levels of military development, democracy, Western values, and moderation. Yet, on some issues, Brazil will pursue quite independent policies. On the whole, much more substantial U.S. differences with Brazil are likely in bilateral or global multilateral matters than from Brazil's role in general South American affairs or in relations with third countries there.

Notes

1. An overview of this period is found in Wayne A. Selcher, "Recent Strategic Developments in South America's Southern Cone," in Heraldo Muñoz and Joseph Tulchin (eds.), *Latin American Nations in World Politics* (Boulder: Westview Press, 1984), pp. 101–118.

2. Roberto Russell, "Argentina y la política exterior del régimen autoritario (1976–1983): Una evaluacion preliminar," *Estudios Internacionales*, no. 66 (April-June 1984), pp. 170–201.

3. The settlement of this major longstanding irritant in Southern Cone international politics is recounted in James L. Garrett, "The Beagle Channel Dispute: Confrontation and Negotiation in the Southern Cone," *Journal of Interamerican Studies and World Affairs*, vol. 27, no. 3 (Fall 1985), pp. 81–109.

4. Cynthia A. Watson, "Alfonsín's Foreign Policy: Argentina Charting a New Course?" Paper presented at the International Studies Association Meeting, Washington, DC, April 15–18, 1987, pp. 20–21.

5. Roberto Russell, "El caso de Argentina," in Monica Hirst and Roberto Russell, *Democracia y Política Exterior: Los Casos de Argentina y Brasil*, vol. 4, no. 12 (Buenos Aires: FLACSO, Programa Buenos Aires, April-June 1987), p. 106.

6. Oscar Camilion, "Tres años de política exterior argentina," *América Latina/Internacional*, FLACSO, Programa Buenos Aires, vol. 4, no. 12 (April-June 1987), p. 106.

7. Heraldo Muñoz, "Chile's External Relations Under the Military Government," in J. Samuel Valenzuela and Arturo Valenzuela (eds.), *Military Rule in Chile: Dictatorship and Oppositions* (Baltimore: Johns Hopkins University Press, 1986), p. 310.

8. Waltraud Q. Morales, "La geopolítica de la política exterior de Bolivia," Documentos de Trabajo PROSPEL, No. 2, September 1984 (Santiago, Chile), p. 20.

9. Mladen Yopo, "Paraguay: Transición o reacomodo?" *Cono Sur*, vol. 6, no. 3 (June-July 1987), pp. 2-4.

10. Joseph Tulchin, "Uruguay: The Quintessential Buffer State," in John Clay and Thomas E. Ross (eds.), *Buffer States in World Politics* (Boulder: Westview Press, 1986), pp. 213-229.

11. The remainder of this chapter builds on ideas originally developed in Wayne A. Selcher, "Current Dynamics and Future·Prospects of Brazil's Relations with Latin America: Toward a Pattern of Bilateral Cooperation," *Journal of Interamerican Studies and World Affairs*, vol. 28, no. 2 (Summer 1986), pp. 67-99.

12. Robert D. Bond, "Brazil's Relations with the Northern Tier Countries of South America," in Wayne A. Selcher (ed.), *Brazil in the International System: The Rise of a Middle Power* (Boulder: Westview Press, 1981), p. 132.

13. For an overview, see Wayne A. Selcher, "Brazilian-Argentine Relations in the 1980s: From Wary Rivalry to Friendly Competition," *Journal of Interamerican Studies and World Affairs*, vol. 27, no. 2 (Summer 1985), pp. 25-53; Monica Hirst and Miguel Lengyel, "Brasil—Las relaciones con Argentina: Primeros sintomas de un acercamiento estable," *América Latina/Internacional*, FLACSO, Programa Buenos Aires, vol. 2, no. 6 (October-December, 1985), pp. 119-122; Institute for European–Latin American Relations (IRELA), *A New Phase in Latin American Integration? The 1986 Agreements between Argentina and Brazil* (Madrid: IRELA, December 1986); "El programa de integración argentino-brasileña," *Integración Latinoamericana* (INTAL), Year 12, Number 122, entire issue; and Renato Baumann and Juan Carlos Lerda (eds.), *Brasil-Argentina-Uruguay: A integraçao em Debate* (Brasilia: Editoras Marco Zero-Universidade de Brasília, 1987).

14. Monica Hirst, "Democratic Transition and Foreign Policy: The Experience of Brazil," in Heraldo Muñoz and Joseph S. Tulchin (eds.), *Latin American Nations in World Politics* (Boulder: Westview Press, 1984), p. 223.

15. On Brazil's cautious diplomatic style and the reasons behind it, see Wayne A. Selcher, "Brazil in the World: Multipolarity as Seen by a Peripheral ADC Middle Power," in Elizabeth G. Ferris and Jennie K. Lincoln (eds.), *Latin American Foreign Policies: Global and Regional Dimensions* (Boulder: Westview Press, 1981), especially pp. 98-101.

16. David J. Myers, "Threat Perception and Strategic Response of the Regional Hegemons: A Conceptual Overview," Paper, Northeast Political Sci-

ence Association, Philadelphia, November 14–16, 1985, especially the country listings in Table 1.1.

17. Inter-American Development Bank, *Economic and Social Progress in Latin America—Economic Integration* (Washington, DC: IDB, 1984), p. 104.

18. Ibid., p. 117.

19. Ibid., pp. 112–114.

20. Assoçiaco Brasileira de Engenharia Industrial, *Exportaçaao de Servicos de Engenharia-Levantamjento Preliminar* (Rio de Janeiro: Mimeographed, May 1982).

21. Robert M. Plehn, "International Trade: Economic Integration of the Argentine Republic and the Federal Republic of Brazil," *Harvard International Law Journal*, vol. 28, no. 1 (Winter 1987), pp. 193–194.

22. The evolution and potentials of the River Plate Basin subsystem are considered in John D. Wirth, "Brazil's Role in the New World Regions," in John D. Wirth, Edson de Oliverira Nunes, and Thomes E. Bogenschild (eds.), *State and Society in Brazil: Continuity and Change* (Boulder: Westview Press, 1987), especially pp. 273–284, and Carlos de Meira Mattos, *Estratégias Militares Dominantes* (Rio de Janiero: Biblioteca do Exercito, 1986), pp. 85–87.

23. Monica Hirst, "Brasil—Balance y perspectivas de la política exterior brasileña," *América Latina/Internacional*, FLACSO, Programa Buenos Aires, vol. 1, no. 1 (July-September, 1984), p. 14.

24. Some of the ways in which chronic internal weaknesses and demands for entitlement carry over into weaknesses of Argentina's foreign policy regarding international interdependence are discussed in Edward S. Milenky, *Argentina's Foreign Policies* (Boulder: Westview Press, 1978), pp. 293–304.

25. The effects of these events on Brazil's foreign policy are analyzed in Wayne A. Selcher, "Brazil's Foreign Policy: More Actors and Expanding Agendas," in Jennie K. Lincoln and Elizabeth G. Ferris (eds.), *The Dynamics of Latin American Foreign Policies: Challenges for the 1980s* (Boulder: Westview Press, 1984), pp. 116–121.

26. *O Estado de São Paulo*, December 11, 1985, p. 7.

27. Carlos Moneta, "Las fuerzas armadas y el conflicto de las Islas Malvinas: Su importancia en la política argentina y en el marco regional," *Foro Internacional*, vol. 23, no. 3 (January-March 1983), pp. 282–285.

28. Alexandre de S.C. Barros, "Brazil," in James E. Katz (ed.), *Arms Production in Developing Countries: An Analysis of Decision Making* (Lexington: Lexington, 1984), p. 83.

29. Alexandre de S.C. Barros, "The Future of United States–Brazilian Relations: Political and Security Issues and Opportunities," Paper, Seminar on the Future of the United States–Brazilian Relations, Center for Strategic and International Studies, Washington, DC: September 26, 1985, p. 6.

30. "Sarney arma seu ciclo," *Veja*, September 9, 1987, pp. 18–19.

5

U.S. Interests in South America

Morris J. Blachman

From the beginning of the American Republic, key U.S. leaders have coveted Latin America. Thomas Jefferson wrote in the late 1780s that it was in the interest of the United States "to gain it (Latin America) from them (Spain) piece by piece."[1] He saw the region as "essential to our tranquility and commerce. . . . Our strength will permit us to give the law of *our own* hemisphere."[2] As if to echo that notion, Secretary of State William Seward in 1846 promised that he would "engage to give you the possession of the American continent and the control of the world."[3] In 1895 Secretary of State Richard Olney, at the behest of President Grover Cleveland, made it clear that U.S. hegemony in the Western Hemisphere had become a matter of policy as well as reality. He said:

> Today the United States is practically sovereign on this continent, and its fiat is law upon the subjects to which it confines its interposition. Why? It is not because of the pure friendship or good will felt for it. It is not simply by reason of its high character as a civilized state, not because wisdom and justice and equality are the invariable characteristics of the dealings of the United States. It is because, in addition to all other grounds, its infinite resources combined with its isolated position render it master of the situation and practically invulnerable as against any or all other powers.[4]

Secretary Olney was correct in the sense that the power of the United States to enforce its will was enormous. The United States came to exercise virtual control over the internal affairs of certain regimes in the Caribbean region by becoming the dominant trading partner, inserting and withdrawing troops, and making and breaking governments. In addition, the United States sought to set the limits of "legitimacy" for the foreign policies of other countries in the hemisphere. U.S. displeasure carried a high cost for certain Latin American nations.

For most of the nineteenth century, the United States exercised little direct influence on the Southern Cone nations or Brazil. The cloak of the Monroe Doctrine provided little coverage during that period. Ironically, it was the United States that in the mid-1800s refused to respond to requests from Brazil and other South American nations to defend the position of the Monroe Doctrine. By 1898, when the United States was on the threshold of becoming the dominant military power in the Circum-Caribbean region, its reach was still limited and its touch relatively light with regard to the Southern Cone and Brazil. The type of intervention so commonly wielded by the United States in its contiguous areas was not found in the farther reaches of the South American continent.

Indeed, if one examines the period between the first and second world wars, U.S. policy often corresponded to the interests of South American nations as they defined it themselves. In many of the most delicate and volatile situations of boundary disputes, the United States joined with South Americans in supporting multilateral diplomatic efforts for the pacific resolution of disputes. On occasion the United States offered its good offices to assist in resolving a particular crisis. This was the heyday in the region of respect for and adherence to the precepts of international law, mutually accepted in Latin America and the United States.

Though the overwhelming majority of heavy-handed U.S. activity in the region took place in the Circum-Caribbean, the South American nations were also covered by the hegemonic veil. U.S. influence in that part of the hemisphere gradually increased during the twentieth century, reaching its peak in the post–World War II era. While military troops have been used dozens of times in the areas geographically closer to the United States, instruments of economic, political, and military cooperation have been the typical coins of the foreign policy realm in U.S. relations with South America.

U.S. Hegemony and National Security

The U.S. hegemonic ambition has been an established fact throughout the twentieth century. It is well recognized and often deeply resented in Latin America. In the United States, academics were writing about hegemony, imperialism, and empire within a decade of the Roosevelt Corollary to the Monroe Doctrine. Walter Lippmann pointed out clearly in 1927, however, that overt acknowledgement of hegemonic behavior by North Americans themselves was nearly inconceivable. According to Lippmann:

All the world thinks of the United States today as an empire, except the people of the United States. We shrink from the word "empire," and insist that it should not be used to describe the dominion we exercise. . . . We feel that there ought to be some other name for the civilizing work which we do so reluctantly in these backward countries. We do not feel ourselves to be imperialists as we understand that word. . . . We have learned to think of empires as troublesome and as immoral, and to admit that we have an empire still seems to most Americans like admitting that they have gone out into a wicked world and there lost their political chastity.[5]

Regardless of the term used to describe the control exercised by the United States in the Western Hemisphere, there could be little dispute that its behavior fit the definition of a hegemonic power. Hegemony, as described by Bergsten, Keohane, and Nye, is a condition when "one state is able and willing to determine and maintain the essential rules by which relations among states are governed. The hegemonical state not only can abrogate existing rules or prevent the adoption of rules it opposes but can also play the dominant role in constructing new rules."[6]

The difficulty Lippmann foreshadowed was exhibited some sixteen years later, when Yale's distinguished diplomatic historian, Samuel Flagg Bemis, published his classic study, *The Latin American Policy of the United States: An Historical Interpretation.* Bemis painfully recognized the dominion exercised by the United States, but he went on to accept it as a justified aberration with no significant consequences with these words:

That the United States has been an imperialistic power since 1898 there is no doubt, although that comparatively mild imperialism was tapered off after 1921 and is fully liquidated now [1943]. A careful and conscientious appraisal of United States imperialism shows . . . that it was never deep-rooted in the character of the people, that it was essentially a protective imperialism, designed to protect, first the security of the Continental Republic, next the security of the entire New World, against intervention by the imperialistic powers of the Old World. It was . . . an imperialism against imperialism. It did not last long and it was not really bad.[7]

The events of the ensuing forty five years suggest that this "protective imperialism" of the Western Hemisphere was less than aberrational, had long-term consequences, and not only has not been liquidated but a version of it extended to the entire globe. The United States had special responsibilities in the world deriving from and spurred on by the notion that, as Arthur Schlesinger, Jr., puts it, "in the United States of America the Almighty had contrived a nation unique in its virtue and magnanimity, exempt from the motives that governed all other states." Schlesinger goes on to argue that one "strain" competing for the control of American foreign policy had been ascendant in the post–World War II period: that of the redeemer, "commissioned to save humanity."[8]

President Truman advised Americans to "take the lead in running the world in the way that the world ought to be run." President Johnson declared that "history and our own achievements have thrust upon us the principal responsibility for protecting freedom on earth." President Ford let us know that we had "a unique role in the world, a heavy responsibility for insuring a stable world order." President Reagan, with a view harkening back to Teddy Roosevelt's acceptance of the role of an international police power in the Western Hemisphere, asserted that U.S. policy commitments were necessarily global. Reagan said that "we in this country, in this generation, are, by destiny rather than choice, the watchmen on the walls of world freedom."[9] Schlesinger, cited above, says that President Reagan "represented a mighty comeback of messianism in foreign policy." Reagan viewed the Soviet Union not only as the enemy, but "the focus of evil in the modern world", the United States was in a struggle "between right and wrong and good and evil" and the Soviets were behind global unrest. "If they weren't engaged in this game of dominoes," President Reagan said, "there wouldn't be any hot spots in the world."[10]

This set of views had important consequences for U.S. policies toward the nations of South America. It led to an overriding concern with short-range security considerations, relegating other U.S. foreign policy goals to low priority and focusing them primarily on what Americans were against.[11] South Americans responded by telling the United States that they distrusted U.S. policy. Argentine scholar Guillermo O'Donnell reflected this view when he said: "For current or future Latin American democratic governments, the cancellation of their mistrust for the content and goals of U.S. policy will have to interact closely with concrete signals from the U.S. government that it is abandoning its hegemonic and paternalistic temptations regarding Latin America."[12]

Changing Realities and Changing Needs

The post–World War II period has been a tumultuous one for the Southern Cone nations and Brazil. Argentina, Brazil, Chile, and Uruguay have each gone through wrenching experiences with new forms of repressive military authoritarian rule. The roles of their armed forces have undergone profound shifts as they were directly involved in the direction and management of their respective societies, undertaking responsibilities well outside the realm of legitimate military roles in democratic theory. The changes wrought in the polity have been matched by dramatic shifts in the economies. Greater integration into the world economy has been accompanied by increasing complexity in the domestic economies, along with the development of a technically sophisticated technocratic class. The accumulation of a massive debt and economies that fail to keep pace with the needs of the population have placed heavy strains on the burgeoning states, already encumbered by commitments they cannot meet.

The "experiments" of military rule around South America failed to deliver on the promise of efficient economic growth. Societal complexities proved just as difficult to manage for the technocratically-oriented military elites. Efforts at consolidating the transition from military to civilian democratic governance (or in the cases of Chile and Paraguay of beginning a transition) have revealed the nature, breadth, and depth of the challenges facing South American countries.

The problems confronting these nations are not amenable to simple solutions, nor are they resolvable solely through their own internal actions. They require the cooperation and assistance of outside powers, but, most importantly, they require a recognition that circumstances have changed over the past several decades. Former President Raúl Alfonsín of Argentina warned that the new realities call for new solutions, since it was "no longer possible to apply old formulas or to repeat routines." Alfonsín also complained that "the developed and prosperous democracies look at us with fondness but with no imagination," responding "to us in a routine manner, as if nothing had actually or could possibly change." He argued that "we know that it is not so, that in the last years substantial changes have taken place," concluding that "today, as forty years ago in Europe, the fate of a continent is at stake: will the rich and developed democracies of today have the imagination and audacity of yore?"[13]

Alfonsín's remarks take us to the heart of the matter. Regardless of one's assessment of past U.S. relations with South America, there is widespread recognition that the policies of the past are inappropriate for today's realities.[14] What, then, are the appropriate policies for the United States to pursue in South America? The response to that question depends on one's understanding of U.S. interests in the region.

National Interest and National Security

The notion of national interest has been a favorite for explaining and justifying U.S. foreign policy. It and its half brother, national security, are among the most used and abused terms in the U.S. foreign policy lexicon. Political leaders use the concepts to rationalize and justify policies. Academics use them to explain certain foreign policy behaviors. Yet the terms have no generally accepted meaning, despite the fact that they are central concepts in the dominant realist paradigm that informs both the theory and practice of international relations.

Hans Morgenthau wrapped the concept of national interest into a theory of international politics that provided the basis of the realist school to which virtually all U.S. policymakers adhere. In an earlier evocation of the idea of U.S. national interest, Charles Beard in 1934 stressed economics as the essential substantive basis of American interests. In the aftermath of World War II, however, and through the influence of Morgenthau's book titled *Politics Among Nations* (first published in 1948), the "Realist School" became dominant. At the same time, the notion of "national security" came to be considered more and more as functionally equivalent to "national interest."[15] Morgenthau himself seemed to advocate this view when he said that "the national interest of a peace-loving nation can only be defined in terms of national security, and national security must be defined as integrity of the national territory and of its institutions." Morgenthau concluded that national security was "the irreducible minimum that diplomacy must defend with adequate power without compromise."[16] This view is stated even more forcefully in Morgenthau's book, *In Defense of the National Interest* (1951), which Arnold Wolfers called "the most explicit and impassioned recent plea for an American foreign policy which shall follow but one guiding star—the National Interest." While Morgenthau is not so explicit about the meaning he attaches to "national security," it becomes clear in the few pages devoted to an exposition of this "perennial" interest that the author is thinking in terms of the national security based on power.[17] Furthermore, as the national interest in essence became national security, the latter became "locked into an East-West perspective."[18] In substance U.S. policy became oriented primarily around anticommunism.[19]

With reference to U.S. interests and actions in Latin America, the anticommunist national security mentality led the thinking of U.S. policy makers to revolve around the intentions of the Soviet Union. As Lars Schoultz puts it, Latin America became an "inert, passive object of no intrinsic value, a place where the United States and the Soviet Union play out the drama of international politics." Schoultz finds it "difficult to overemphasize how policy makers' dominant concern for security leads to the debate over Soviet intentions." Schoultz goes on to say that the reductionism of national interest to national security to anticommunism to keeping the left out of power and ultimately to distrusting any situation of instability as potentially leading to Soviet expansionism has led to a policy posture that "has the singular defect of being unalterably negative." Consequently, "it provides an answer to the question of what the United States does *not* want Latin America to be but no satisfactory, realistic vision of the type of relationship the United States should attempt to develop with the nations of the region." This lack of vision not only reaffirms how Latin Americans see and react to the United States, but also affects U.S. officials who are involved in the Latin American policy process. "There is no vision, no *elan vital*." In sum, the policy of containment provides no guidance for a creative vision.[20]

Many Latin Americans also refer to national interests and national security as interchangeable. The content of national security for them, however, is considerably different than its meaning in the United States. As Chilean writer Sergio Bitar notes, "Latin American security historically has been closely linked to domestic political unity, social progress, and economic development. . . . Latin American proposals regarding hemispheric security have repeatedly emphasized concern with economic development."[21] The point is made most succinctly in the 1983 report of the Inter-American Dialogue:

> When Latin Americans think of security, most of them think of the internal challenges of national unity and development, of border issues with neighboring states, and, in some cases, of the possibility of intervention by the United States. In the United States, the focus on security is external, global, and strategic. . . . The United States generally seeks to assure political stability abroad, sometimes by supporting the *status quo* under sharp internal or regional challenge. Many Latin Americans feel that profound change is inevitable in their region, and that an emphasis on immediate stability is therefore misguided.[22]

Gabriel Marcella also emphasizes the importance and persistence of the differences in the meaning of security for the different parties. "Asymmetrical perceptions on security," he says, "will persist as long as the United States remains locked into an East-West perspective on national security." In Marcella's view, "the United States needs to accept Latin American security concerns and be prepared to deal with an agenda that stresses interdependence in economic affairs as a central element of security."[23]

Latin American political leaders, and analysts from both continents, have been saying for years that such a narrowly based U.S. policy is inimical to both U.S. and Latin American interests. Alfonsín addressed the threat posed by the U.S. conception of national security when he said that "it is indispensible to prevent the political and military aspects

of the global ideological confrontation from dominating the internal
scenario of our countries."[24] In a review of thirty-eight studies dealing
with the Malvinas/Falklands conflict, written mostly by Latin Americans, Joseph Tulchin reports that "all of the Latin American specialists
are convinced that the Malvinas episode demonstrates once and for all
that the inter-American system does not work, except for the convenience of the United States, and that the future security of Latin
America can be guaranteed only through regional organization without
the United States, economic integration of the region, and a new
economic order."[25]

Other studies since World War II have come to the similar conclusion
that the United States must get beyond its hegemonic strategic vision
to see its national interests in a new and different way.[26] In 1969 Nelson
Rockefeller reported to President Nixon that "the kind of paternalistic
relationship the United States has had in the past with other hemisphere
nations will be increasingly costly and counter-productive in the years
ahead. We believe the United States must move increasingly toward a
relationship of true partnership, in which it will cooperate with other
nations of the hemisphere in those areas where its cooperation can be
helpful and is wanted."[27]

The National Interest Reconsidered

Is it in the national interest of the United States to change its policies
as has been urged by so many Latin Americans and by regional analysts
in the United States? This is a difficult question to answer since
confusion exists as to what the national interest is. Scholars and practitioners have debated extensively what should constitute the national
interest and how it should be determined. Some of them have argued
that the term is used in so many different ways and is so imprecise
that it should be discarded as a prescriptive guide. Nevertheless, the
currency that the concept has in the thinking of political leaders and
the writings of academics suggests that however vague it might be it
in fact provides some sense of direction for foreign policy. While this
essay is not the place to conduct an extended assessment of the concept
and its theoretical utility, a few comments are in order to establish
that the concept does have some value.

Generally speaking, five basic approaches to determining U.S. national interest may be gleaned from the literature. Each of them is
fraught with difficulty.

The first method is to infer the national interest from actual state
behavior. This approach teases out the central tendency found in that

behavior and assumes that policy outcomes represent policy intentions. This "you are what you do" approach emphasizes a systematic flow of the cross pressures, influences, and power that are brought to bear in successive stages of the policy process. The major categories are policy conceptualization (the goals to be achieved), policy implementation (the instrumentalities to be used in pursuing the policy), policy output (the conduct of the policy), and policy outcomes (the results of policy in its operational environment).

The second method sees national interest as the aggregation of all the specific interests in society, while the third approach corresponds to a Rousseauvian idea of the general will. These two ideas have a certain aesthetic appeal and are conceptually clear, but are operationally very difficult to measure and to determine with any precision.

The fourth method is, as Fred Sondermann says, what most of us do most of the time—that is, to accept the definition of the national interest provided by state policy makers.[28] Aside from the fact that political leaders often use the term as part of an attempt to gain popular acceptance of their particular version of the national interest, there is a serious flaw in this method. If the national interest is whatever policy makers say it is, then by definition they would be acting in the national interest regardless of what they do. Were this the case, one could never assert that any administration, policy maker, or policy was not in the national interest. The concept would be void of any descriptive, explanatory, or prescriptive value.

The final approach involves the effort to define the national interest in terms of the enduring values for which the nation stands. The obvious difficulty with this technique lies in how one determines values that are enduring and in assuming that because a value is enduring it is desirable.

None of these five versions constitutes a fully satisfactory way to determine the national interest. They do provide, however, some guidelines about how to think in national interest terms. Despite the differences in the five methods, they all assume that pursuit of the national interest is the essential thing for states to do. There is also an at least implicit and sometimes explicit theme running through most of the literature that active pursuit of the national interest will benefit the nation and that, conversely, not doing so will be deleterious.[29] A useful approach is to think about the national interest in terms of determining general societal values held in common by most members of the nation as its basis. While this lead still provides no clear solution, it gives some footing for the conception of national interest as rooted in a consensus about national values.

The U.S. National Interest

A value statement of the fundamental national interests of the citizenry of the United States was provided by the Framers of the Republic. It constitutes a part of the social contract recorded in the Declaration of Independence and in the Preamble to the Constitution. The former has no legal claim on citizens, although it rests on the underlying philosophical justification for the existence of the nation and for the generic conception of the system of governance. The latter, while not having the legal force of the body of the Constitution, carries sufficient weight to be cited for support in Supreme Court decisions.[30] Thus the Declaration and the Preamble provide a useful starting point to discern the consensual U.S. national interest.

The Declaration makes clear the commitment to the universality of certain rights of individuals at the same time that it recognizes the legitimacy and individuality of governments. The affirmation of the right and duty to overthrow tyranny accrues to a country's citizens. The Declaration does not establish, however, a transnational right of one people to play the role of judge, jury, or policeman for others.

The Preamble establishes the specific array of interests to be pursued with no distinction made between domestic and international interests. In the Preamble the expression of these national interests is to "establish justice, insure domestic tranquility, provide for the common defense, promote the general welfare and secure the blessings of liberty to ourselves and our posterity." The presumption is one of a federal system that pursues all the interests as appropriate. These interests as set out in the Preamble have been regularly reaffirmed when officials of the United States government have taken the oath of office: They swear to uphold and defend the Constitution.

When we consider the Preamble and then look to the literature, we find a considerable degree of congruence in specification of the national interests to be pursued in U.S. foreign policy. These interests can be summed up in four categories: (1) democracy; (2) peace; (3) security; and (4) broadly shared development. Each of them is important in its own terms, but they are not meant to stand alone. These interests are mutually reinforcing and it is essential that they be pursued simultaneously. We have considerable experience to evaluate the consequences of not doing so.

Perhaps it is not surprising that there has been such an overemphasis on the dimension of security for the past forty years. The hegemonic strategic vision guiding U.S. policy in Latin America since the turn of the century generated a legacy in which the United States sought to exercise a veto control over certain facets of Latin America's domestic and foreign policies.[31] This traditional hegemonic view, articulated by Theodore Roosevelt, was given great impetus with the onset of the Cold War. The overselling of the threat of communism with its concomitant demonization of the new enemy was conducive to the notion of a life and death struggle between good and evil (as, especially, Secretary of State John Foster Dulles saw it).[32] Security became the all-encompassing interest to be pursued.[33] Other interests were acknowledged but subordinated. The view of the international arena as nasty and brutish, in which the conflict of national interests was largely a zero sum game, was compounded by the nature of the perceived communist threat spearheaded by the Soviet Union. The Cold War was seen as permanent and high levels of threat and conflict as inevitable.

This image overlay U.S. relations with South America as it did other parts of the world. The United States saw "threats" to its "security interests" in the region. Democracy, peace, and broadly shared development were generally acknowledged and on occasion given great play. When the chips were seen to be down, however, as for example in Allende's Chile, they were unquestionably subordinated to security concerns. The rationalization that in the short term the security issues must be given priority and the responsibility for doing so fell to the United States; in the medium and longer terms, democracy, peace, and development would come into play. Henry Kissinger made this point when he indicated that it was up to United States leaders to "set the limits of diversity." "I don't see why," he said, "we have to let a country go Marxist just because its people are irresponsible."[34] The penchant for intervention was noted by Tom Farer, former chairman of the Organization of American States' Commission on Human Rights. Reflecting on his experience in that position, he said that Americans did not ask whether or not it was a good idea to intervene; rather, they asked how best to do it.[35]

The problem with the above rationale is the inability to escape and get beyond the short term that has so long characterized policy. To do so requires a realistic appraisal of actual conditions in the region. There are no imminent threats to U.S. security in the Southern Cone or Brazil. No nuclear Sword of Damocles hangs over the head of the United States or any other country in that region. (This is not to discount the importance of the nuclear developments, especially those in Brazil and Argentina that pose potential threats; but the presence of democratic civilian governments probably provides a buffer against the manufacture of nuclear weapons.) The presence of the Soviet Union is muted. Little sympathy exists in South America for the Soviet Union or for Cuba.[36] Chilean scholar Augusto Varas finds that "the Soviet model of interregional relations excluded any threat to the military security of the United States and was not designed to destabilize U.S. hemispheric security."[37] Robert Evanson's assessment of the political uses of trade by the Soviets in the area should also lay to rest fears concerning a significant spread in their influence by that route. Evanson's study "illustrates the fact that the USSR lacks the capacity and the will to spend a great deal of its resources for political purposes in Latin America." It predicts that trade will remain at modest levels; "any large future increase in Soviet–Latin American trade will be the product of changing perceptions of mutual economic advantage, not political."[38]

The principal threat to security in the region comes not from communism or the Soviet Union. As the U.S. Department of Defense itself noted, the major threat comes from the oppressive conditions of poverty and inequity in which so many South Americans live. Specifically, the challenges "are not primarily military in nature, but rather take the form of political instability and the potential exploitation of political instability generated by serious economic and social problems."[39]

Other essays in this volume help provide a fuller picture of the economic drama in South American countries. What is important for the purposes of the present discussion is to appreciate the degree to which economic problems pose a threat to South Americans and are of paramount concern to their political leadership and, therefore, to U.S. interests. During a conference on the transition to democracy in the Southern Cone at the University of South Carolina in March 1987, political practitioners from Argentina, Chile, and Uruguay were emphatic in arguing that resolving the economic crises of debt and development were crucial to the survivability of democracy in the region.[40] Osvaldo Hurtado has stated the issue in stark terms, saying that what is at stake is social peace and the stability of the democratic system itself.[41] Peruvian President Alan García has referred to what he calls the strangulating effects of the debt crisis, confronting the nations of the region with choosing between debt or democracy.[42] The nature of tensions in Brazil was assessed in a document published by the Brazilian National Council of Bishops; it spoke of national dissatisfaction so great that it "could well explode with catastrophic consequences for the country."[43]

The key to meeting economic threats lies in supporting regional neighbors by actively pursuing the multiple U.S. interests in peace, democracy, and broadly shared development. Doing so would help to meet the real security interest of the United States in the region by addressing the major causes of disruption and instability.[44] It would also mean reassessing and changing policies that exacerbate the crisis. This latter process could be greatly facilitated by listening to, and taking seriously, the evaluations of the democratic political leadership in the region. The willingness to consult has not been a strong characteristic of U.S. policy. In 1916, former U.S. Ambassador to Argentina Charles H. Sherrill lamented that the United States had almost never "taken into account the viewpoint of the South American, nor considered whether our actions pleased him or whether our suggestions were formulated in accordance with his views." Sherrill asked: "Why have we throughout all our history constantly disregarded the opinion of our Latin sister republics, and failed to take them into our councils? Why have we so persistently, so ignorantly, so blunderingly disregarded *their* point of view, even carelessly neglected to study it?"[45] Similar sentiments were echoed by Ambassador Sol Linowitz nearly seventy years later. He argued that the strains affecting U.S. relations with Latin America "reflect a lack of communication and empathy that is rooted in neglect, or, at times, in paternalism. We seem to ignore the fact that constructive relations with Latin America are as important for the United States as they are for Latin America."[46]

What is it that South Americans are telling the United States? They are saying that the best way to stabilize their societies and provide for their respective populations is to establish and consolidate democratic institutions, values, and practices. The new democratic leadership agree with Alfonsín's vision of democracy's freedom, tolerance, and pluralism as the best means to assure peaceful and civilized coexistence within the South American nations: "Only democracy can secure the consensus and flexibility required by the deep changes we must produce."[47] They also argue, however, that democracy cannot flourish in conditions of economic impoverishment. Broadly shared development is crucial to give the people a stake in the system, to remove the conditions of cultures of poverty that may lead people to embrace authoritarianism of whatever ideological stripe.[48] Such development cannot come solely from within; it requires the cooperative support of the international financial community and, especially, of the United States.

National Interest and the Current Agenda

The United States has a strong interest in seeing the South American region at peace with democratic governments and populations enjoying the fruits of development. The current moment is a delicate one. Military rule has been widely discredited, but the fragility of the democracies stands them on the edge of a precipice of renewed intervention. That contingency in Argentina, Brazil, and Uruguay depends on the ability of the fledgling democratic governments to deliver adequate economic and political benefits to the broader population. The unfolding of events in the three democracies will affect the transition processes in Chile and Paraguay.

Among the lessons issuing from the University of South Carolina conference on the transition to democracy in the Southern Cone (cited above) were several directly applicable to supporting the democratization process. They provide guidance for U.S. policy and fit well within the bounds of U.S. national interest. Three essential components of the process are to consolidate civilian control, respect human rights, and institute a system of accountability. In this regard, demilitarization must be clearly distinguished from democratization. Demilitarization is a necessary but by itself an insufficient condition. Likewise, the installation of structural mechanisms of formal democracy, such as the holding of elections, must be clearly distinguished from more broadly functioning democracy. U.S. condemnation of all human rights violations, in a consistent manner, provides much needed support to internal groups to facilitate the transition and consolidation processes.[49]

The United States can respond to the current issues on the regional agenda in ways that mutually maximize its own interests with those of its South American partners. To do so means U.S. support of South American efforts to strengthen their democracies and to restructure their economies. This will require working with them in a cooperative fashion. The United States simply cannot exercise the kinds of control it used to do, especially in the new South American environment. The changes in the world, in the United States, and in the region have bypassed that era. "Because both American power and American wisdom are limited," Arthur Schlesinger, Jr., says, "an effective foreign policy requires the cooperation of allies."[50]

While the United States cannot act at will in the region, it is still the most important external power. Its actions, both intended and unintended, have great consequence for the future there. The stability of the region in the fullest sense requires serious attention to the issues currently on the agenda, what have been referred to as the "four Ds": debt, democracy, development, and drugs. We have already addressed democracy and development. The United States has an obvious interest in seeing a rapid and reasonable resolution to the debt crisis. As long as the debt situation exists in its current state, broadly shared development will remain only a long-term aspiration and the financial squeeze on the national economies is likely to go unabated. All of them long ago passed the point of debt service payments in excess of twenty percent, the traditional rule of thumb for determining creditworthiness.[51] Their societies have gone through considerable trauma in the attempt to get the problem under control. While considerable progress can be achieved through internal changes in government policy, it must be recognized that this is not just a national problem, but a transnational one that ultimately can be resolved only through multilateral cooperation. The United States could provide the leadership for creating a viable alternative that escapes the trap of the "bandaid" approach and focus on growth for development, not merely to pay the debt. Part of that alternative would be to remove the protectionist restrictions on access to markets in the developed countries, particularly those in the United States.[52]

The suggestion has been made that the single most important factor in generating economic recovery in Latin America lies not in the capitals south of the Rio Bravo, but in Washington, D.C. In November 1985, at a University of South Carolina conference on the debt issue, William Brock, then-Secretary of Labor, put forth this view:

> [The] most important single step the United States can take to solve its problems and the problems of its neighbors is to get rid of its own deficit. . . . It's inexcusable that we seem to lack the political will or the integrity, if you will, to live within our collective means. . . . So while we're very fulsome in our praise of ourselves and very quick with our criticism of others, I think we had better look into our own house and clean up our own nest because we are the largest single problem for everyone and only we can solve that.[53]

The narcotics traffic has developed into a major issue in the Southern Cone area and Brazil. The expansion of coca production southward from Colombia, Peru, and Bolivia into Argentina, Brazil, and Paraguay will embroil them in the most rapidly growing issue in the hemisphere. Handling it will be particularly difficult for the United States as it is seen as impinging directly on its national security interest. The debate in the United States over how to handle the drug problem and what to do about the *narcotraficantes* raises many of the same warning flags as earlier fears of communism. This could easily lead to unilateral responses, relying heavily on coercion and the use of military force. Some members of congress are seeking to place heavy responsibility in the "war" against drugs in the hands of U.S. armed forces.

The drug problem also highlights the importance for the United States of broadly shared development. One of the reasons the drug chiefs have been able to get such broad cooperation in their own countries is because they are providing employment and high wages in economies that present little or no alternative. Much remains to be learned about the dimensions of the problems surrounding this issue.[54] It needs to be approached by maximizing cooperation among the governments concerned.[55]

There are other issues more long-term in appearance and consequence. They have received scant attention, except from special interest groups. These include a wide range of ecological issues that will grow in importance and should be addressed before they become crises. This is especially the case for Brazil.

Finally, it would be naive to believe that because there is a mutuality of interests between the United States and its South American partners that conflict will disappear. Even under the best of circumstances there will be tensions in the relationships. Some will come, no doubt, through continued misunderstanding or even from bad policy decisions on the part of one or another government. Structural aspects of conflict, especially in economic relations, involve clashing short-term national interests. This is true of virtually all international relationships (including those of the United States with its European allies). In South America the United States must learn to respect these differences and seek to resolve them in ways that are as mutually beneficial as possible. The key is to approach disagreements with a willingness to negotiate seriously and not to act within the context of a hegemonic vision. In the longer run, differences that are settled through the arrival of mutually acceptable accords will be more lasting and serve to strengthen rather than weaken ties. It will also build respect in the hemisphere for the United States and permit it to reassume the kind of moral authority it had during the Good Neighbor and Alliance for Progress eras.

Conclusion

In 1927 Walter Lippmann warned of the dangers of not looking "the whole thing squarely in the face and to stop trying to deceive ourselves. We shall persuade nobody abroad by our words. We shall merely acquire a reputation for hypocrisy while we stumble unconsciously into the cares and the perils of empire."[56] Hegemony no longer works, whatever value one may believe it had in the past. Basing policy on an outmoded vision is dangerous to the United States and to the South American states. President John Kennedy understood the danger of assuming that kind of mantle. He urged the nation to reject simplistic views of international life such as the one calling for a mission to remake the world in the American image.[57]

South America presents an opportunity for U.S. foreign policy. That policy has been less encumbered by the ravages of the East-West conflict that have so distorted the playing out of political forces in Central America. The result of this lesser intensity in the imposition of the Cold War on the southern continent has been that the United States can design policies for the region without having to filter the reality through that set of lenses. On the other hand, the problem has been to place the Southern Cone and Brazil on the agenda of high priority issues and to do so before the crises grow worse. Unlike Central America, the combination of the Cold War perspective and the hegemonic strategic vision that have elevated that region to a central spot on the foreign policy agenda are missing in the South American region.

By its actions and its rhetoric, which all too often have not been synchronized, the United States will meet or fail the challenges of the next decade. "The United States failed," wrote Herbert Matthews in 1959, "the tidal wave of democratic idealism that swept over Latin America in the 1950s."[58] As the United States enters the 1990s it has another chance. By pursuing its true national interests in the region—in security based on democracy, peace, and broadly shared development—and by working with the South American nations in a truly multilateral way, the United States can avoid the failures of the past, help its Latin neighbors reach for their own national goals, and regain its moral authority in the hemisphere by virtue of its example.

Notes

1. Saul Landau, *The Dangerous Doctrine: National Security and U.S. Foreign Policy* (Boulder: Westview Press, 1988), p. 14.

2. Morris J. Blachman, William LeoGrande, and Kenneth E. Sharpe (eds.), *Confronting Revolution: Security Through Diplomacy* (New York: Pantheon, 1986), p. 330. Emphasis added.

3. Charles W. Kegley, Jr., and Eugene R. Wittkopf, *American Foreign Policy: Pattern and Process,* 3d ed. (New York: St. Martin's Press, 1987), p. 38.

4. Thomas Karnes (ed.), *Readings in the Latin American Policy of the United States* (Tucson: University of Arizona Press, 1972).

5. Quoted in Robert Leiken and Barry Rubin (eds.), *The Central American Crisis Reader: The Essential Guide to the Most Controversial Foreign Policy Issue Today* (New York: Summit Books, 1987), pp. 81–83.

6. Cited in Bruce Russett and Harvey Starr, *World Politics: The Menu for Choice* (San Francisco: W.H. Freeman and Company, 1981), p. 429.

7. Samuel Flagg Bemis, *The Latin American Policy of the United States* (New York: Harcourt Brace, 1943), pp. 385–386.

8. Arthur M. Schlesinger, Jr., *The Cycles of American History* (Boston: Houghton Mifflin Company, 1986), pp. 16, 54–55.

9. Kegley and Wittkopf, p. 43.

10. Schlesinger, p. 55.

11. See Edwin Lieuwin, *U.S. Policy in Latin America: A Short History* (New York: Frederick A. Praeger), 1965, p. 133; and William R. Kintner, "A Program for America: Freedom and Foreign Policy," *Orbis,* Vol. 21, No. 1 (Spring 1977), pp. 139–140.

12. Guillermo O'Donnell, "The United States, Latin America, and Democracy: Variations on a Very Old Theme," in Kevin J. Middlebrook and Carlos Rico (eds.), *The United States and Latin America in the 1980s: Contending Perspectives on a Decade of Crisis* (Pittsburgh: University of Pittsburgh Press, 1986), p. 375.

13. Raúl Alfonsín, address to a conference on "Reinforcing Democracy in the Americas," Atlanta, Georgia, November 17, 1986.

14. Alfred Stepan, "The United States and Latin America: Vital Interests and the Instruments of Power," *Foreign Affairs*, Vol. 58, No. 3, (1979), p. 692. Also see Hans J. Morgenthau, *Politics Among Nations: The Struggle for Power and Peace*, 3d ed. (New York: Alfred A. Knopf, 1962), p. 156. In the midst of an argument of "typical error[s] imparing the evaluation of national power," he states: "There is a seemingly ineradicable inclination in or attitude toward the Latin-American countries to assume that the unchallengeable superiority of the colossus of the North, which has existed since the nations of the Western Hemisphere won their independence, was almost a law of nature which population trends, industrialization, political and military developments might modify but could not basically alter."

15. Charles A. Beard, *The Idea of National Interest* (New York: Macmillan, 1934). In addition to Morgenthau's *Politics Among Nations*, see his *In Defense of the National Interest* (New York: Alfred A. Knopf, 1951). Also see Joseph Frankel, *Contemporary International Theory and the Behaviour of States* (New York: Oxford University Press, 1973); Donald E. Nuechterlein, "Foreign Policy in the 1980s: In Search of the National Interest," *Foreign Service Journal* (May 1981), pp. 17–41, and *America Overcommitted: United States National Interests in the 1980s* (Lexington: University of Kentucky Press, 1985); Thad D. Smith, "A Methodological Note on Reconceptualizing National Security: Interests, Priorities, Threats, and Opportunities," paper presented to the International Studies Association Annual Meeting in Washington, D.C., April 1987; P. A. Reynolds, *An Introduction to International Relations*, 2d ed. (London: Longman Group Limited, 1980); Fred A. Sondermann, "The Concept of the National Interest," *Orbis*, Vol. 21, No. 1 (Spring 1977), pp. 121–138; Alan Tonelson, "The Real National Interest," *Foreign Policy*, Vol. 61 (Winter 1985-86), pp. 49–72; and Arnold Wolfers, *Discord and Collaboration: Essays on International Politics* (Baltimore: Johns Hopkins University Press, 1967).

16. Morgenthau, *Politics*, p. 562–563.

17. Wolfers, 148–149.

18. Gabriel Marcella, "Defense of the Western Hemisphere: Strategy for the 1990s," *Journal of Interamerican Studies and World Affairs*, Vol. 27 (Fall 1985), pp. 1–25.

19. Kegley and Wittkopf, pp. 45–68; and Blachman, LeoGrande, and Sharpe, Chapter 13.

20. Lars Schoultz, *National Security and United States Policy Toward Latin America* (Princeton: Princeton University Press, 1987), p. 325, 328, and 329.

21. Sergio Bitar, "Economics and Security: Contradictions in U.S.-Latin American Relations," in Middlebrook and Rico, p. 594.

22. "The Americas at a Crossroads," report of the Inter-American Dialogue, Woodrow Wilson International Center for Scholars, April, 1983, pp. 40–41.

23. Marcella, p. 18.

24. Alfonsín, p. 13.

25. Joseph S. Tulchin, "The Malvinas War of 1982: An Inevitable Conflict that Never Should Have Occurred," *Latin American Research Review*, Vol. 22, No. 3 (1987), p. 137.

26. See, for example, *The Rockefeller Report on the Americas, The Official Report of a United States Presidential Mission for the Western Hemisphere*, by Nelson A. Rockefeller; The New York Times Edition (Chicago: Quadrangle Books, 1969); "The Americas At a Crossroads," *The Miami Report*, published by the Graduate School of International Studies of the University of Miami, 1983; and *The Americas in 1988: A Time for Choices, A Report of the Inter-American Dialogue* (Lanham, Maryland: University Press of America), 1988.

27. *Rockefeller Report*, pp. 40–41.

28. Sondermann, p. 132.

29. Conceptually speaking, the first approach is a notable exception to these comments. There is also an important division in this literature between those who often equate the national interest with the interest of the "state," and those whose interpretation of "national" inheres in some conception of the citizenry—it may be at the individual level as Reynolds argues or with some larger grouping as Wolfers maintains. Does the national interest necessarily mean, as Osgood said, "a state of affairs valued solely for its benefit to the nation. The motive of national egoism, which leads men to seek this end, is marked by the disposition to concern oneself with the welfare of one's own nation: it is self-love transferred to the national group." Quoted in Fred A. Sondermann, "The Concept of the National Interest," *Orbis*, Vol. 21, No. 1 (Spring 1977), p. 124. Or must it take account of the interests of others as Sondermann and, at certain times, Morgenthau argue?

30. See, for example, "Texas Against White," 7 *Wall* 700 (1869); and "Martin Against Hunter's Lessee," 1 *Wheatten* 304 (1816). I want to thank Prof. Glenn Abernathy for bringing this to my attention.

31. Blachman, LeoGrande, and Sharpe, Chapter 13.

32. Jerry Sanders, *Peddlers of Crisis: The Committee on the Present Danger and the Politics of Containment* (Boston: South End Press), 1983.

33. Professor James Crown of New York University observed that it was precisely when the United States became most insecure that it began to adopt the terminology of security most strongly. He suggested that it could be useful to think of the famed 1947 act as the "national insecurity act" and to think of policy as being justified in terms of "national insecurity."

34. Michael H. Hunt, *Ideology and U.S. Foreign Policy* (New Haven: Yale University Press, 1987), p. 184.

35. These comments were made at the conference "Reinforcing Democracy in the Americas."

36. Howard J. Wiarda, "United States Policy in South America: A Maturing Relationship?" *Current History*, Vol. 84, No. 499 (February 1985), p. 36.

37. Augusto Varas, "Soviet–Latin American Relations Under the U.S. Regional Hegemony," in Augusto Varas (ed.), *Soviet Latin American Relations in the 1980s* (Boulder: Westview Press, 1987), p. 35. See also the corpus of works on this subject by Cole Blasier.

38. Robert K. Evanson, "Soviet Political Uses of Trade with Latin America," *Journal of Interamerican Studies and World Affairs*, Vol. 27, No. 2 (Summer 1985), pp. 118–119.

39. Varas, p. 35.

40. "The Challenge of Transition: Democracy in the Southern Cone," held at the University of South Carolina, March 22–27, 1987.

41. Riordan Roett, "Democracy and Debt in South America: A Continent's Dilemma," *Foreign Affairs*, Vol. 62, No. 3 (1983), p. 720.

42. Lester R. Brown, "Special Supplement: New Dimensions of National Security," in *American Defense Annual 1986–87*, p. 219.

43. *The Latin American Weekly Report*, February 18, 1988. The March 31, 1988 issue quotes David Rockefeller as saying: "In all my visits to Brazil, I have never before come across such desperate poverty."

44. Marcella, p. 19 says: "A broader view of security recognizes the mutual interests of all nations of the region, such as resolving the debt crisis . . . and strengthening fragile democratization. . . . Short-term *ad hoc* responses to crisis are no longer good enough for dealing with the complex challenges being made to the region's security.

45. Charles H. Sherill, *Modernizing the Monroe Doctrine* (Boston: Houghton Mifflin Company, 1916), pp. 53–54 and 58–59.

46. "The Americas at a Crossroads," p. 66.

47. Alfonsín, p. 6.

48. See Joseph Tulchin, Riordan Roett, and Alfred Stepan, "The United States and Latin America: Vital Interests and the Instruments of Power," *Foreign Affairs*, Vol. 58, No. 3 (1979), pp. 659–692.

49. Michael Francis quotes Alfonsín in a related matter as referring to the importance of the kind of stance the United States takes on human rights. Alfonsín said that Carter was to be acclaimed for "letting human rights activists know they were not alone; for putting the military on warning about human rights violations; and, most importantly, for saving hundreds, if not thousands of lives." In "Reagan and Latin American Democracy: The Cases of Argentina and Chile," presented to the International Studies Association Convention in St. Louis, March, 1988, p. 23.

50. Schlesinger, p. 59.

51. Brown, p. 212. The participants in the transition conference at the University of South Carolina in March 1987 expressed considerable concern about the relationship between economic problems and democracy. One of the lessons of the conference was that the severity of economic problems that confront the countries threatens to undermine the consolidation of democracy and trigger another military intervention.

52. President Alfonsín commented on this problem at the conference on "Reinforcing Democracy in the Americas." He said: "It is a bitter paradox that

the advanced democracies—which encourage us to consolidate our reborn democracies—also chastise us through trade discrimination, through the lowering of the price of our exports by subsidizing products that compete with ours, harshly demanding payment of a debt that is bleeding us, undermining—in summary—the meager possibilities we have to alleviate a crisis that threatens the survival of the same democracy they encourage us to sustain." (p. 13).

53. Remarks at the conference, "Progress Toward Prosperity."

54. See, for example, Bruce Michael Bagley, "The New Hundred Years War? U.S. National Security and the War on Drugs in Latin America," prepared for the conference on "The Latin American Narcotics Trade and United States National Security," Mississippi State University, June 1988. Also see Jonathan F. Galloway and Maria Vélez de Berliner, "The Worldwide Illegal Cocaine Industry," presented to the International Studies Association Convention in Washington, D.C., April, 1987.

55. There has been an important and discernible growing trend of cooperation on development and other projects among these nations. See Gratzia V. Smeal, "Cooperation for Development in Latin American Countries: A New Perspective," M.A. Thesis, University of South Carolina, 1986. One very important area of movement in this direction has been the exchange of visits between Alfonsín and Sarney to see each other's nuclear laboratories.

56. Lippmann, p. 82.

57. Charles W. Kegley, Jr., "The Lost Legacy: Idealism in American Foreign Policy" for the symposium on "Evangelicals in American Foreign Policy," Calvin College, September 1988, p. 7.

58. Herbert Mathews (ed.), *The United States and Latin America* (2d ed. Englewood Cliffs: Prentice-Hall, 1963), p. 173.

6

Extrahemispheric Interests and Actions

Georges A. Fauriol

In a development likely to reshape global power relationships, South America has become a permanent fixture of the international diplomatic and economic scene. This new situation differs from the experience of the nineteenth century or the interwar period in the present century when South America was principally the object of attention by European powers and the United States. In the late 1980s, however, the region has become an active participant in global affairs. The emergence of South American influence is the product of the convergence of new regional dynamics, radically altered U.S. relations with the rest of the Western Hemisphere, and the ensuing growth of extrahemispheric interests.

A critical source of the region's changing environment is found among South America's vigorous major actors, notably Brazil and Argentina. Brazil is now ranked as one of the world's top ten nations across an array of economic and political-geographic attributes, while Argentina has claimed international attention in a number of economic, political, and defense areas. Other regional states are also significant. Chile and Peru, following radically different paths, have structured a complex web of international relationships that range from Chile's ties with the People's Republic of China to Peru's radical positions on national debt-restructuring questions. Even the Southern Cone's smaller players have in recent years established a sharper multinational focus, as exemplified by Uruguay's involvement in the "Group of 8" support effort to the Central American peace process.[1]

A second source of Latin America's global growth has been the result of the region's difficult functional agenda, such as debt and unstable polity questions. These issues have galvanized international interest to the point of blurring relevant distinctions between Caribbean Basin crises and various South American challenges. Regardless of the negative aspects of this agenda, the industrialized world's contortions regarding South American financial issues and domestic political development have produced a deeper engagement by the regional states in global affairs. South American states (with the qualified exception of Brazil) are not yet global players, nor are they fully integrated in the international trading and political system; but the level of their interaction in the economic arena, and the intensity of extra-hemispheric actors in South America's political development, suggest a rapidly changing environment.

Finally, a source of expanding South American international links is to be found in the relative decline of U.S. preponderance in regional affairs. The United States is being displaced not because of its inherent weakness but by virtue of the extraordinary recovery and growth of Western Europe, Japan, and the Western Pacific rim nations, and, as suggested above, by developments in South America itself. Contrary to what is often postulated, the relative decline of Washington's influence is not the result of a defeat of American "imperial" policy; it is the product of a deliberate and sustained U.S. cooperative initiative undertaken globally since the end of World War II.[2]

These developments in the South American subsystem suggest a challenging but fundamentally positive basis for U.S.–South American relations. The new regional dynamics are not the result of profoundly bitter competition; they are the outcome of cooperative U.S. policies (which, admittedly, have often been less than attentive). Consequently, Western Hemispheric relations appear to be reaching a more mature plateau. The elements of U.S. relations with the region's most important actors, Brazil and Argentina, provide the key variables in the evolving environment. These South American actors have the potential for considerable external outreach; conversely, their very potential implies that they are likely to attract extra-hemispheric interest well beyond the present level, and to continue to affect the character and quality of relations with the United States (which remains the hemisphere's premier power).

The factors identified above represent a potent problem for the United States if they are allowed to evolve in an unstructured manner. The presence of extrahemispheric actors in itself is not necessarily a harmful development for Washington, unless it involves powers strategically hostile to the Western Alliance. The role of Cuba and the Soviet Bloc in regional affairs has in the last three decades become an area of concern, in a manner akin to Germany's penetration of South American economies and politics in the 1930s. On the other hand, the involvement of European states and transnational actors, particularly if pursued in parallel with similar U.S. goals in the region, has potentially positive consequences for all concerned.

This aspect of hemispheric relations is as much a challenge for South American nations as it is for the United States. With significant nuances, such as the degree of diplomatic cooperation with Castro's Cuba, the strategic gap between Washington and South American capitals has widened only marginally. The widening has so far occurred largely as a result of the newly revived South American sense of autonomy rather than any significant affinity for the Soviet bloc or rejection of cooperation with the United States. In this regard, as a matter of comparative judgement, erosion of the U.S. position in Central America in the 1980s may be greater than its loss of prestige or influence in South America. In the long run, the danger for the United States will be that a decline of its position in one portion of Latin America will have repercussions in other parts of the region.

Finally, the growth of South American global politics is not only the product of a shift away from traditionally passive roles but the result of increasing interaction between external and internal dynamics. A number of examples illustrate this point.

The transformation of most South American states from authoritarian politics and military regimes to more open societies and representative governments has altered the character of their interaction with the rest of the world. If nothing else, an easing of South American domestic political tensions has mitigated serious points of contention for many countries in the industrialized world (human rights being especially important among them).[3] These domestic political developments have also allowed non-governmental international relationships to evolve further and more openly than had been possible under the more constrained environment of the past. These external sub-national relationships now incorporate a broad web of interaction that includes transnational political party connections, labor union association, church-related activities, human rights and electoral reform activities, and cultural and scholarly exchange, in addition to the long-standing forms of economic and business transactions. Relationships with transnational actors have enriched the fabric being woven by South America's dynamic societies with the rest of the world.

Conceptualizing South America's
External Relations

South American international relations impinge on the way individual national foreign policy establishments collectively manage a number of occasionally overlapping and conflicting external constituencies. Writing only a decade ago, an analyst could suggest an essentially two-part universe of relevance to the region: the United States and a nebulous "Third World."[4] Today's environment is much more complex and differentiated.

Although the United States remains a leading actor in hemispheric activities, it no longer dominates the South American agenda and is unlikely to do so anytime soon. In an evolving structure likely to be sustained into the foreseeable future, the United States shares the limelight with at least three sets of other actors of salience to South American politics: the rest of the industrialized world, the Soviet bloc, and the Third World.

The Industrial World

Interacting in different ways, the European Community (EC)—its members also operating on a bilateral basis—Japan, and to a lesser degree Asia's Newly Industrialized Countries (NICs), form an important external grouping in the South American subsystem. Depending on the economic or strategic considerations at stake, these extrahemispheric actors now operate autonomously from the United States in the trade or investment arena or as uncomfortable adjuncts of a U.S.-led Western alliance. In this regard, Western Europe's interaction with South America is much broader in scope and degree of independence than the relationship it entertains with the Caribbean Basin; in the latter instance, the geostrategic interests of the United States intrude much more strongly into the policies of allied extrahemispheric states.[5]

Most observers underline the singularly economic character of much of Europe's and Japan's interests in South America. Conversely, the regional states' outreach beyond the United States toward Western Europe and Japan is likewise economically motivated, with the resulting South American psychological sense of political autonomy generating increased diplomatic byproducts in the extrahemispheric relations.

The Soviet Bloc

While not a new element in South America, the role of the Soviet Union and its East European partners is increasingly important and changing in nature. Within the Soviet bloc grouping, South American ties with the Soviet Union form the most important factor. The Soviet Union's long-standing ignorance of Latin America in general has not implied disinterest in South American affairs. Since the days of Lenin, the basic notion of Soviet interest in Latin America, to include its perception of South America, has been based on the concept of the region as the "soft-underbelly" of the United States.[6] Prior to World

War II, Soviet ties involved mostly political party affiliations organized in the Moscow-controlled Comintern organization. After the war until the Cuban Revolution, the Soviet Union seemed to accept its isolated position with regard to the Western Hemisphere. In recent years, however, the Soviet Union has significantly broadened its hemispheric ties.

Unlike the Caribbean Basin and Mexico, where East Bloc activities operate under closer U.S. scrutiny, the South American environment is not only geographically but politically more distant for the United States. Nevertheless, aside from salient diversions from the norm (such as Allende's Chile), most South American economic and even political concerns have remained tied to the United States and the Western world's industrial community. What has changed is a growing sense within South American governments that despite the East Bloc's marginal relevance to their day-to-day concerns, ties with Moscow are neither diplomatically irrelevant nor politically menacing.[7]

The Third World

The notion of the Third World in the South American context has been variously construed to imply non-aligned politics in East-West conflict, development diplomacy in the North-South debate, and developing country relations in a South-South context. In the case of Brazil, bilateral diplomacy with Africa and the Middle East has been a special consideration. The depth of this environment is relatively shallow, prone to rhetoric and "points-on-the-compass" symbols rather than precise structures or concrete actions.

Nevertheless, most South American foreign ministries have engaged in some sort of "Third World" diplomacy consisting of a hybrid of nationalism, anti-Yankee feelings, developing world "solidarity," and bona fide sympathy for demonstrations of independence on the part of the Third World. From the early 1940s through the early 1960s, Peron's Argentina and Goulart's Brazil produced independent and nationalistic diplomacy with a non-aligned orientation. More recently, the Third World debt crisis has brought to the surface a degree of confrontational economic diplomacy in which South American nations (most prominently Brazil, Argentina, and Peru) have been major players. This crisis has inspired a degree of rhetorical cooperation between South America, Africa, and Asia in areas of common economic and political concern.

Yet other developments in recent years have limited the scope even of this arena of relations. Few of the grand designs of the 1970s, such as the New International Economic Order (NIEO) and the North-South dialogue, have generated significant results upon which to expand interregional activity. Furthermore, the logic for Third World policies has declined in importance as South America's more advanced nations have become more integrated in the international economic system—although that logic has clearly not disappeared in South America's popular consciousness. For Brazil, Argentina, and Chile, for example, any commonality of views with the Third World is in fact shared with other NICs, such as South Korea and India, and less with the bulk of the developing-country community.

In fact, the distance of the major South American nations from the bulk of the "Third World" is growing to the degree that the latter remains a ward of development assistance largess while the former seeks some degree of competitive integration—preferably on its own terms—into the First World's economic system. Brazil particularly in recent years has devoted a significant portion of its foreign relations to such interests. Brazil has focused attention on Africa's former Portuguese colonies as well as commercial prospects in other parts of the continent; it has also directed attention to the Middle East's arms procurement needs partly out of economic necessity to boost exports and partly as a result of technological developments well-suited to Third World military needs.[8]

To examine in detail the myriad and overlapping bilateral and transnational relationships the South American region has developed with the extrahemispheric community would be a gargantuan task—and thus well beyond the limits of this chapter. At this juncture, instead, let us examine the general parameters of some of the more critical relationships—with Western Europe and transnational players, Japan, and the Soviet Union.

Western Europe

Despite a lengthy history of bilateral exchanges between Western Europe and South America, relations between these two actors in the early post–World War II period reached a low ebb. The principal reason for this phenomenon related to European perceptions of national interests; namely, during a period of reconstruction and recovery, South America barely factored into the European national interest equations. Instead, European attention focused closely on its recovery from the war and the development of relations within the emerging superpower relationship and the ensuing NATO framework. For some, especially the British and French, the aftermath of World War II also brought to the fore decolonization challenges—drawing attention to Africa and Asia, not South America. Ultimately, attention was drawn to efforts at integration culminating in the formation of the EC.

By the 1960s Europe's political, military, and economic position had been successfully reestablished. A renewed interest in South America was generated, exemplified through expanded diplomatic contact (for example, French President de Gaulle's highly publicized tour of the region in 1964) and economic assistance programs. However, in so doing, Europe was only attempting to regain the considerable ground lost to U.S. economic and diplomatic influence since the 1930s. Considering the latter's preponderance, the major feature of European involvement was not that it remained secondary, but rather that it began to include a broader range of governmental and non-governmental contacts.

European involvement was tempered by several considerations that continue to shape current interests. Because of geostrategic distance between the two regions, South America has not been important to European security interests. As a corollary, Europeans realize that South America, while no longer under U.S. hegemony, is, nevertheless, a higher strategic priority to the United States than to Europe. In a different arena, European economic and development assistance programs to the Third World have been prioritized on the basis of economic and political factors. South American nations are by no means among the poorest in the "developing world"; aid flows have focused on Africa, the Middle East, and Asia. West Germany was an exception, and instead upgraded its economic presence in South America as soon as it was able to do so.

After the 1960s, Europe in general increased its position in response to very practical economic considerations. Latin American economies, to a degree casting aside ill-suited economic policies of import substitution, became an inviting site for investment and trade. The region enjoyed many years of high growth levels.[9] With the recycling of petrodollars, this continued to the late 1970s. Commercial investments, concessionary loans, and trade credits produced a boom environment in which Europe became a major player—a boom that went bust in the 1980s; and also began to face competition from Asia. Thus, although the EC is South America's largest trading partner after the United States, by 1987 South American countries accounted for only 8 percent of EC exports and 11 percent of its imports.[10]

What are the factors that have shaped this mixed European–South American record? Despite South America's impressive growth rates in the 1970s, the onset of the debt crisis underscored the region's fragile economic environment. Business enthusiasm for South America quickly soured. These tensions have to a degree fueled problems involving general agreements on trade and investment policies, bilaterally or within the framework of GATT. More narrowly, Europe's assistance programs (and perhaps particularly those of the EC) have been motivated more by self-interest than altruism. Translated into practice, European aid has been primarily channelled toward its own export potential, based more on a concern to improve the European balance of trade than to promote South American economic development. Thus, credits and loans may have been granted more often to finance South American purchases of European products, rather than specifically to serve South American developmental purposes. When combined with the debt crisis of the 1980s, and European concerns posed by excessive exposure to South American financial liquidity problems, European–South American economic relations have faced their share of challenges.

These developments in the economic sphere have overlapped with political and occasionally even diplomatic and military agenda.[11] The metamorphosis of most South American nations from military regimes and authoritarian politics to civilian, democratic governments and more representative societies in the 1980s has altered the character of the region's foreign policy interactions. As a byproduct of these considerations as well as of developments elsewhere (especially in Central America), European attention has begun to acquire a formalized quality. That is, the diplomatic consolidation of the EC has generated a semblance of a "Latin American" policy with a focus on democracy, human rights, debt, and development. This political focus has capitalized on the historical cultural bonds in addition to a vague notion of desired autonomy from U.S. policies and actions. As an alternative, South America's policy communities look to Europe for moral and political support.

Complications have arisen, however, particularly in the security or defense arena. An example of this was the Falklands/Malvinas conflict in 1982. When the United Kingdom pressed for a broad range of economic sanctions against Argentina, the EC as a whole agreed (sometimes reluctantly) to give its support. Although Ireland and Italy were unwilling to make political and economic sacrifices and hence withdrew from the sanctions policy, France and West Germany—who seemed to have more to lose than many others—did not oppose the action. Overall, the European reaction was driven by commitment to Britain, not by a fundamental reassessment of its ties with Argentina or South America as a whole. Except for the unresolved Argentine-U.K. dispute, the broader context of economic and political relations has glossed over any damage that might have been produced by the 1982 crisis.

Focus on the Falklands/Malvinas war also brings to light another aspect of South American ties with Europe—namely, commercial arms sales. This sector of the relationship, although less active in the 1980s than before, has been conditioned by South American armed forces' appetites for modern equipment and European desires to expand a lucrative trade. U.S. policies beginning in the mid-1960s and further emphasized in the latter half of the 1970s, contributed to the development of this phenomenon. In particular, the Carter Administration's emphasis on human rights and nuclear non-proliferation led to changes in South American financing and sourcing of weapons.

South American nations turned to Western Europe. The United Kingdom and France pursued policies of virtually unrestricted arms sales in the rather profitable South American market. Ironically, France supplied the Argentine Navy with the Exocet missiles that sank British warships during the Falklands/Malvinas war. As the major South American powers have modernized their armed forces establishments, however, a reverse flow has also developed. Brazil, Chile, and Argentina have themselves entered the arms export market, manufacturing primarily for Third World markets. Brazil's Tucano military trainer aircraft contract with the British Royal Air Force is a significant symptom of the degree to which this aspect of cross-Atlantic relations has changed.

This changing environment has spawned the involvement of a series of transnational actors. Much of this new involvement has occurred at the non-governmental level, and has been associated with political party and electoral reform activity, labor unions, human rights groups, and church-related activities. With similar political traditions and structures, Europe's parties have found fertile ground in South America's troubled political developments. Several democratic European international political party organizations—the Socialist International (SI), competing with the Christian Democrats and the Conservative Union—have inserted themselves in a wide variety of local issues. Although not alone, the West Germans have developed the most extensive political network in this regard.

Germany's four major political parties—the Social Democratic Party (SDP), the Christian Democratic Union (CDU), the Christian Social Union (CSU), and the Free Democratic Party (FDP)—each maintain federally and privately funded foundations—respectively, the Friedrich Ebert, Konrad Adenauer, Hans Seidel, and Friedrich Naumann foundations. All maintain overseas contacts and offices, geared toward funding, assisting, and inviting political groups in South America into a network of political activity shaped by the particular foundation's philosophy or political orientation. The fairly broad ideological spectrum this network represents has enabled a continuous German presence almost regardless of the particular regime in power in South American capitals. The success of this approach has been viewed by some as the inspiration behind the United States' own effort at projecting democratic political development through the National Endowment for Democracy.

An important development immediately facing biregional relations is the impact of EC economic integration in 1992. At this juncture, some concerns have already been expressed by South American leaders that this intense market integration could inhibit the very concept of trade and open markets that the region's economic survival is so dependent upon. In contrast, voices within the EC discount these concerns.[12] South American interests are likely to see further bilateral lobbying as well as involvement in broader forums (such as GATT) designed to insure an open multilateral trade environment. These are also issues of significant interest to the United States.

Japan

The environment shaped by geography, culture, and world politics that has long isolated Asia from Latin America is changing dramatically. The dynamic presence of Japan alone is expanding to the point where it has a major stake in Latin American regional trade patterns ($15 billion), is the second largest aid donor to a half dozen Latin American nations, and is creditor for 20 percent of the region's $420 billion external debt. In fact, direct Japanese investments in Latin America and the Caribbean ($20 billion in 1987) rank closely behind Japanese investment in Asia ($21 billion) and far ahead of Japan's position in Europe ($14 billion). Likewise, Japanese manufacturers have in recent years taken a careful look at new regional trade provisions, particularly the Mexican *maquiladora* border plant concept and the Caribbean Basin Initiative. Asia's NICs, and even China, are following suit.

This Asian–Latin American relationship has not transferred into the political or strategic arena, yet one can easily conceive of growing interests in these areas—Japan, for example is not only a major user of the Panama Canal, but also a formal player (by treaty) in any future plans regarding the management or modification of isthmus transportation issues. Latin Americans, from the Southern Cone to Mexico, cannot but appreciate the salience of these expanding relationships.

Japan's position in Latin America, and particularly in South America, is principally a post–World War II phenomenon.[13] Furthermore, the South American presence is built in large part on an extraordinary relationship with Brazil. The latter has attracted immigration from Japan since the turn of the century. By the 1980s, Japanese migrants and their descendants numbered about one million people, the largest expatriate implant of ethnic Japanese anywhere in the world. This well-established community provided an initial point of departure for Japanese economic activity in Brazil after 1945. In 1949, even while Japan was still under U.S. military occupation, a Japanese trade mission visited Brazil. This was followed in the 1950s by a resumption of Japanese migration, the opening of trading offices in Brazil, and after 1955 what is described as the "first rush" of Japanese investment.

During the 1960s and 1970s, Japan became a leading participant in Brazil's boom years. For the first time, the semblance of a formal framework in the relationship began to take shape. Regular joint economic meetings were held, and increasingly large Japanese commitments were made to Brazil's economic development. This was backed up by senior level diplomacy. In 1974, Prime Minister Kakuei Tonaka visited Brazil; in 1975, his successor, Takeo Fukada, followed suit. The following year, Brazilian President Ernesto Geisel visited Japan. This active form of Japanese-Brazilian ties continued into the mid-1980s— for example, in 1982, Prime Minister Zenko Suzuki visited Brazil, and President Joao Figueiredo visited Japan in 1984. Nevertheless, the relationship remains primarily a product of economic interests and private sector contacts. Although both countries recognize each other's strategic salience, neither military nor cultural considerations motivate much activity.

Japanese economic expansion in Brazil rests on a striking economic complementarity involving trade, investment, and technical and financial assistance.[14] On one hand, Japan needs raw materials and food, while the Brazilian economy requires their export; on the other hand, Japan's modern industrialized economy must export large quantities of its manufactured goods, for which Brazil provides promising markets. Japan has aimed its investment, as well as financial and technical assistance, at the development of Brazil's agricultural and raw materials export sectors. Brazil then uses the foreign exchange generated by these exports to buy Japanese goods. Japanese trading companies have played a role in the distribution of services to Brazilian exporters in both conventional and countertrade transactions, thereby further expanding the volume of Brazilian exports. Japanese assistance in the expansion of Brazil's export sector has probably served Japan's interests elsewhere in the world. One might argue that by increasing the world supply of key primary-sector products, Japan's import costs from the United States and elsewhere has remained competitive.

For Brazil, Japan also provides an important basis for an economic diplomacy of diversification. Nationalist sentiments in Brazil might define this as an attempt to lessen the traditional dependence on U.S. commercial and financial power. In some areas this has led to discriminating differentiations on the part of Brazil vis-à-vis trading practices. The highly visible bilateral tension with the United States over protectionism, with both sides making charges and counter-charges, is much more subdued in the ties with Japan, despite the latter's high barriers to Brazilian imports. Likewise, while Japan's development aid effort has often been viewed as less than altruistic, in recent years Tokyo's debt-related aid-recycling packages to Latin America (and the Third World) have to a degree limited any political exposure Japan faces in Brazil and elsewhere.

The positive aspects of Japan's relations with Brazil, however, remain tempered by the pragmatic views that Japanese business holds of Brazil's economic and political difficulties in the late 1980s. Although Brazil is already the largest recipient of Japanese direct investment, and the country remains a favorite of Japan's trading community, the recent political and financial precariousness has placed a damper on Japanese enthusiasm.[15] After the mid-1980s a "go-slow" approach was adopted by Japanese interests, awaiting a resolution of the Brazilian crises. This in part hinged on Japan's approach to debt and other financial matters and Japan's perceptions of how successful Brazil will be in liberalizing its economic and foreign trade sector.

Brazil's declaration of a moratorium on its commercial foreign debt interest payments in 1987 further damaged its image in Japan—which holds 10 percent of Brazil's external debt. Given the traditionally cautious nature of Japanese investors, their renewed interest cannot be expected to take root until issues relating to Brazil's economic and political uncertainty are resolved. This is unlikely to occur until well into the 1990s.

The Soviet Union

South American expansion of relations with the Soviet Union have been pursued primarily to enhance an independent posture from the United States. From the Soviet perspective, however, relations with South America have remained a fairly low priority. Nevertheless, by establishing a stable and slowly widening relationship with South American states, the Soviet Union is in a position to advance its presence more than ever before.

Historically, the Soviet Union had little contact with the South American subsystem. Its policy views were affected by perceptions of geographic distance and U.S. hegemonic influence.[16] During the 1917–1933 period, most South American governments followed the lead of the United States in refusing to grant official recognition of the new Soviet government. The few Soviet links that did exist were managed under the auspices of the Comintern. With the exception of a temporary increase in official diplomatic recognition during the 1930s and 1940s, it is only since the 1960s that South America has reappeared on Moscow's foreign policy map. The Cuban Revolution did much to draw

Soviet attention to Latin America; subsequently, with superpower detente in motion, relations with South America slowly expanded once again. Today, the USSR remains a marginal, yet very visible, actor in the South American affairs.

In the 1980s, Moscow's objectives have appeared to be shaped by limited expectations—to expand its position in an arena until fairly recently dominated by the United States, but within the limits of modest political and financial cost and risk. The Soviet Union has shown limited ability to exploit differences between Washington and the capitals of South America. For example, on the debt question, Soviet appeals for long-term relief have fallen on deaf ears. On South American trade and technological needs, the USSR and its allies—unlike Europe or Japan—have had little to offer. In the political arena, Washington's differences with Latin America as a whole (for example, over Central America, and, at least temporarily, over the Falklands/Malvinas crisis) have not readily provided Moscow with a practical basis from which to deploy its influence beyond the rhetorical level. A worrisome possibility is the less visible but potent East Bloc support of radical groups and terrorism. The South American view of the USSR is a generally nebulous and tolerant one, skeptical of the notion of "communist encroachment" but aware that Moscow offers little in practical terms.

While Soviet–South American relations can be interpreted as a convenient marriage of reciprocal political and economic interests, they are ultimately conditioned even more by the state of the superpower relationship and the tone that relationship develops in regional affairs.[17] It is evident that the Soviet Union tends to perceive its relations with South America as derivative of its relationship with the United States. Translated into practice, the recent warming of relations between Moscow and Washington has provided the opportunity for the former to upgrade its ties with the capitals of South America. In general, the United States presently views the Soviet approach to South America as less threatening than it previously perceived Soviet advances in the region.

The Soviet Union has achieved certain political gains through the symbolic gestures represented by high-level visits. In September 1987, Eduard Shevardnadze became the first Soviet foreign minister to make an official visit to South America, touring Argentina, Uruguay, and Brazil. Argentine President Raúl Alfonsín reciprocated this gesture as the first South American president officially to visit the Soviet Union. In 1986, Uruguayan Foreign Minister Enrique Iglesias also visited Moscow; Brazilian President José Sarney travelled to the Soviet capital in October 1988. So far, these visits have not produced further substantive bilateral consequences.

Both South America and the USSR wish to advance ties without provoking alarm in Washington. Some observers point to Moscow's decision not to seek overtly political capital during the 1982 Falklands/ Malvinas war. On the other hand, one can point to Soviet intelligence provided to Argentina and the latter's expanded sales of grain to the USSR after the 1979 U.S. grain embargo as indicators of Soviet agility in gaining advantages wherever possible.

If the Soviet Union has achieved some diplomatic and political successes, the Achilles Heel of Soviet potential in the region remains economic. Over the years, trade missions and demonstrations of technological performance have paraded throughout South America, but Moscow has little to show for it except for some measure of goodwill and a modicum of cultural exchanges. With some imagination under the circumstances, varying forms of barter offers, low-interest loans, bargain-basement pricing, even tripartite merchandise flows (U.S.-South America-USSR/Soviet Bloc) have been promoted. But the Soviet desire to cultivate South American business has not been matched by any enthusiastic response. Three reasons account for this state of affairs: (1) the Soviet Bloc has little to offer nations such as Brazil or Argentina that have already developed a modern technological base of their own; (2) conversely, the Soviet Bloc is not yet a promising market for South American goods; and, (3) Soviet motives regarding Western know-how complicates trading with South American nations.

What Moscow has been able to offer has been of marginal consequence to the real-world problems of the region. In Peru, the use of countertrade practices led the USSR to accept shipments of footwear, foodstuffs, and textiles in exchange for a portion of Peru's debt related to Soviet arms sales. The Soviet Union has promoted the idea in which it is compensated for technical and material assistance in development-related projects with indigenous staples and manufactures. Over the years, there has been discussion of natural resource (mining).investment projects in Brazil, but no agreements have been reached. South American economic managers have looked at the Cuban and Nicaraguan experiences with the Soviet Union and have hardly been encouraged by Moscow's offers of trade and other help.

In the arena of arms transfers, where the USSR holds a major global market-share, Peru is the only South American nation with which the Soviets have a significant relationship. During the early 1970s, preliminary Soviet-Peruvian commercial and economic cooperation agreements opened the door for the 1973 development of bilateral military relations. This remained in place in the 1980s, including a large mission of Soviet military personnel stationed in Peru, although Peruvians have not been entirely satisfied with the quality of equipment they have received. Argentina indicated an interest in purchasing military hardware from the Soviet Union until the return of democracy to Argentina and its chronic economic difficulties curtailed the arms sales potential. In this area, Moscow has yet to overcome fully the security risk image that it represents for most of the region's anti-communist armed forces establishment.

In the final analysis, Soviet policy in the region remains opportunistic, pragmatic, and cautious.[18] The Soviet Union appears unwilling to become entangled in either regional or international conflicts involving South America. At the cost of a modest trade deficit, the Soviet Union is achieving its foreign policy objectives in South America of widening its diplomatic contacts and garnering goodwill. By projecting itself as a viable, albeit limited, alternative to the United States without appearances of ideological strings attached, the Soviet Union has caused the South American capitals to regard Moscow as a useful, if marginal, counterbalance to U.S. influence. If nothing else, for governments such as Brazil or Argentina, these ties are indicative of their own growing maturity and visibility in the international community beyond the Western Hemisphere.

Conclusion

South America has become a permanent fixture of the global diplomatic and economic scene. The principal reason for this phenomenon relates to changes both within the region and the international arena: The convergence of altered regional power dynamics, developments in relations with the United States, and the ensuing growth of extrahemispheric interests in an era of ever-increasing interdependence.

The ability of South American nations to exploit this expanding environment is obviously fraught with problems to overcome. In the case of the European Community, although relations in the 1980s have reached new heights, the market integration of the EC in 1992 may prove to be a major hurdle to be overcome before biregional relations can further grow. In looking to Asia, particularly Japan's relationship with Brazil, much has been accomplished in the economic realm. Brazil's management of its external debt crisis, however, has made the Japanese increasingly cautious, and there has been little carry-over of this bilateral relationship into the political sphere. Soviet relations with South America have also moved forward, but limited Soviet financial resources have not allowed them to move beyond generally modest levels. Because Soviet–South American relations are derivative of the global superpower relationship, their further development will remain tied to the nature of the working relationship between Moscow and Washington.

The increased intensity of extrahemispheric relations within the South American subsystem in the 1980s has posed new challenges to U.S. policy. The question remains of how the United States will come to terms with the new regional realities. Washington clearly no longer has the opportunity to act in a nearly unilateral fashion in designing its relations with South America. The U.S. stance on regional developments has become a complex agenda of conflicting priorities requiring unprecedented material and policy resources. This has also become an agenda inextricably intertwined with the interests and actions of a broad array of extrahemispheric actors.[19]

Notes

1. In fact, Uruguay has in the past also played an active role as a participant in United Nations peace-keeping efforts.

2. Zbigniew Brzezinski articulates this very simply: "The relative decline in American global economic preeminence occurred not in spite of America but because of America," in "America's New Geostrategy," *Foreign Affairs* (vol. 66, Spring 1988), p. 693.

3. One has to be more cautious when suggesting that the appearance of democratic governments in the 1980s has also produced an expanded level of activity of South American foreign policies. More democratic governments, by their very nature, tend to generate a more pluralistic approach to foreign policies. Domestic consensus and consistency regarding these policies is another matter.

4. See Gregory F. Treverton's *Latin America in World Politics: The Next Decade* (Adelphi Papers #137, London, IISS, 1977).

5. These points are well laid out in a number of analyses: William Perry and Peter Wehner (eds.), *The Latin American Policies of U.S. Allies* (New York: Praeger, 1985); Esperanza Duran, *European Interests in Latin America,* Chatham House Papers 28 (London: Routledge and Kegan Paul/The Royal Institute of International Affairs, 1985). For Japanese relations, see also "The Japanese Challenge," *Latin American Special Reports* (August 1986).

6. See Stephen Clissold (ed.), *Soviet Relations with Latin America, 1918–68* (New York: Oxford University Press, 1970).

7. See Ilya Prizel, "Gorbachev's 'New Thinking' and Latin America," paper presented at the CSIS Conference, Soviet Studies Program, December 1987; for a Latin American perspective, see Augusto Varas (ed.), *Soviet–Latin American Relations in the 1980s* (Boulder: Westview Press, 1987); an assessment somewhat sympathetic to Soviet views is found in "The Other Superpower: The Soviet Union and Latin America, 1917–1987," in NACLA *Report on the Americas* (vol. XXI, Jan./Feb. 1987), pp. 10–40.

8. "Latin America's Relations with Israel and the Arab World," *Latin American Special Reports* (November, 1985). Bishara Bahbah, *Israel and Latin America: the Military Connections* (New York: St. Martin's Press, 1986).

9. Latin America enjoyed growth rates in the 1970–74 period averaging 7 percent, and in the 1975–80 period, 4.9 per cent.

10. South America does receive a proportionally higher level of exports from the EC than other Less Developed Countries (LDCs)—attributable to the fact that it represents by far the most advanced LDC region.

11. For a survey of these growing linkages, see Wolf Grabendorff's "European Community Relations with Latin America," *Journal of Interamerican Studies and World Affairs*, Volume 19, Number 4 (Winter 1987-1988), p. 69–87.

12. See, for example, *The IDB Monthly News* (from the Inter-American Development Bank), December 1988.

13. For a more detailed discussion of the development of this relationship, see Peter Wehner and Eric Fredell, "Japanese Involvement in Latin America," in William Perry and Peter Wehner (eds.), *The Latin American Policies of U.S. Allies* (New York: Praeger, 1985).

14. For a discussion of the current status of Japanese involvement in Brazil, see "The Japanese link—an update," in *Latin American Special Reports*, August 1988.

15. Comparatively, by the mid-1980s, Brazil represented 6 percent (and third in ranking) of total Japanese direct foreign investment. In contrast, Brazil represented about 4 percent (and ranked sixth) of total U.S. direct foreign investment. See Leon Hollerman, *Japan's Economic Strategy in Brazil* (Lexington: Lexington Books, 1988), pp. 196–97.

16. For a discussion of the concept of overwhelming U.S. regional influence, see Augusto Varas, "Soviet–Latin American Relations Under the U.S. Regional Hegemony," Augusto Varas (ed.), *Soviet–Latin American Relations in the 1980s* (Boulder: Westview Press, 1987), and Robert Leiken, *Soviet Strategy in Latin America* (New York: Praeger, 1982).

17. Further discussion of this topic can be found in Augusto Varas (ed.), *Soviet–Latin American Relations in the 1980s* (Boulder: Westview Press, 1987).

18. For an elaboration of this theme, see Robert Leiken, *Soviet Strategy in Latin America* (New York: Praeger, 1982).

19. For an in-depth discussion of this idea, see Georges Fauriol, *The Third Century: U.S. Latin American Policy Choices for the 1990s* (Washington, D.C.: Center for Strategic and International Studies, 1988).

7

The Political Economy
of South American Debt

William Guttman

This chapter's theme is that the early 1990s, with the inauguration of the Bush administration in the United States and the worsening condition of the South American debtors, is an uncertain transition period in the regional debt crisis.[1] It contains an analysis of the history of South American external indebtedness and some suggestions as to what courses of action might be adopted in the near future. The first section outlines the nature of the problem; it is followed by a summary investigation of the roots of the crisis and of the initial responses to it on the part of the various actors involved. Subsequent parts of the chapter examine in greater detail the nature of the crisis. A concluding section examines possible multilateral, private sector, creditor government, and South American actions that may help to resolve the debt dilemma.

The Nature of the Problem

Financial turmoil in South America in the 1980s has settled into what might be aptly termed "permanent crisis." Repudiation, default, bankruptcy, and systemic collapse are said to hang over the global financial community, South American countries, and the world economy. Even more than the financial system, however, is at stake. Parts of South America face extreme poverty, plummeting wages, and little prospect of economic growth. Many people in the Andean region see emigration or the cultivation and distribution of illegal drugs as the most promising options left open to them. In the Southern Cone region, political parties of the extreme right and left gain support by attacking "excessive" cooperation with the International Monetary Fund (IMF) and the World Bank. Some leading candidates for high office have threatened to declare debt moratoria and cease cooperating with creditors should they be elected. In such an atmosphere, incumbent governments find it increasingly difficult to sustain austere economic policies or to negotiate in good faith with foreign lenders.

The largest South American debtors face a variety of problems. Brazil's 1988 moratorium on debt repayment is perhaps something of the past, but the potential for further conflict with creditors is not. After a brief victory over inflation in 1986, price increases in Brazil returned with a vengeance. Annualized inflation rose to nearly 1,200 percent, with the Brazilian currency devalued against the U.S. dollar at the rate of one percent every day. The fiscal deficit as a percentage of Gross Domestic Product (GDP) continued to increase significantly, despite an IMF plan to reduce the fraction to 4 percent. The economy as a whole remained stagnant, with industrial output falling and likely to register negative growth for the near-term. Longer-run investment was discouraged by high domestic interest rates, and the increasing rates of interest on Brazil's foreign debt added $1 billion to debt service for every one point rise. All of these disappointing indicators boosted the popularity of left-wing populists aiming to ascend to the country's presidency in late 1989.

In Argentina, the collapse of the "Austral Plan" brought the return of severe inflation, with prices rising at an annual rate of more than 1,000 percent. GDP is likely to grow only slightly or not at all into the next decade. The trade surplus should show improvement to about $3 billion annually, but this compares with nearly $5 billion in hard currency requirements for debt service. Argentina is already $1 billion in arrears, and long overdue on payments, which could force U.S. banks to declare Argentine loans as non-performing. The IMF cancelled a $450 million tranche because of the government's consistent failure to meet fiscal targets. The Peronists, enjoying resurging popularity under the leadership of Carlos Menem, charged that the ruling Radical Party had favored the banks' interests over those of the nation.

Peru's economy again faltered in 1988 after two years of booming consumer spending and 8 percent growth. Inflation neared 400 percent and GNP growth became marginal. Foreign exchange reserves were entirely depleted, and access to capital markets was cut off as a consequence of President García's 1986 decision to limit interest payments to 10 percent of export earnings. García's 1987 expropriation of private banks was widely unpopular. The United Left coalition and its Marxist leader, Alfonso Barrantes, will continue to take political advantage of the situation, raising the specter of a military takeover.

Chile was South America's economic bright spot, but its politics remained fragile. Inflation was reduced to 16 percent, with GDP rising 5 percent in each of the last three years. Foreign investment tripled in 1987 from the average for the previous four years, and was likely to increase another 50 percent in 1988. The government expected a record trade surplus of $1.9 billion and a fiscal deficit of 1 percent that would meet the IMF's target. However, real wages fell by nearly one-fifth since the beginning of the decade, and many Chileans made clear their disenchantment with the political system. Moreover, Chile's economic success raised a troubling question for its neighboring democracies: is it possible to pull out of economic decline without the strong economic hand of political authoritarianism?

South American debtors have taken surprisingly little action to correct the generally weak condition of their economies. This is not, however, for lack of ideas or of abundant advice. A variety of individual and institutional sources have made literally dozens of proposals. Resistance from one or more of the interested parties, however, has prevented the adoption of reforms. This failure results more from the political shortcomings than the economic deficiencies of the proposals.

One of the most serious impediments to the adoption of reforms is that the content of reforms themselves make explicit the grave nature of the problems faced. A consequent danger is the temptation to abandon financial institutions during the implementation of extensive reform, which would be a catastrophic turn of events. Another flaw in many proposals is that the suggested reforms damage one party or another rather than equitably allocate the burdens of adjustment. Other proposals spend public money too freely. Even when politically and economically realistic proposals appear, they may threaten existing bureaucracies or fail to gain public support. More radical proposals for comprehensive reform are presented in an "implementation vacuum"—they focus on the desirable with inadequate reference to the possible. Public policy constraints, such as the U.S. budget deficit, are generally overlooked.

Roots of the Crisis

The fact that remedies for the enormous South American indebtedness are based on widely differing premises makes assessment of them difficult. Each of the major actors in the debt drama has its perception of and explanation for the causes of the crisis and offers its own justification for resisting accountability. It is much easier to engage in "debt demonology"—to blame the irresponsibility of the borrowing countries, the blindness of the banks, or the greed of the oil producers—

than to accept compromise solutions that may involve dispersed costs and sacrifices on the part of all actors. Proposals to "resolve" the crisis have often been little more than political manifestos that seek to shift the burden onto other actors.

While each of the parties involved in borrowing, lending, and regulating bears a certain degree of responsibility for the present situation, surely none can be held exclusively accountable. It is important to acknowledge the overlapping responsibilities in order to get beyond finger-pointing and make the collective sacrifices needed to stabilize international financial interactions. A brief survey of the events leading to the 1982 debt crisis indicates the complexity of its causes.

The Oil Producing Countries

The oil producing countries, either as members of the Oil Producing and Exporting Countries (OPEC) or following OPEC's lead, bear a large share of responsibility. The two most recent global recessions can be traced in large part to the two oil price shocks of the 1970s.[2] With recession as a demand-side shock (reduced orders for the exports of the developing countries) and oil price hikes as supply-side shocks, the need for foreign capital in South America was sharply increased.[3] While OPEC intensified the need for capital flows to the non-oil-exporting developing world, however, they hardly generated the problem. In fact, one could argue that the oil exporters simply resolved their own development capital shortages. Nevertheless, the decade's cumulative total additional expense for oil imports among the developing countries was almost $260 billion, or roughly half of the total increase in debt by Less Developed Countries (LDCs). This figure does not include the expenses involved in borrowing the money or the cumulative debt-service expenditures. The level of oil as a percentage of LDC imports rose from less than 6 percent in 1973 to 21 percent in 1981. Thus, one must point to oil as one of the most important contributors to the debt crisis. The OPEC barons of the 1970s have their own agenda of problems for the late 1980s and 1990s, and are unlikely to contribute in any significant way to the resolution of the debt problem.

The Bankers

The mantle of villain has also been rendered unto the international banking system. While the banks are not blameless in the debt crisis, they were more its transmitters than its generators. Nonetheless, the banks voluntarily and enthusiastically increased their exposure to massive levels in the LDCs. The most important question from the standpoint of responsibility, however, is whether the big banks irresponsibly allowed themselves to become vulnerable to collapse through LDC lending. To the contrary, it is notable that the banks did everything they could to protect themselves from just such a contingency.

When Walter Wriston became Chairman of Citibank in 1968, he promised shareholders that he would deliver 15 percent earnings increases each year. Such a high growth policy would, he said, require "aggressive exploitation of earnings opportunities" and "constant pressure to expand volume."[4] In short, bankers would be aggressive salespersons and look to foreign customers to satisfy the required increased diversification in their loan portfolios. As a result, even before the first oil shock in 1973, the banks had become even more intensely internationalized. In addition, banking innovations such as loan syndication and Eurocurrency instruments appeared. Finally, removal of capital controls by Western governments became widespread. The stage was set to increase assets and profits prodigiously when OPEC provided the script.

Between 1974 and 1977, the banks performed lending services that other institutions, both public and private, did not want to undertake. They were handsomely rewarded for their efforts. The nature of the "new" banking industry is indicated by a review of the lending that took place between 1977 and 1982, when the crisis ensued. Even though the surpluses in the OPEC countries had settled by 1977, international liquidity surged over the next few years. This came about because of the increasing U.S. current account deficit and low demand for loans in industrial countries.

Shifts in supply attest to bank inconsistency toward borrowers; they also prove that bank officials were focused on short-term profitability and burden-shifting. This statement is confirmed by three sets of evidence. First, the overwhelming majority of loans to LDCs were denominated in dollars; banks structured loans in dollars in order to avoid losses from local currency exchange depreciation. Second, almost all of the post-1973 loans carried variable interest rates, which protected the banks' earnings from fluctuation due to interest rate changes in the United States. Finally, the maturities of loans to LDCs were set at short intervals, so that a bank would have frequent opportunity to review them before refinancing. Thus, the maturities had little to do with individual countries' ability to pay off loans.

On the surface, the banks seemed to have dealt effectively with identifying individual country risks and camouflaging changes in the international economy through variable interest rates, enough so that they were comfortable in lending heavily to the LDCs. What their executives did not deal with effectively—what, in fact, they largely overlooked—was systemic crisis. Few of them seem to have considered that a crisis in several of the larger borrowing countries could spill over into the entire developing world. Like the South American countries, banks for the most part were taken by surprise by the shifting macroeconomic variables. The camouflaging of such fundamental changes in the world economy through clever loan terminology misled the banks into thinking that they were protected from those changes when, in fact, they were the most likely victims.

The Debtor Countries

If the banks provided easy access to credit, the South American countries were grateful for it. In most cases, they were faced with three unpleasant means to deal with the deficits created by the oil shocks: To finance, to restructure, or to deflate. Financing meant simply borrowing or selling reserves in the hope that balance of payments deficits were temporary. Restructuring was a supply-side measure that meant reducing oil consumption and developing new exports and export markets. Deflation was a demand-side measure that would minimize the need for external borrowing by depressing consumption, investments, and imports. South American leaders tended to choose the financing option; they viewed the prevailing real negative interest rates as favorable but without fully realizing the consequences of potential upward revision in the interest rates. When interest rates finally increased in 1981, any recessionary decline in South American liquidity would dramatically alter their capacity to pay.

Of greater concern, in the context of responsibility, were South American policies for using the recycled capital. They were often incoherent or nonexistent. In large part the loans resulted in massive government spending on inefficient public enterprises. Some governments used the new capital to boost their domestic popularity by granting wage hikes. Such government policies often led to inflationary spirals, high import consumption, and waves of speculation in property and construction. Worse, the widespread lack of exchange controls and the depreciation of national currency by inflation led to capital flight. All of these policies had the same result of making repayment of external obligations more difficult and a payments crisis more likely.

The Creditor Countries

The last entities to which some responsibility can be ascribed are the governments of the industrialized countries, in particular of the United States. Immediately after the first oil shock in 1973, the international community could conceivably have designed some mechanism to ease the weight of the newly intensified deficit burden. It did not, however, want to face up to the question of who would pay. Furthermore, many senior U.S. Treasury officials were "market-oriented"—they believed that the best means of recycling the OPEC surpluses was to let the market take its course. At the time, this policy of "neglect" removed almost all governmental responsibility for adjustment while at the same time giving the government, through its national banks, leverage over the LDCs. The U.S. government also objected to increasing the resources available to the IMF in case of financial crisis.

The U.S. decision to attack inflation through a tight monetary policy was probably the most important creditor-government contribution to the crisis. While politically necessary and even laudable from a domestic standpoint, the policy drove up the interest costs of South American loans dramatically. It also contributed to the global recession that caused commodity prices to drop nearly 40 percent from their peak in 1974 and international trade to contract sharply. As a result, South American foreign exchange earnings were reduced, diminishing the resources with which the loans could be serviced. Finally, the stunning U.S. budget deficits during the Reagan Administration crowded out private borrowers, including the South Americans, by absorbing an unprecedented amount of world liquidity.

The central conclusion to be drawn from this recapitulation is that responsibility must be shared for the emergence of the debt crisis. That shared responsibility is one of the main arguments for even-handedness in the construction of proposals for relief.

Initial Responses to the Crisis

The initial responses to the Mexican payments crisis and its spillover into the rest of Latin America were ad hoc; they failed to incorporate long-term strategies that addressed the issues of growth, equity, and systemic deficiency. For all these shortcomings, however, the early actions of the IMF, the U.S. Treasury and Federal Reserve Board, and the Bank for International Settlements kept the financial pipeline to the South American countries from shutting down completely. A $26 billion reduction in debt service payments was achieved in twenty-five IMF-sponsored reschedulings in 1982 and 1983. Unfortunately, the systemic goal of continued interest payments on the outstanding debt without substantial flows of new credit had perverse effects in both South America and the world at large. As Robert Samuelson poignantly noted, "Latin countries are impoverishing themselves so that [the United States] can enjoy higher unemployment and protectionist pressures. They have had to export more and import less to generate trade surpluses in dollars to repay dollar debts."[5]

The consortium of interest groups advocating the sanctity of debt payments has placed the burden of adjustment to the debt crisis most heavily upon the people of South America. The recent trade surpluses of Brazil and others were achieved through the sharp devaluation of national currencies, elimination of many public sector subsidies, wage cuts, and import restrictions. Per capita consumption in South America declined an average of 3.3 percent annually between 1980 and 1984. Gross domestic investment plunged an average of 11.2 percent per annum in the largest Latin American debtor countries during the same period. While exports grew at an average rate of 2.3 percent, imports declined significantly faster, at a rate of 10.8 percent, suggesting that the trade surpluses were less an indication of increased success in penetrating overseas markets than in learning to live without foreign goods, some of them critical to sustained growth.

The basic flaw in the ad hoc strategy was the lack of new money with which to invest and import producer goods. Banks, even with IMF persuasion, were unwilling to maintain, let alone increase, their exposure to problem countries in real terms. This made it significantly more likely that their South American loans would become worthless. Indeed, debtor adjustment and bank intransigence combined to produce the "transfer paradox," whereby capital-importing developing countries transfered net capital (interest and amortization less new lending) to the capital-exporting industrial countries. Net outflows from heavily indebted countries amounted to nearly $100 billion between the start of the crisis and the end of 1987. In such an environment, "interest payments . . . are really financed by a mortgage on future standards of living and on the debtor's growth potential."[6]

By 1985 it was clear that the economic position of the borrowers was stagnating or deteriorating. Banks were less willing to participate in "involuntary" lending exercises. The OECD countries were growing at a rate of less than 3 percent. South American economies and exports were growing at a rate below their real interest costs, resulting in increased debt-to-GDP ratios. In mid-1984 a severe downturn began in non-oil commodity prices, followed in 1985 by the commencement of the oil glut. The terms of trade deteriorated for all South American countries.

These inauspicious signals heralded the birth of the Baker Plan, the namesake of U.S. Treasury Secretary (later Secretary of State) James Baker. The plan, introduced in 1985, was designed to address directly the issue of new money. It set a figure of $29 billion for flows to heavily indebted countries, and threw the weight of the United States behind both involuntary lending efforts and increased balance of payments disbursements by the World Bank. The Baker Plan was not a major departure from the conceptual underpinnings to debt management that had preceded it. In fact, the timely payment of interest remained an explicit goal, even if debtor growth was added to the list of objectives. The Baker Plan was quite modest compared to other plans that had been suggested, but it recognized, at least implicitly, that the U.S. government had a role to play, that U.S. interests beyond bank profits were at stake, and that danger was reflected in debtor country officials wondering out loud about the rationale for staying the course. Indeed, one analyst considers the main impact of the plan to have been to "defuse any discussion of a debtor cartel in Latin America."[7]

The period since the Baker Plan's promulgation has been difficult for its presumed beneficiaries, leading to its dismissal in some quarters as a well-intentioned failure.[8] Others have noted that not only has the $29 billion in new capital not been forthcoming, it was an inadequate amount in the first place. Indeed, the yearly lending targets represented a decrease in both real lending and in bank exposure.[9] Before dismissing the plan, however—as would those who prefer to write off the debt— it is only fair to note that it succeeded in at least one instance in extending the conceptual boundaries of debt management. The multi-party rescue package for Mexico in 1986 included a number of innovations: (1) arranging cofinancing with the World Bank, including partial Bank guarantees on the commercial portion of a $1 billion facility to develop non-oil exports; (2) offering a $1.2 billion facility linked, through the IMF, to potential shortfalls in oil receipts; and (3) providing $500 million of "growth continuity financing," available for disbursement if the Mexican economy failed to reach agreed growth targets.[10] However, this single country, eighteen-month package accounted for over 40 percent of the three year target for all heavily indebted countries, suggesting that the plan's financing goals were inadequate.

Perhaps the most telling criticism of the Baker Plan was that the crisis continued to be as serious as ever. Net capital flows remained negative, economic growth in the OECD countries persisted at low and uneven levels, protectionism remained a threat, and real interest rates were above their historical average and continued to rise. In addition, the debtor countries suffered from "debt fatigue" insofar as their "good behavior" (in the form of financial austerity and continued willingness to pay interest) failed to produce renewed voluntary lending. Brazil's temporary moratorium on interest payments, and the lending banks' decision to set aside significant amounts as reserves against potential losses in South America, suggest that the central parties to the crisis are less than sanguine about the chances for repayment under existing terms.

In short, the crisis has entered a new phase. It is becoming more widely recognized that even sustained growth in the industrial countries and continued Baker-style rescue packages will not produce positive net transfers to the South American debtors. The fragile democracies in the region are under pressure to take unilateral action to achieve relief. Several U.S. senators and congressmen have proposed legislation to transfer the debt burden from the South American countries to international taxpayers, multilateral institutions, or banks. The banks themselves are exploring innovative means to diversify and secure their risks, such as the notable auction of Mexican bonds organized in spring 1988 by Morgan Guaranty Bank.

The road to recovery continues to run up against a sociopolitical time clock. By seeking to defuse, in 1989 the United States amended existing policy regarding the Third World debt. The response became the Brady Plan and was shaped by developments in Latin America. The most significant departure from previous U.S. positions was the adoption and approval by Washington of debt reduction measures.

Nature of the Crisis

Before one can prescribe effective means to ease the current crisis, it is necessary to define precisely what the crisis is. In sum: (1) the predicament is not a global one or even a plight of the international financial system; (2) significant differences exist among those countries and institutions that do suffer from the crisis; (3) a significant foreign debt, per se, is not necessarily a bad thing; (4) such crises are not unique; and (5) because the concerned parties have interests beyond the debt itself, crisis resolution takes on aspects of a public good.

As to the first point, the crisis of national governments unable to pay interest to commercial banks is limited for the most part to a group of relatively wealthy developing countries and several large international "money center" banks. The total developing-country long-term debt outstanding for ninety market economies in 1986 was about $655 billion. Of that sum, well over half was concentrated in only seventeen countries (classified by the World Bank as "heavily-indebted countries"), of which nine were in South America; and nearly half of this amount (approximately $160 billion) was owed by the four largest South American debtors—Brazil, Argentina, Venezuela, and Chile. The average per capita income of these four countries was more than $2,000, compared to the global developing country average of $610. Furthermore, several South American countries classified as heavily indebted have managed to retain at least respectable growth rates during the decade of crisis. On the credit ledger, almost half of all loans to South

America emanated from the United States. In addition, the nine money-center banks held about two-thirds of all U.S. bank exposure in South America.[11]

It may be noted that few South and East Asian countries have had problems servicing or rolling over old debts. African debt is mostly official, fixed-interest, and concessional. Their problems, while serious, do not emerge from the same sources as the South American crisis, do not threaten the international financial system, and can be addressed in terms of humanitarian official transfers. It seems reasonable to argue, therefore, that the crisis is not systemic but geographically restricted. Consequently, transferring scarce international resources to South America would require explanations to India, Korea, Thailand, and other countries as to why they were being penalized for their successful financial management.

Even among the South American countries significant differences are found in their ability and willingness to cope. The ratio of debt outstanding to GNP in 1986 ranged from 41 percent in Brazil to 138 percent in Chile.[12] The ratio of interest payments to exports ranged from 15.3 percent in Uruguay to 33.1 percent in Argentina.[13] The ratios of potential losses on LDC debt to reserves are similarly diverse among the nine largest U.S. banks, ranging from Bank of America at 266 percent to 153 percent at First Interstate, with Citibank, Chase, and Manufacturers bunching about halfway between the two extremes.[14] Some countries and banks are more in need of relief or restructuring than are others.

The point must be emphasized that the overall position of a country is more important in determining the existence and nature of a crisis than any particular ratio or ceiling. That is, no objective basis exists for determining how much debt or interest a country can afford. Debt-to-GNP and interest-to-export ratios are simply rules of thumb and should not be arbitrarily applied. Indeed, a senior banker recently noted: "The South American debt will never be repaid; it will become larger, although at a reduced rate. But the U.S. government's debt also will not be paid, nor will the AT&T debt."[15] Debt should relate to potential rather than present GNP or exports. Indeed, if debt is used to invest in new plants, the resulting production and exports will not appear in the statistics for some time. Capital flows from industrial to developed countries have been, and will remain, part of an efficient allocation of global resources.

Another important point is that debt crises are not unique. Many debt crises have appeared through the centuries, including two previous defaults in South America. Even such industrial countries as Britain and France defaulted on U.S. loans in the 1930s. What is unique in the current situation is that the world is "trying to deal with an excess of debt without the historical context of repudiation, inflation, or some kind of revolution."[16] In South America, the debt accumulated by the end of the nineteenth century was reduced in real terms by the postwar inflation of the 1920s. An awareness of the precedent-setting quality of emerging from the crisis without a shock is critical. Further, as a former Colombian finance minister has noted, "the experience of the 19th century shows that it takes decades of muddling through and renegotiation before creditors and debtors can agree on the relief measures that are adequate to overcome the debt hurdle. A genuine solution . . . only became feasible when the Latin American countries achieved high growth rates in a period of open and profitable trade markets."[17]

Finally, indebtedness has developed into a crisis largely because implicit interests have gone well beyond the specific issue of debt. Many global issues have never received the kind of attention focused on the South American debt, and the reason is fundamentally political. The geographic proximity of South America to the United States makes the problems of these countries appear more urgent than the human tragedies of Sub-Saharan Africa. Furthermore, there is a desire to aid the South American democracies by recognizing the political constraints on the ability of governments to impose austerity. As Stanley Fischer notes: "Given long enough, and given a government powerful enough to reduce living standards sufficiently, [South American] countries would be capable of generating the trade surpluses that would enable them to regain normal access to the capital markets."[18] But what form would such a government take? Most likely, one that did not share Western democratic values, ruling a country "with no private sector, no middle class and a resentment level ready to explode at any time in the face of [American] national security."[19] Thus, a stable, democratic South America seems to have the characteristics of a public good, and therefore suggests the applicability of public intervention.

Proposed Initiatives to Ease the Crisis

Multilateral Institutional Initiatives

A number of multilateral initiatives have been proposed that revolve around the functions of existing institutions—the World Bank and the IMF—rather than any new entities. The suggested courses of action are modular; that is, none needs the execution of any other, although some may require cooperation between creditors and debtors.

The IMF and World Bank have played valuable roles in international economic interaction for forty years and have adapted well, though not always without a struggle, to changing conditions in world markets. With the acquiescence of the major contributors and increased assistance from regional organizations, internal facilities could be developed to help increase flows to the South American debtors and help them cope with future adverse shocks on equitable terms. The IMF, the World Bank, and their related agencies should not participate in efforts to reduce the outstanding debt. The following recommendation has merit:

> Multilateral institutions, which are not supposed to serve any individual country's national interest, should base their policies on criteria of global equity and efficiency. On those grounds, the major beneficiaries under the Baker . . . proposals should not in fact be given relief in preference to countries that are poorer and/or have pursued superior policies.[20]

In other words, the foreign policy goals of the United States (or any other country, for that matter) should not be addressed by multilateral lending policy but rather by explicit arrangements on a bilateral basis. Several neutral proposals have been offered:

(1) Agreement to Regularize SDR Allocations. Lessard and Williamson argue that the Special Drawing Rights (SDR) system should be "used for the purpose for which it was invented, namely to permit nonreserve centers to build up their reserves without the need to run payments surpluses."[21] Their suggestion of annual allocations of $9 billion is probably unworkable, however, because of industrial country concern that such increases in liquidity would spur inflation. An alternative would be to agree on an allocation formula related to the income velocity of money or other leading indicators of inflation; when liquidity was artificially low, SDRs would be issued automatically, and when the global money supply grew too rapidly, allocations would be reduced or cease. Such a policy, or some variation on it, would not require new powers or additional bureaucracy for the IMF.

(2) New General Contingency Facility. A new financing mechanism, perhaps called the General Contingency Facility (GCF), could be established to deal with adverse changes in world macroeconomic variables—such as real growth in the industrial countries, barriers to trade, and exchange-rate fluctuations. The GCF could be financed out of a general increase in quotas or, more usefully, from contributions based on the level of each country's foreign exchange reserves, which are a function of trade and payments surpluses. Unlike suggestions of a fund based on trade surpluses, however, which make politically unacceptable demands on successful exporters like Japan and Germany, a reserve-based fund would only require substantial commitments from reserve-

hoarders who diminish world liquidity. The moral hazard inherent in this proposal—that countries would attempt to reduce their reserves—actually works to its benefit. In addition, SDRs could be exempted from the accounting, both to reduce LDC exposure to facility contributions and to provide an incentive to use the SDR as a unit of account.

(3) New Consultative Risk Committee. A multilateral "credit committee," possibly denominated the Consultative Risk Committee (CRC), would provide capital markets with an enhanced capacity to judge risks and debtors with the ability to hold rational interest rate expectations. It would do so by setting out appropriate criteria for different interest spreads. This would be analogous to Moody's bond ratings or the Standard & Poor's ratings of corporate debt. Arguments against such a rating system are based on the fear that it would lead to tighter credit rationing.[22] This eventuality is likely if the debt instrument of a country is rated poorly and the country does or can do nothing to improve it. However, in a phased system the country would be subject to a higher risk premium rather than denied credit; its instruments could conceivably trade as "junk" (see below). In fact, informal ratings are already available in the market; Standard & Poor's itself calculates "shadow" ratings of debt that are released to financial institutions with country approval. In the prospective CRC system, spreads would be linked to performance and potential performance by including ongoing productive investment and resource-shifting in the matrix of spread criteria.

The World Bank, like the IMF, cannot focus too heavily on debt already incurred. It can, however, play a leading role in the restoration of positive capital flows to South America. Several of the proposals outlined below could be accomplished internally, but some would also require cooperation with banks or regulatory coordination with creditor governments.

(4) Co-financing and Guarantees. One of the most significant means by which the World Bank can increase commercial bank lending in South America is by participating in new loan packages with its own money and, in certain instances, with partial guarantees. With respect to the former, what is most important is the Bank's good name and the precedent among developing countries of prompt repayment of World Bank loans. In fact, during the 1987–1988 Brazilian repayment moratorium, loans co-financed by the Bank were specifically excluded.[23] The first voluntary commercial lending to South America since the onset of the crisis was in the form of a $45 million commitment to an Uruguayan hydroelectric project, matched by $45 million from the

Bank. The offering was heavily oversubscribed and included a significant number of new lenders.[24]

As noted above, the World Bank provided partial guarantees for a $1 billion facility for Mexico as part of that country's 1986 rescue package. In cases where capital is needed to develop economically sound projects, but is not forthcoming from commercial banks, such guarantees may be essential. A valuable aspect of the Bank's implicit and explicit guarantees is that they effectively subordinate old loans and thus encourage additional flows.

(5) Innovative Lending Policies. The World Bank can have an enormous impact on the policies of commercial lenders by introducing new loan instruments. The present Bank lending policies are rather conservative in this regard. A partial consequence has been that commercial lenders have been hesitant to adapt innovations from within the domestic market to South America, disinclined to utilize such means as variable payment loans (wherein interest payments are constant and maturity fluctuates) and price level adjusted debt (which shifts a portion of the interest increase risk to the lender).[25] By taking the first step, the World Bank might be able to help overcome resistance to such innovative instruments.

(6) Public Good Transfers. The World Bank is the appropriate body to address issues related to the destruction of world natural resources. The Bank could swap its own debt or administer a special facility, financed by industrial members, to acquire long-term leases on threatened resources, such as endangered species and tropical rainforests. Several private foundations, the World Wildlife Fund among them, have already used the swap market to purchase four million acres of tropical forest in Bolivia and 40,000 acres of dry forest in Costa Rica.[26] The resources available to these private groups, however, are very limited. Moreover, the increasing threat to non-renewable resources stems at least in part from the process of economic development that the Bank has actively encouraged. In more than one sense, then, the Bank has an obligation, which it has only recently begun to fulfill, to help countries develop adequate environmental management. In that process, it must recognize that the economic wherewithal to protect natural resources on a large scale will not exist for the foreseeable future.

(7) Low-Interest Instruments. The Bank should be authorized to issue tax-free bonds at below-market rates of interest, with the savings passed on to its borrowers.[27] Like tax-free municipal bonds in the domestic market, the proceeds would be used to create needed public infrastructure in the developing countries. The tax-free aspect would create incentives for new non-bank lending, with industrial-country costs lim-

ited to foregone tax revenues. These instruments would be an important element in addressing the transfer paradox discussed above.

In sum, these seven multilateral initiatives, if adopted, would provide a significant buffer for the international financial system in case of future shocks. To a more limited extent, they would help to restore normal transfers from capital-rich to capital-poor countries. It should be recognized, however, that even in the unlikely event that all of the above recommendations were to be implemented, the resources of the Bank and the Fund would remain relatively limited. Thus, significant independent contributions to crisis resolution would also have to be made by private sector entities and member governments.

Commercial Banking Initiatives

Commercial banking transactions can be categorized in one of three ways: (1) unilateral actions by banks to rationalize or reduce exposure; (2) trading debt for securities or equity (swaps); and (3) new money innovations.

The choice by banks to rationalize or reduce their exposure is problematical and, in this author's view, an unwise action. Three international financial actions aimed at such ends—increasing individual bank loan–loss reserves, making loans to secondary market prices, and reducing LDC exposure—suggest a conclusion on the part of commercial banks that the crisis cannot be resolved and that the only option is to cut losses and move on to other business. The argument was made above that the crisis is not terminal; therefore, these three actions are not constructive.

Trading debt for securities or non-debt assets has productive potential. Equity swaps would address the consequences of a central problem in international capital markets, namely limited risk sharing. Lessard says this:

> The character of loans to developing countries implies that specific lenders have little or no stake in the success or failure of specific undertakings since their recovery of the amount lent depends only on borrowers' overall payment performance. . . . Thus, the bank that lends money for the purchase of armaments is in the same position as the bank that funds an industrial project.[28]

Equity positions are, conversely, largely dependent on the project's success or failure. In addition, bankers have looked differently upon losses sustained as a result of swapping. Citibank Chairman John Reed recently said that "a loss on a debt-equity swap would have no impact on our advancing new money to a country that adopted sound, growth-oriented policies."[29]

A large variety of swaps have been proposed over the last few years, and several South American countries have adopted extensive swap programs. They are described in two major categories:

(1) Debt/Debt Swaps. Bank debt is exchanged for bond debt with longer maturities and lower interest payments. A lower interest rate is applied because bonds have historically had preference to bank debt in repayment priorities. The 1988 Morgan-Mexico bond auction, which could serve as a precedent for South American programs, illustrates both the potential and limitations of such swaps. The Mexicans were able to retire a sizable (but nevertheless disappointing) fraction of their outstanding debt at a discount of just over thirty percent. The new bonds were poorly subscribed despite the fact that they were partially collateralized with U.S. Treasury notes. Furthermore, the collateral required an advance transfer of $2 billion from Mexico's foreign exchange reserves. Only a few countries have the wherewithal to pursue this swap approach.

(2) Debt/Equity Swaps. Bank debt is exchanged for an interest in a local firm. Chile has been the most active in swapping debt for equity, converting about $2.2 billion into domestic enterprises through mid-1988. Most such swaps involve a third party—usually a multinational corporation—which buys the debt at a discount and exchanges it with the relevant central bank for local currency. Recently, however, banks have engaged in such transactions for their own accounts. The process is attractive insofar as the banks rid themselves of a portion of their exposure outside the weak secondary market, the multinationals get local currency at a discount, and the South American debtors pay off the loan in local currency.[30] On the other hand, interest payments are replaced by dividend or profit remittances, domestic debt (fiscal deficit) is increased by the discounted purchase price, and the country transfers a portion of its capital stock to foreigners.[31] Because of these limitations, it is likely that the value of these transactions will remain marginal relative to the total South American debt, with turnover on the order of $10 billion annually.

Various alternatives in the debt/equity category are possible. They include swapping debt for:

(a) Government Property. Large amounts of virgin and developed land are owned by South American governments. While a sizeable fraction is of little commercial value, the land as a whole represents a significant non-income producing asset. Debt could be traded for portions of land, with discounts on the face value of the debt provided for development variances, the creation of special economic zones, or the provision of infrastructure.

(b) Trade Credits. Banks could swap discounted debt to national export credit institutions, which would offer to retire the debt or forgive annual interest payments if enough goods were imported into the relevant country.[32] This would reduce both South American debt and industrial country trade deficits that were created by South American payments constraints.

(c) "Class B" Shares in Protected Industries. Companies such as Petrobras (Brazil's state-owned petroleum enterprise) would be snapped up by foreign investors if put on the market, which is why they are not. As an alternative, banks could receive non-voting stakes and/or provide new money covenants to the firms in return for profit participation. The Scandinavian Airlines System recently paid $204 million for a 40 percent share of the state-owned Aerolineas Argentinas. Iberian Airlines is engaged in talks with the Uruguayan government about the purchase of a significant minority interest in Pluna, Uruguay's state-owned air carrier.

(d) Escrowed Export Proceeds. Bank debt could be traded for the foreign exchange earned from particular projects. This scheme draws on the concept of exchange participation notes, whereby a country's debt is transformed into a commitment to transfer a percentage of its total foreign exchange earnings.[33] However, this more limited proposal could be instituted on a case-by-case basis and not require the multi-party coordination and strict conditionality of the broader concept.

The final area for private sector initiatives—new money—is also the most important. While the restructuring inherent in the proposals outlined above may increase capital transfers to a limited extent, the scale would not be nearly large enough to promote a return to pre-crisis South American growth rates. For this to occur, as much as $15 billion of new capital will be required annually. Alternative instruments that would be useful in raising this amount include:

(a) Non-Bank Investment. The creation of mutual funds to trade in South American stock markets, such as those pursued by the International Finance Corporation (IFC), could be duplicated by private money managers. Return on investment has historically been higher in emerging than in mature markets; and most South American markets, moving countercyclically to industrial country markets, allow for risk-hedging. In addition, price/earnings ratios in South American stock-markets are extremely conservative, averaging about half those of developed markets. These arguments, with proper marketing, could attract investment from pension funds and insurance companies. Lessard and

Williamson suggest that flows from these new sources could amount to $1 billion annually.[34]

(b) Loan Insurance. An area with great unexplored potential is the commercial guarantee of new lending. Citibank and Cigna failed to agree on coverage terms during an aborted negotiation in 1984, but this, at least in part, was because past loans with a high likelihood of non-performance were to be covered. Risk premiums charged by insurance companies would probably not be prohibitive if new insured lending were conducted on a specific project basis.

(c) Junk Bonds. Venezuela issued the first South American junk bonds in February 1988, with the proceeds to be used to improve export sector infrastructure. The bonds paid nearly a fifty percent premium over five-year U.S. Treasury bonds, enough to generate full subscription to the $100 million issue. This suggests that if South American countries have investment projects with strong export-enhancing or generating potential, it may be worth the premium to attract new finance. Moreover, major players in junk, such as Drexel Burnham Lambert, have recently begun to take a keen look at South America. The Japanese, once ultra-conservative but now flush with capital, have begun to enter the junk market. The projects to be financed must, however, be strong foreign exchange earners if junk is not to sink the South Americans into a deeper hole than they have experienced to date.

(d) Shared Appreciation Loans. Adapted from the home mortgage market, shared appreciation loans would carry below-market rates of interest in return for a performance-based dividend at maturity.[35] In essence, this is a new money/equity swap. Another advantage over debt/equity, aside from the new money itself, is that no specific ownership interest is implied and no ownership distinction (as suggested in relation to Class B shares) would be required. Such an instrument might also be attractive to non-banks wishing to enter into production-sharing agreements with South American manufacturers.

In all, these commercial initiatives show the way toward market-based resolution of the transfer paradox and, to a limited extent, reduction of the debt overhang. The private sector, like the multilateral institutions, is not usually the appropriate party to address previously incurred debt. This can be best approached politically, and this is where the creditor governments enter the picture.

Creditor Government Initiatives

Analysts often point out that the givens for any resolution to the debt crisis are (1) strong OECD country growth, (2) restriction of protectionist impulses, (3) reduction of fiscal deficits to sustainable levels, and (4) relatively stable exchange rates. These four elements are more important to the South American debtors than any number of lending innovations. Unfortunately, they are not assured. Because there is no way to adequately address these broad issues in a single chapter, suffice it to say that industrial country macroeconomic policy should take the interests of South American countries seriously. The debt crisis itself proves that ill-conceived or abrupt policy changes that damage South American economies have negative long-term consequences for global finance and trade.

Creditor governments also need to address a number of other central issues. First, export credit relative to GDP has contracted sharply in most countries. This contraction may help ease short-term pressure on fiscal accounts but, in the long-run, it impedes trade flows to South America and reduces their ability to receive transfers of technology and skill. Second, a variety of industrial country guidelines have the effect of reducing the pool of financial resources available to South American debtors. Regulation "K" in the United States sets time limits on bank ownership of South American non-bank companies, and allows them to be acquired only if they are being privatized and are worth less than $15 million or 5 percent of the bank's capital. Japan's $300 billion postal savings fund cannot be invested in South America. Similar oddities abound in other OECD countries, making it more difficult to conduct swaps or tap new sources of funding.

The United States has a dominant role to play in addressing these and other debt-related issues. Despite reports of ill U.S. economic health, other OECD countries still look to the primus inter pares to promote new initiatives (even if they often fail to agree on their implementation). If the United States, with the most at stake politically in South American countries, cannot or will not make significant interventions on their behalf, what would prompt others to do so? Therefore, the next U.S. administration should try its hand at several endeavors, explicitly recognizing that U.S. interests in drug enforcement, illegal migration, and democracy are indivisible from the debt crisis. The United States can reward performance in one of its interest areas with relaxation of demands in others, and is free to subordinate fairness and "the market" to political necessity.

A number of constructive U.S. initiatives could be considered. Among them are:

(1) Capital Increases for Multilateral Institutions. The most obvious and perhaps most helpful initiative would be the approval of a general capital increase for the World Bank, the IMF, and the IFC. The IMF's paid-in quota, in the case of the United States, has dropped by nearly

two-thirds relative to GDP since the Fund's creation.[36] Japan's quota was cut by almost four-fifths, by the same measure, since its admission.[37] One consequence is the Fund's own transfer paradox; capital flows into the Fund from the South American debtors.

With new capital at its disposal and $15 billion of already outstanding borrowings, the IMF could explore a variety of useful facilities directed toward easing future shocks. As for the World Bank, the proposed $75 billion capital increase would go a great distance toward the replacement of private capital flows. Because of their limited resources and conservative lending policies, the Bank and the Fund together have been able to cover only about one-fifth of the decline in commercial bank lending. Without a capital increase the negative transfers from the South American debtors to the Bank will continue.

(2) G-7 Coordination. The debt crisis has shown little sign of coordinated efforts among the Group of Seven countries. A few words were spoken on the crisis at the most recent industrial country summit, but joint action has not been forthcoming. It is conceivable that the limitations of individual countries, in terms of both resource and policy constraints, have precluded the development of a unilateral plan to ease the crisis. In limited circumstances, however, individual countries have shown remarkable creativity. The rescue package for Mexico and France's forgiveness of one-third of its African debts are points of reference. Rather than attempt joint efforts, it may be more productive to make a de facto allocation of spheres of interest that could draw in other important countries to the reform process, particularly West Germany and Japan.

(3) Strategic Stockpiling. As with the advance U.S. purchase of Mexican oil as part of a bridging package, creditor governments could reserve important commodities in South American countries, both as a political prop and as an effective hedge against future price increases. With a higher degree of coordination (a much longer-term option), this might be an effective route to commodity price stabilization in politically pressured South American countries.

(4) Good Offices. The United States and other creditor governments should be doing more to investigate innovative proposals to ease the crisis. A particularly useful initiative would be to bring together a small number of representatives from each interest group (debtors, banks, multilateral institutions, and G-7 governments) to discuss the dozens of technical proposals outstanding. Though this might not produce any sort of agreement, it would serve to provide notice on what each group finds unacceptable, and so lead to more effective proposals in the future.

These initiatives are not as radical as other quasi-political proposals receiving favorable attention, such as the creation of a new multilateral institution or asking international taxpayers to foot the bill for the crisis. The central difference is that most of the initiatives outlined above are designed to help the South American countries resolve the crisis themselves.

South American Initiatives

The debtor countries can help themselves at least to a limited extent by applying voluntarily, and by means of their own devising, the strict conditionality that has thus far been forced upon them by outsiders. "Self-conditionality" suggests the institution or continuation of a variety of policies. They include the following initiatives:

(1) Reducing Public Sector Economic Activity. Despite the austerity measures in South American countries, fiscal deficits remain among the highest in the world. In part, this is because they retain significant subsidies, particularly on foodstuffs. In Argentina, for example, these subsidies have led to rural-urban tensions. Furthermore, South American countries have historically relied on controls and pursued inward-looking policies traceable to the interwar period that are hardly appropriate to today's economic realities. The past emphasis on state-run enterprises should be reexamined, especially in light of the evidence that these companies were the most profligate borrowers during the 1970s. To the extent that it is politically viable, many state enterprises should be privatized.

(2) Encouraging Foreign Competition and Investment. Such a policy would be aided by eliminating non-citizen barriers to withdrawal of profits, and restrictions on foreign ownership for all but the most politically sensitive industries. At the same time, South American governments should consider policies for the return of the $100 billion or more of flight capital—especially stable and appropriately valued exchange rates and positive real interest rates. Amnesty should be avoided because of its inherent moral hazard.

(3) Offering Innovative Financial Market Instruments. The governments of South America should encourage their financiers to master the technicalities of international financial markets and offer investors sophisticated new instruments that have emerged in the main trading centers. The South American countries should move with these markets to more reliance on bond issuance, and less on straight commercial lending.

Above all, the debtors should rule out default as an option. The not-so-pleasant results could be the termination of lending, default interest, termination of trade credit, withdrawal of export insurance, curtailment of bilateral aid, import bans, legal action, seizure of foreign assets, and economic blockage.[38] Aside from bringing on punitive actions from the industrial countries, default carries with it the same implication as a unilateral writedown by the banks—that the crisis is intractable to anything but extreme action. Angus Maddison has pointed out that the "clearest signs that [default] is not regarded favourably are the action which was taken jointly by Brazil, Colombia, Venezuela and Mexico to lend $500 million to Argentina to prevent it falling into interest arrears, and the fact that communist countries with severe payments difficulties such as Cuba and Poland have not repudiated their debts."[39]

Even the example of Peru, which limited interest payments to ten percent of export earnings, is unlikely to be followed. Although Peru managed a temporary spurt in annual growth to 8 percent, in the year following its action economic expansion faded from lack of foreign exchange and external capital resources. The South American countries seem to have decided, rightly, that it is in their own long-term interests to negotiate with creditors. While more radical winds have begun to blow in the region, this decision should hold firm. Its indefinite continuance, however, can be counted upon only if some measure of effort to ease their distress is forthcoming from the international financial community.

Conclusions

Debt crisis expectations involve a hierarchy of three elements: (1) The risk of unilateral or multilateral suspension of debt repayment; (2) the risk of widescale creditor bankruptcy through payment collapse; and (3) the risk of a broad downturn from structural weaknesses exacerbated by bank failure. It is reasonably safe to say that such fearful expectations are exaggerated. However, there are other problematic sub-crisis concerns about the debt and the transfer paradox: (1) political turmoil as a result of imposed austerity; (2) the consequences of reduced capital inflows on development; (3) the risk of new, imposed regulatory policies on foreign lending; (4) trade disruptions through impoverishment of South American markets; and (5) threats to hemispheric security concerns and other U.S. interests (such as drug enforcement).

These dilemmas demand attention, although exactly what kind of attention is a matter of debate. It has been argued in this chapter that radical comprehensive plans are unworkable, primarily because of moral hazard, unfair shifting of scarce international public resources, and the probable lack of bank and debtor government support. Instead, a number of alternatives to ease the crisis have been offered in each of four categories: (1) Multilateral initiatives to create internal facilities to increase world liquidity, lend in crisis, improve information available on debtors, and provide for public good credits; (2) commercial initiatives to increase the flow of new money on commercial principles; (3) creditor government initiatives to increase resources available to international institutions to combat debt crises on an equitable basis and to improve coordination; and (4) South American initiatives to reduce the role of the state in economic activity and reduce the need for external policy dictates.

The adoption of a sizable fraction of these proposals would immediately affect the condition of South American debt. However, the course and progress of reform measures since the beginning of the crisis in 1982 does not suggest a willingness to undertake the measures proposed. Perhaps the adoption of many new initiatives is not required to head off a breakdown of the existing system; perhaps economic growth in the OECD will increase and commodity prices will recover; perhaps Western leadership can adopt the rapidly fading disposition of the South American governments, and simply hope for the best. But by relying on such hope, the South American debt crisis has already been more costly than the world can continue to afford.

Notes

1. The author would like to express appreciation for the helpful comments and suggestions provided by M. Delal Baer, Norman Bailey, Reginald Brown, Georges Fauriol, Robert Hormats, Jean Rosenheim Lange, Thomas Reckford, Kristine Rigopulos, and Penelope Hartland-Thunberg. This chapter draws on material in the author's "Between Bailout and Breakdown: A Modular Approach to Latin America's Debt Crisis," a study prepared for the CSIS Latin American Program.

2. For a concise analysis of the relationship between the oil shocks and debt, see William R. Cline, "International Debt and the Stability of the World Economy," *Policy Analyses in International Economics* 4 (Washington, DC: Institute for International Economics, September 1983), pp. 20–22.

3. Mexico, Ecuador, and Venezuela, it should be noted, received a substantial windfall from OPEC's actions. However, they borrowed on the assumption that oil prices would rise or at least remain stable, and were hurt badly when prices began to drop.

4. Quoted in John Makin, *The Global Debt Crisis: America's Growing Involvement* (New York: Basic Books, 1984), p. 145.

5. This situation is not unlike that of the United States itself in relation to its major creditors in Europe and Japan. Importantly, the South American example shows that it may be quite counterproductive to rapidly force down consumption in a debtor country. The Samuelson quote can be found in Robert

A. Pastor, "Planning for the Future," in Robert A. Pastor (ed.), *Latin America's Debt Crisis: Adjusting to the Past or Planning for the Future?* (Boulder: Lynne Rienner, 1987), p. 139

6. Rudiger Dornbusch, "Our LDC Debts," National Bureau of Economic Research Working Paper #2138 (Cambridge: January 1987), p. 21.

7. Christine A. Bogdanowicz-Bindert, "The Debt Crisis: The Baker Plan Revisited," *Journal of Interamerican Studies and World Affairs* 28:3 (Fall 1986), p. 41.

8. See for example Peter Hakim, "The Baker Plan: Unfulfilled Promises," *Challenge* 29:4 (September/October 1986), p. 56.

9. Patricia Wertman, "The International Debt Problem: Options for Solution," *Economic Development in Latin America and the Debt Problem* (Washington, DC: USGPO, October 29, 1987), p. 120.

10. Bogdanowicz-Bindert, op. cit., p. 35.

11. Data on money-center banks is taken from Jeffrey Sachs, "International Policy Coordination: The Case of the Developing Country Debt Crisis," National Bureau of Economic Research Working Paper #2287 (Cambridge: June 1987), Table 8.

12. The specific debt/GNP figures are: Argentina, 65.8 percent; Bolivia, 118.8 percent; Brazil, 41 percent; Chile, 138.8 percent; Colombia, 46.8 percent; Ecuador, 83.5 percent; Peru, 62.4 percent; Uruguay, 63.4 percent; Venezuela, 70.8 percent.

13. The specific interest/export figures are: Argentina, 33.1 percent; Bolivia, 31.5 percent; Brazil, 30.2 percent; Chile, 29.5 percent; Colombia, 16.6 percent; Ecuador, 24.4 percent; Peru, 29 percent; Uruguay, 15.3 percent; Venezuela, 22.5 percent.

14. Richard Evans, "New Debts for Old—And the Swapper Is King," *Euromoney* (September 1987), p. 86.

15. Terence C. Canavan quoted in discussion in Robert A. Pastor, "Planning for the Future," in Pastor, *Latin America's Debt Crisis: Adjusting to the Past or Planning for the Future?* (Boulder: Lynne Rienner, 1987), p. 63.

16. Fishlow in Ibid., pp. 117–118.

17. Roberto Junguito, "Letter from Latin America," *The International Economy* (May/June 1988), p. 17.

18. Stanley Fischer, "Resolving the International Debt Crisis," National Bureau of Economic Research Working Paper #2373 (Cambridge: September 1987), p. 12.

19. The phrase is borrowed from Norman Bailey's comments on "permanent" austerity in the Latin American countries quoted in Anatole Kaletsky, *The Cost of Default*, A Twentieth Century Fund Paper (New York: Priority Press, 1985), p. 51.

20. Willem H. Buiter and T.N. Srinivasan, "Rewarding the Profligate and Punishing the Prudent and Poor: Some Recent Proposals for Debt Relief," *World Development* 15:3 (1987), p. 416.

21. Donald R. Lessard and John Williamson, "Financial Intermediation Beyond the Debt Crisis," *Policy Analyses in International Economics* 12 (Washington, DC: Institute for International Economics, September 1985), p. 108.

22. See, for example, Simonsen, op. cit., p. 122

23. Economist Intelligence Unit, *South America: Economic Structure and Analysis* (London: Economist Publications, 1987), p. 10.

24. C. Fred Bergsten, "The Responsibilities of the Industrialized Countries and the Need to Strengthen the World Bank," in Robert A. Pastor (ed.), op. cit., p. 100.

25. These and other lending innovations in the domestic mortgage market are described in detail in Laurie S. Goodman, "Alternative Design for LDC Loans: Lessons from the U.S. Home Mortgage Market," *Bankers Magazine* 167:3 (May/June 1984), pp. 66–72.

26. United Nations, *Development Forum* 15:8 (October 1987), p. 1.

27. This concept was broached in Simonsen, op. cit., p. 123.

28. Lessard, "International Financing . . . ," op. cit., p. 20.

29. Quoted in Anatole Kaletsky, "Banks Face the Facts at Last," *Financial Times* (May 21, 1987), p. 17.

30. Dornbusch, op. cit., p. 43.

31. Ibid., pp. 43–44; Edmar Bacha, "Next Stop in Debt Crisis—Is Confrontation Inevitable?" *The International Economy* 1:1 (October/November 1987), p. 57; and Graham Bird, "Debt Conversion in Principle and Practice," Banco Nazionale del Lavoro, *Quarterly Review* 161 (June 1987), pp. 183–195.

32. Richard Rothstein, "Give Them a Break," *The New Republic*, vol. 198 (February 1, 1988), p. 24.

33. Norman A. Bailey, "A Safety Net for Foreign Lending," *Business Week* (January 10, 1983), p. 17, and Norman A. Bailey, David Luft, and Roger W. Robinson, Jr., "Exchange Participation Notes: An Approach to the International Financial Crisis," in Thibaut de Saint Phalle (ed.), *The International Financial Crisis: An Opportunity for Constructive Action* (Washington, DC: Georgetown University, Center for Strategic and International Studies, 1983).

34. Lessard and Williamson, "Financial Intermediation . . . ," op. cit., pp. 85–101.

35. For an explanation of the domestic instrument, see Goodman, op. cit., p. 68.

36. From 0.96 percent, to 0.35 percent of GDP in 1986.

37. From 1.05 percent, to 0.22 percent of GDP in 1986.

38. Richard L. Bernal, "Default as a Negotiating Tactic in Debt Rescheduling Strategies of Developing Countries: A Preliminary Note," in Antonio Jorge and Jorge Salazar Carrillo (eds.), *Foreign Investment, Debt, and Economic Growth in Latin America* (London: Macmillan, 1988), p. 46.

39. Angus Maddison, *Two Crises: Latin America and Asia, 1929–38 and 1973–83* (Paris: OECD, 1985), pp. 79–80.

8

European and South American Perspectives

Wolf Grabendorff and Roberto Russell

Abstract

This final chapter addresses the implications of the changing realities of South America's international relations from a European and a South American perspective. It is divided into two parts. The first section is written by Wolf Grabendorff and provides an expert European outlook on the subject. The second section, authored by Roberto Russell, presents the views of a noted South American scholar and policy analyst. They both explore the changing South American scene in terms of West European and South American policies, respectively, with comments about the corollary meaning for those of the United States.

A European Perspective

Future possibilities of European–Latin American relations are understood to a considerable degree in terms of traditions. It seems that most U.S. officials tend to have little historical perspective when thinking about South American relationships, forgetting that prior to World War I the major outside powers in South America were European, and that Europeans were as important in the region as the United States until World War II. The current U.S. role as a major power is a recent phenomenon. Furthermore, many South Americans today are in various ways turning back to Europe, often building on past relations to realize their desire for a more diverse international structure in which Europe plays a comfortable role. The point is that this is nothing new; South Americans are attempting to redress the balance with the United States by, among other things, reviving their European relations.

It is important to recognize this fundamental reality of inter-American relations: The United States interacts with the highly diverse grouping of South American states both as a global superpower and a key subregional actor. These relations are inherently asymmetrical.

South Americans resist this general fact of international life by attempting to redress the balance in specific areas. That is, they understand that the more dependent they are in a general sense, as in the fundamentally important economic arena, the more important it becomes to them to find some segment of the relationship, some smaller but important area, where they can distance themselves from the United States. They might decide, for example, to recognize Cuba or give fishing rights to the Soviet Union in order to demonstrate some freedom of action. In this regard, future South American relations with Europe will be on a more equal footing than those with the United States, partly because Europe is seen as less willing and less capable to intervene.

Europe and South America have certain commonalities that facilitate cooperative international relations. Both regions must deal with the United States as a major partner, seeking adjustments that involve a combination of costs and benefits. Many South American politicians find it easier to discuss certain issues with European than U.S. politicians. A case-in-point is the recent past when South American military dictatorships were prevalent and thousands of South American political exiles went to Europe. Those exiles found that the experience of persecution in their own countries was viewed sympathetically by many of their French, German, Spanish, and other colleagues, since Europeans had undergone similar experiences in the past fifty or sixty years. On the other hand, South Americans found that the lack of such experience in the United States made it more difficult for North Americans to understand their political problems.

A degree of a common political culture also exists between Europeans and South Americans that facilitates communication on certain issues. Political diversity is a concept well understood in both South America and Europe. For example, a South American social democrat looking for ideas may examine more than one European model to find that which is most relevant or congenial—the various European models of social democracy demonstrate a great deal of diversity. On the other hand, the South American finds that in the United States the similar orientation of Republicans and Democrats offers little to choose from. Therefore, European pluralism, both within individual countries and, especially, within the community of Western Europe, offers South Americans a variety of choices with regard to social security systems, trade practices, state enterprises, and so on.

The importance of European–South American relationships on the substate level should be emphasized. South Americans have been given good access to European political parties, trade unions, churches, and professional organizations across the spectrum from left to right. These transnational relations are much more symbiotic than are those with U.S. entities. The strongest transnational relationship in the case of the United States and South America is the business community, not the trade unions, political parties, professional associations, or even the churches.

Other factors, however, tend to complicate European–Latin American relations. The mixed nature of European perceptions of South America sometimes leads to contradictory European policies. They see the continent simultaneously as part of the Third World, of the Western world, and of international political party movements (especially the Socialist and Christian Democratic internationals). South America is included in the Western world and, therefore, alongside Europe in East-West conflict. As part of the Third World, however, South America is involved in the North-South debate on the other side. For Western Europeans, South America is the only continent in the Third World that seemingly has similar political structures and processes, even though, in fact, their political values are far from identical. Thus, when dealing with the single South American region, Europeans variously address the East-West dimension, the North-South dimension, or the ideological dimensions of party relationships. This mixed view sometimes makes Europeans unhelpful to South Americans.

Another problem is the European trend to compartmentalize their South American interchanges with little coordination between the various kinds of relations. Transactions take place principally on three levels: (1) the supranational level of the European Community, which deals mainly with biregional trade and development issues; (2) the national level, which is very strong between certain countries like Germany and Brazil and Italy and Argentina; and (3) the transnational level (discussed above). European actions are very particular on each level with little correlation between them; as a result, South Americans often see disarray in European endeavors.

With regard to specific current issues, Europeans emphasize two of concern on the South American scene: The debt crisis and democratization. Difficult questions arise regarding European policies in both instances. On the debt question several European governments are sympathetic to the problems raised for South American societies but they resist dealing with the problems at the expense of their taxpayers. A great deal of public sympathy is also found in Europe with regard to democratization and an assumption that democratization can proceed successfully only if it is helped economically. But who will assume the economic costs of Latin American democratization? Should it be left to the United States because of its interest in a stable region? The considerable European sympathy evidenced in these issues is always tempered by considerations of domestic costs.

In the future, Europeans will deal increasingly with South America without necessarily coordinating with the United States, an unthinkable approach even a few years ago. The strong possibility exists for the creation of a mechanism for regular consultations between European foreign ministers of the European Community and of the Group of Eight. Europeans could improve their approach to South America in a number of ways, some in the economic field and many in the cultural and political field. They could be especially helpful by offering their own political experiences to help construct working democracies; certain Europeans can understand South American problems because, in a historical sense, they have only recently established their own democracies. It would be unfortunate if the extension of this kind of European "know-how" about running democratic countries were perceived by the United States as malicious meddling. To the contrary, there needs to be a mutual understanding that both Europe and the United States have potentially constructive roles to play in South American political and economic development.

A South American Perspective

South America has experienced significant changes in the past twenty-five years. The domestic socio-economic alterations that have occurred throughout the continent, whether positive or negative, have made the character of the region markedly different from that of the 1950s. In order to fully comprehend the international relations of South America into the 1990s, it is essential to weigh the impact that current internal dynamics have had on the foreign policies of the region's major actors. The new South American internationalism is also the consequence of reduced bipolarity and increased transnationalization of the international political system, and the correspondingly altered policies of the United States. Relative U.S. global power eroded after the mid-1960s; this trend continued during the Reagan Administration despite its attempts to reassert U.S. power and influence, and will continue into the future with a significant impact on inter-American relations. These systemic modifications importantly affect South American relations with the United States.[1]

A major change on the continent has been the decline of what was called the "new South American authoritarianism." Chile is the exception to the unravelling of the system launched by the 1964 military coup in Brazil. The principal consequence of this unravelling process has been the rebirth of representative political structures, which in turn has opened up unprecedented prospects for change in the foreign policies of the South American states and for their increased coordination.[2]

For the South American states, the advent of democracy, drastic external vulnerability, and increasing difficulties in defining and protecting interests in North-South disputes have led them to emphasize their own unique policies. It logically follows that the South American nations would search for new forms of intraregional cooperation in an attempt to transcend the inoperative economic integration efforts that characterized the region's international relations over the past several decades. The current foreign policy designs of the region's major actors highlight the need to explore new mechanisms for selective integration and to move toward precise coordination of their common foreign policy interests. Under the military regimes, South American international action was completely devoid of a coordinated strategy.[3]

The majority of the countries in the region have developed their policies with the following objectives in mind: (1) to set in motion the process of selective integration; (2) to reactivate regional institutions; (3) to strengthen peace in the region and put a halt to arms races on the continent; (4) to oppose any doctrine that subordinates South American interests to the strategic objectives of either superpower; (5) to establish policies that will permit regional conflicts to be identified as such and to develop appropriate regional solutions; and (6) to strengthen the system of representative government throughout the continent.

The clearest example to date of South American cooperation surfaced out of the regional initiatives that led to the formation of the Group of Eight. Likewise, the recent Argentine-Brazilian agreements that followed close on the heels of democratic transition in both countries offer a prime example of selective integration. The agreements signified that the traditional rivals were moving closer to the rapprochement envisioned in 1979, which, among many other things, put an end to their long-standing dispute over the use of common natural resources. The rapprochement further resulted in Brazil's diplomatic gestures to support Argentine claims of sovereignty over the Malvinas/Falkland Islands, and to coordinate positions in international forums such as the United Nations General Assembly, UNCTAD, and GATT. Other issues—the debt crisis, trade protectionism practiced by the industrial world, and general East-West conflict—have further encouraged South American governments to speak with one voice.

This new framework for regional cooperation could facilitate the development of the conditions needed to advance changes in traditional Latin American geopolitical thinking toward topics that stress cooperation and integration. The peaceful resolution of the Beagle Channel conflict between Argentina and Chile, and their subsequent signing of the Treaty for Peace and Friendship, demonstrate that South Americans are already headed toward a new era of cooperation. Despite the suspicions of important sectors in the Argentine and Brazilian armed forces, the strategic requirements of the foreign policies of both states and their new bilateral relationship indicate that they are opting for cooperation over conflict. It seems reasonable to assume that a new hypothesis of convergence is emerging that will ultimately override the longstanding secular hypothesis of conflict that led to the well-known South American "armed peace" policies pursued by the military regimes.

Understanding the profound transformations occurring in the South American subsystem requires acknowledging the new environment of cooperation. Some analysts exaggerate the prevalence of realpolitik, border issues, and irredentism in the region, and overstate the situation with the argument that Argentina's claims to the Falkland/Malvinas Islands are symptomatic of the potential for interstate conflict. It is crucial to separate interstate conflicts of a strictly South American nature from a conflict between a Latin American nation and an extra-regional power. A strong Latin American consensus supports Argentine claims to sovereignty in the Malvinas; it is unlikely that this issue will unleash interstate conflicts on a regional level.

The delicate and complicated evolution taking place today in the very meaning of democracy in key Latin American social and political sectors merits special comment. The redefinition of democratic concepts does not imply that mere "formal" democracy will come back into vogue. Instead, the notion is undergoing a profound transformation. President Raúl Alfonsín of Argentina captured the essence of this phenomena when he said: "The construction of democracy is not merely a restoration process. Instead, it signifies the creation of new institutions together with the exercise of new routines, new habits and new patterns of human interaction."[4]

It is important to point out that the reevaluation of political forms demands the reformulation of democracy *qua* democracy. It would be a mistake for North Americans to perceive a South American hostility toward the United States or its political institutions. South Americans do sense that the European experience serves as a better model for their democratic transition than the North American political experience; but this is due more to the greater degree of political and parliamentary structural similarities than anti-United States nationalist sentiments.

Furthermore, we should distinguish the crucial difference—well understood in South America—between the United States as a society and the United States as a superpower. Current political debate demonstrates that South America is fundamentally reevaluating the merits and virtues of both the North American political system and important aspects of its own social and economic development. This debate does not exclude rejection of specific U.S. international actions in response to its interests as a superpower. Opposition on the part of the lesser powers to the policies of the greater powers is a permanent feature of international politics. Again quoting President Alfonsín, from an address at Yale University, there exists "a scandalous incongruence between the principles that many industrialized democracies consider valid to govern their own internal affairs and the principles that they apply in the conduct of their international affairs."[5]

The failure of military regimes to resolve national problems—particularly in the cases of Argentina and Uruguay—and the violence and repression that many South American people suffered under these governments, are closely tied to the reevaluation of democracy. These experiences have significantly transformed the South American political-cultural realm by strengthening the democratic process. A prime example of this shift is the willingness demonstrated by today's major political actors to share the stage with a multiplicity of players. Along the same lines, political debate has taken on a much more realistic tone: South American leaders and populations are increasingly suspicious of the simplistic ideological proposals of the past and are rejecting them. More and more South Americans are concluding that pragmatic, pluralist, generally centrist regimes will serve them best; in my view, they would also be good for U.S.–South American policies.

South Americans seem to have exercised a greater degree of pragmatism in inter-American relationships than has the United States. This is not surprising when one considers the shifts in South American attitudes over the past few years, especially the fact that current South American political discourse tends to emphasize moderation. At the same time, the region as a whole is developing more sophisticated, pragmatic, and incrementalist foreign policies, carried out with a more polished diplomatic style. The Reagan administration, on the other hand—not surprisingly to South Americans—"Central Americanized" all of its Latin American policy. That is, policy was based on an ideological and ethnocentric vision of the world that assumed the East-West conflict pertained to the entire universe. Consequently, U.S. policies toward South America were unimaginative, focused on narrow military strategic concerns to the detriment of pressing socio-economic problems.[6]

The Latin American economic crisis, especially the external debt, is the most salient problem on the U.S. agenda. But the United States is overlooking the long-term impact the crisis could have on its own security interests, inasmuch as the principal threat to democratic processes stems from the economic predicament. Should the emergency continue, the governments of the region will not be able to provide the minimum level of economic growth needed to respond to the increasing social demands of the neediest sectors of their populations. This eventuality would be devastating for democratic prospects. A strong correlation exists between the socio-economic development of a country and the prospects for successfully implementing representative government.

If one holds the assumption (as I do) that democracy, more than any other political system, best serves U.S. strategic and other interests, then the debt issue will be of the utmost importance for the future of U.S.–South American relations. Consequently, two suggestions seem to be in order. First, the United States should pay more attention to the region's financial crisis and the attendant problem of economic growth in the region. The debt situation could reach crisis proportions, the result more of circumstances than a deliberate Latin American policy of confrontation. Second, the United States should fully and wholeheartedly support the redemocratization in South America, not only for ethical reasons but because it serves U.S. national interests.

The era of automatic Latin American alliance with the United States has come to an end. This situation is the product of the structural changes discussed above, and is unrelated to the democratic or authoritarian nature of the region's political regimes. In fact, South American differences with the United States transcend the character of political systems. Instead, the discrepancies stem from conflicting national interests such as Latin American positions on the debt crisis, trade issues, or the various proposals for settling the Central American crisis.

History is full of examples illustrating that U.S. policy for South America is crisis-oriented. Whether we like it or not, South America occupies a low priority position on the U.S. strategic agenda compared to other parts of the world, including the northern portion of Latin America, and there is little reason to expect that the old patterns of crisis and response will change. South America will warrant increased attention from the United States only at moments of crisis, regardless of who is in the White House. Incidents that might provoke heightened concern include a state threatening to turn socialist, the adoption of confrontational attitudes regarding the debt crisis, or a major threat to U.S. interests such as drug trafficking. It is useless to point out the need for Washington to change its traditional approach, since this scenario is unrealistic except when "normalcy" is threatened.

Most South American governments and people today clearly favor pluralist and capitalist political-economic systems. The fact that the region has made this choice minimizes the risk that threats of an East-West nature will surface or develop. In other words, there are no significant challenges to U.S. global concerns emerging from the region, including the primary U.S. concern of the expansion of communism. In this context, existing discrepancies between the United States and South America consist fundamentally of questions that normally fall in the realm of North-South issues involving essentially economic questions.

While South America ascribes culturally to the West, the region also attempts to separate the ideological components of the East-West conflict from those that are specifically military-strategic in nature. This distinction is made because the region perceives the strategic dimension of the ongoing confrontation between the United States and the Soviet Union to be the product of two superpowers pursuing global interests. As such, a central aspect of South America's new democratic foreign policies is to prevent the region from becoming another stage for the playing out of East-West tensions. This goal is reflected in actions like the formation of the Contadora Support Group; and support for Brazil's initiative to create a Zone for Peace and Cooperation in the South Atlantic (adopted as a UN General Assembly resolution in October 1986, with the United States casting a negative vote). The Brazilian initiative, contrary to the earlier frustrated proposal for a South Atlantic Treaty Organization, leans toward the creation of a security system for the region once the South Atlantic's identity is properly recognized and the need to keep the area safe from the East-West conflict is acknowledged. These attitudes demonstrate that most South American countries are taking preliminary, although tentative, steps towards disengaging the subregion from U.S. strategic doctrines and advancing toward indigenous South American ideas.

Notes

1. I agree with the editor of this volume that any analysis of U.S.–Latin American relations must differentiate Mexico, Central America, and the Caribbean on the one hand, and most of South America on the other. U.S. priorities in each subregion differ tremendously. These distinctions further provide different frameworks of reference for South American foreign policies. Given the complexity and diversity of South America, my comments refer generally and

primarily to Argentina, Brazil, and Uruguay; I place special emphasis on the impact of democratic transition on their foreign policies.

2. For more information on the concept, see David Collier (ed.), *The New Authoritarianism in Latin America*, Princeton: Princeton University Press, 1979.

3. For further discussion of the fragmented decision making process, see my essay, "Argentina y la política exterior del regimen autoritario (1976–1983); una evaluación preliminar," *Estudios Internacionales*, v. XVII, no. 66 (April/June 1984).

4. *La Nación*, June 21, 1987.

5. *La Nación*, November 19, 1986.

6. It is important to emphasize that neither the Malvinas-Falklands conflict nor the debt crisis—both outside of the East-West orbit—modified these criteria. They may, however, have brought a certain degree of sophistication to the political visions that I have described.

Index